THE REVELATION PROJECT

A Fresh Look at the Last Book

John W. Stanko

The Revelation Project
by John W. Stanko
Copyright © 2010 John W. Stanko

All rights reserved. This book is protected under the copyright laws of the United States of America. This book may not be copied or reprinted for commercial gain or profit. Unless otherwise identified, Scripture quotations are taken from THE HOLY BIBLE: New International Version © 1978 by the New York International Bible Society, used by permission of Zondervan Bible Publishers. Scriptures marked NAS are taken from the New American Standard Bible, Copyright © 1960, 1962, 1963, 1968, 1971, 1973, 1975, 1977 by The Lockman Foundation. Scriptures marked KJV are taken from the King James Version of the Bible. All are used by permission. All rights reserved.

ISBN 978-1-63360-047-8
For Worldwide Distribution
Printed in the U.S.A.

PurposeQuest Ink
P.O. Box 8882
Pittsburgh, PA 15221-0882
412.646.2780

Table of Contents

Study 1: Revelation 1:1-6	1
Study 2: Revelation 1:7-14	5
Study 3: Revelation 1:15–2:3	9
Study 4: Revelation 2:4-8	14
Study 5: Revelation 2:9-12	19
Study 6: Revelation 2:13-17	22
Study 7: Revelation 2:18-22	26
Study 8: Revelation 2:23–3:4	30
Study 9: Revelation 3:5-9	35
Study 10: Revelation 3:10-13	39
Study 11: Revelation 3:14-22	44
Study 12: Revelation 4:1-7	50
Study 13: Revelation 4:8–5:4	55
Study 14: Revelation 5:5-10	59
Study 15: Revelation 5:11–6:3	64
Study 16: Revelation 6:4-11	69
Study 17: Revelation 6:12–7:3	74
Study 18: Revelation 7:4-13	79
Study 19: Revelation 7:14–8:2	85
Study 20: Revelation 8:3-7	90
Study 21: Revelation 8:8-13	93
Study 22: Revelation 9:1-9	97
Study 23: Revelation 9:10-17	103
Study 24: Revelation 9:18–10:7	107
Study 25: Revelation 10:8–11:4	113
Study 26: Revelation 11:5-11	118
Study 27: Revelation 11:12-19	122
Study 28: Revelation 12:1-9	129
Study 29: Revelation 12:10-17	134
Study 30: Revelation 13:1-10	141
Study 31: Revelation 13:11-18	146
Study 32: Revelation 14:1-11	151

Study 33: Revelation 14:12-20	157
Study 34: Revelation 15:1-8	162
Study 35: Revelation 16:1-7	169
Study 36: Revelation 16:8-16	173
Study 37: Revelation 16:17-21	180
Study 38: Revelation 17:1-8	184
Study 39: Revelation 17:9-18	190
Study 40: Revelation 18:1-8	195
Study 41: Revelation 18:9-24	200
Study 42: Revelation 19:1-8	207
Study 43: Revelation 19:9-13	212
Study 44: Revelation 19:14-21	218
Study 45: Revelation 20:1-6	224
Study 46: Revelation 20:7-15	230
Study 47: Revelation 21:1-8	237
Study 48: Revelation 21:9-16	243
Study 49: Revelation 21:17-27	249
Study 50: Revelation 22:1-7	256
Study 51: Revelation 22:8-13	263
Study 52: Revelation 22:14-21	269
Endnotes	276
Scripture References	276

Introduction

I recently taught a Saturday evening course on Revelation at the church where I am a staff member. We have Saturday evening services and then small groups meet after the service. I had 45 people sign up for the class! That is how it is with Revelation. People are interested in it, yet when I asked the class why they don't study it more, these are some of the responses I received:

- It's too scary.
- I don't understand what it all means.
- It's so different from any other book in the Bible.
- I sat in other classes on Revelation and I got confused.
- There seem to be so many interpretations, how do I know which one is true?

Yet on the last night of the class, one of the members who attended every session said, "Now it's starting to come together for me. I remember in the first class when you asked us to hold on and be patient until we reach the last class," she continued. "I'm glad I did because now it all makes more sense."

And that is what I am going to ask you to do as you read this book, along with a few other suggestions that will help you grasp the message and value of this book known as the Revelation of John or the Apocalypse.

When Revelation is taught or mentioned today, too often we immediately divide into camps of interpretation concerning eschatology or the study of the end times. Some are premillennialists, who believe in a literal thousand-year reign of Christ (called the millennium and mentioned in Revelation 20) usually preceded by a Great Tribulation. Others are postmillennialists, who maintain that there will be an increase of godliness leading up to the return of the Lord. Finally, there are amillennialists, who maintain that there is to be no literal thousand-year reign of Christ on earth. There is one more humorous category called the pan-millennialists. They believe that, in the end, everything will just simply pan out!

I suppose it is natural for us to think about the end of time and speculate about what will happen after that. And with the proliferation of teaching tools, the various positions on the end times, using Revelation as the key (along with Daniel, Ezekiel, and some parts of the gospel accounts), it's difficult not to evaluate the material and choose a position that is consistent with your church, your denomination, or your own personal convictions.

Yet as you start this study called *The Revelation Project*, I am asking you to do something completely counterintuitive. I am asking you to suspend any and all preconceived notions that you have accumulated about Revelation, just for as long as you read this book. I don't want you to think as a pre- or post-millennialist. If you don't do that, then you will approach this book or a reading of Revelation looking for what you are familiar with, consequently not seeing what else there may be.

Notice I did not say to suspend your amillennial presuppositions. That is because I am bringing one of the basic tenets of that position forward and that is there will be no literal thousand-year reign of Christ on earth. You may think that unfair, and maybe it is. My reason for asking this, however, is that the doctrine of a literal millennium can so cloud the reading of Revelation so as to preclude any new insight or devotional worth of the book.

That brings me to my main objective in writing this *Project*. I want you to read this book and Revelation, approaching it as a ***devotional*** book. My reason for this is how, at least in part, you approach the other 65 books of the Bible. You usually read those books asking, "What can I learn from this that will help me in my daily walk?" "What can I learn about God's will for my life?" "What can I learn about the Lord Jesus that will enhance my worship and walk with Him?"

Once you suspend your preconceived notions of what Revelation is or how you have interpreted it in the past, here are some other guidelines I have set up as you work through the material, just so you know how I am approaching the *Project*:

1. **Revelation is not a book primarily about the future. It is a book about the past.** This does not mean that there are no future aspects to Revelation. There most certainly are. Yet the other sixty-five books of the Bible primarily explain how God has worked among His people, culminating in the work of Christ on the cross. The Old Testament basically tells us that Christ is coming. The New Testament explains the implications for His finished work and ascension to heaven. Revelation has much to tell us about Christ's work as well.

2. **Revelation is a book about Christ, not the Antichrist.** Yes, Revelation does depict the work of forces that align themselves against

the Lord and His Anointed One, but their actions are shown to be futile in light of God's superior power and authority. To focus on the enemies of God has tended to magnify their power and actions. We are never to magnify the enemy, only God.

3. Revelation had to mean something to the churches that initially received it. The New Testament was written to the Church for all ages, and Revelation is no exception. The gospel of Matthew has meaning for us today, but it also meant something to those for whom it was first written—the Jews of the first century. If we can grasp and recapture some of what Revelation could have meant to them, then we will have a clearer understanding of what it says to us today.

4. Revelation is called the Apocalypse because it is a book that utilizes apocalyptic language and images. The word *apocalypse* literally means "unveiling." It was a genre of literature that was well-known to the early church, but almost a complete mystery to us today. There were specific rules of interpretation for apocalyptic literature then, just as there are for satire and science fiction today. You approach those latter types of literature with certain expectations and rules for interpretation. You must do the same as you read Revelation. Much of Revelation employs graphic and exaggerated symbols and metaphors, intended to give a general bird's eye view of the work of Christ as He rules until all His enemies are His footstool. Those metaphors are not to be taken as literally as some have imagined.

5. Revelation was not intended to generate fear but trust and confidence in God. If the other 65 books of the Bible were intended to teach the fear of God and confidence in His ability to protect His people, then why would Revelation be any different? Yet the Bible and Revelation do tell the sinner—those who are apart from God, those who are in open rebellion—to fear. He will not remain silent forever, and He will eventually rule and judge His enemies, both in this Age and at the Final Judgment. If anyone should fear when reading Revelation, it is not God's people but those who are not.

So there you have my assumptions as we begin our study together. When you have finished, you can decide whether or not to resume or adjust your assumptions about Revelation. In the meantime, this book is written in fifty-two separate studies, which cover a verse-by-verse look at the entire book. You can read these studies one a week for a year to take your time to savor every lesson, or read through it as quickly as you feel comfortable.

The questions I pose are geared to enhance the devotional aspect of your reading. Remember, my goal is for you to read this so that it increases your devotion to Christ and His Word. I do not to try to give a full explanation of things that in my opinion were never intended to have a literal explanation.

Initial responses to this manuscript and my classes in which I have taught from it have been encouraging. People are seeing Revelation in a whole new light. Pastors have gone forth to teach and preach from it, having avoided it altogether for years. Others are more confident talking about Revelation to their friends and associates. Many have reported that their faith has increased and they are more confident in God's future for them and the Church. I trust you will find the same benefits and more as you read and study *The Revelation Project: A Fresh Look at the Last Book*.

One last suggestion before you begin. I would suggest you start a *Revelation Project* journal to record your own impressions as you read Revelation and this book. Perhaps you can answer some of the many questions I pose in my book. Maybe you will want to record your own insights into Revelation as you read. Or maybe you would like to write out your points of disagreement with my premise for this book. Either way, I am confident you will have plenty to enter into your journal if you take this *Revelation Project* seriously. The author of Revelation promised a blessing for anyone who read the book and took it to heart. Use your journal and your time to get a blessing as you embark with me on a magnificent journey through this last book of the Bible in *Revelation Project*.

Study 1: Revelation 1:1-6

1:1 *The revelation of Jesus Christ, which God gave him to show his servants what must soon take place. He made it known by sending his angel to his servant John*

Revelation and insight into the things of God are gifts. There is no reason for pride or arrogance, for God gives insight to whomever He chooses. Anything you see, God has opened your eyes to see. You should not criticize anyone who doesn't see it, because there is a chance that God hasn't opened his or her eyes to see it.

Let's consider some biblical examples of God opening someone's eyes to see something:
- Hagar (Genesis 16:7-16)
- Abraham (Genesis 22)
- Balaam (Numbers 22:21-31)
- Gehazi, Elisha's servant (2 Kings 6:15-17)
- The disciples on the Emmaus road (Luke 24:31)
- The scales that fell from Saul's eyes (Acts 9:18)

This is the revelation "of" Jesus Christ that can be understood in two ways. First, it is a revelation that talks about and shows John and the church more of who Jesus is. Second, the revelation belongs to Jesus. He gives it to whom He wills. Jesus is the source and focus of all revelation, so it is referred to as a revelation "of" Jesus.

Much modern study of Revelation focuses on the end times. The purpose for the book as expressed in this first verse, however, is to reveal what will happen "soon." Is this reference to "soon" figurative for what will happen over the next two thousand years, or does it mean right away?

You cannot understand the book of Revelation, which is a vision, unless you take into account what it meant to the churches to which it was addressed. Therefore, the focus of *The Revelation Project* will not be the end times as traditionally defined, but rather will focus on the possible meaning to the early church and the application of that meaning for your life today.

God the Father gave this revelation to Jesus, who entrusted it to an angel to give to John who in turn wrote it to the church. Revelation is always given to someone and is then to be passed on faithfully. God often gives you something not only because you need it but also because someone you will come in contact with needs it as well.

The word for servant in 1:1 is *doulos*, which means "slave." A slave has one right and that is to know the will of the master. You and I are God's servants; He is not to serve us, we are to serve Him. Do you know His will for your life? Are you doing it?

I have visited the isle of Patmos on three occasions. It is a remote, small Greek island in the Aegean Sea. The island is dominated by one big mountain, where you climb or ride up a winding road to tour an Orthodox chapel at the top that is more than one thousand years old! Then you go down to the famous cave. Tradition has it that the revelation came to John while he was in this cave, and he dictated it to an assistant.

Tradition also has it that the apostle John received the revelation. That is subject to dispute, but for the purpose of this study, we will assume that John, the beloved apostle and gospel writer, received and recorded the revelation. It makes sense that the revelation would be given to John since he was the last surviving apostle. His name would carry a lot of authority then and now.

1:2 *who testifies to everything he saw—that is, the word of God and the testimony of Jesus Christ.*

John "saw" the Word of God. The Word of God gives vision and opens the eyes of your heart to the things of God. John also "saw" the testimony of Jesus. Even though the angel delivered the message, it was a faithful and true account of Jesus' words. Angels are trusted messengers. We are to be faithful messengers as well. The angel isn't the focus; Jesus is the focus. You aren't the focus either. It's always about Jesus! Jesus was also a faithful witness, for He testified faithfully to everything the Father wanted Him to report. He expects His followers to do the same.

1:3 *Blessed is the one who reads the words of this prophecy, and blessed are those who hear it and take to heart what is written in it, because the time is near.*

A blessing is given to anyone who reads the book of Revelation. I don't think that promise is attached to any other book in the Bible; it may be implied, but it isn't written. Further blessing is given to those who take it to heart.

To repeat, we must determine what this book meant to the church of its day in order to comprehend the real meaning of the revelation for us today. It isn't enough to hear the Word, we must comprehend it and take it to heart. Are you only a hearer of the Word, or a hearer and doer? (see James 1:17).

1:4 *John, To the seven churches in the province of Asia: Grace and peace to you from him who is, and who was, and who is to come, and from the seven spirits before his throne*

I have heard it taught that seven is a number of perfection and completion. Therefore, the seven churches could represent the entire church and the seven spirits the fullness of God's Spirit. Remember, the role of the Spirit is to lead the Church into the truth and convict the world of sin. The Spirit with all His power and authority is behind this revelation.

But I tell you the truth: It is for your good that I am going away. Unless I go away, the Counselor will not come to you; but if I go, I will send him to you. When he comes, he will convict the world of guilt in regard to sin and righteousness and judgment: in regard to sin, because men do not believe in me; in regard to righteousness, because I am going to the Father, where you can see me no longer; and in regard to judgment, because the prince of this world now stands condemned (John 16:7-11).

John wished the churches "grace and peace." Revelation has been a source of tremendous speculation and anxiety instead of grace and peace. Therefore, any interpretation of this book that doesn't produce grace and peace in the lives of the hearers isn't the correct interpretation.

Why were these seven churches singled out for this revelation? Perhaps John had a relationship with them after ministering there. Maybe their problems and strengths were representative of the problems of the church in that era. Whatever the reason, it is safe to say that Jesus is concerned with the condition of every church, and these problems were indicative of problems that every church has encountered or will encounter.

1:5 *and from Jesus Christ, who is the faithful witness, the firstborn from the dead, and the ruler of the kings of the earth. To him who loves us and has freed us from our sins by his blood*

The Father and Spirit were mentioned in the previous verse and now Jesus is mentioned. We see three of Jesus' characteristics in this verse, which establish His revelation as supreme to all others. He is:

A faithful witness: A faithful witness tells only the truth, free from deceit, delusion or exaggeration. A faithful witness represents another with integrity, which Jesus did when He was sent from the Father to declare His love.

The firstborn from the dead: If Jesus is the firstborn from the dead, then others are or will be born from the dead after Him. Of course the resurrection is an important part of Jesus' message today and forever. The church in which I was raised seemed to focus more on the crucified Jesus rather than the resurrected Jesus.

The ruler of the kings of the earth: Kings are on the earth; they are part of God's plan for government. Every king has a King over him, however, and that King is Jesus. Jesus is not just over the Church; He has authority over the nations of the world. All kings are expected to rule with Him in mind.

Jesus has titles and authority, but He also loves us and freed us from our sins through His death. Jesus is not aloof, sitting in heaven enjoying His power and prestige. He touched and changed my life, and yours too! What's more, He stays intimately involved. That is why Revelation is a book of worship—not only because of who Jesus is but also because of what He has done for His people.

1:6 *and has made us to be a kingdom and priests to serve his God and Father— to him be glory and power for ever and ever! Amen.*

Not only is Jesus our personal Savior, but He also made us a people united under His leadership. We are saved into a kingdom; that implies that we have a King. We are citizens and part of a heavenly kingdom. Think of what this meant to the early church. They were well acquainted with Rome's kingdom, so they could understand a kingdom culture. Their allegiance, however, was transferred to a higher kingdom and King, even though the Roman kingdom demanded greater loyalty. Jesus had told us that the kingdom of God was within us or in our midst, unlike other earthly kingdoms (see Luke 17:21).

We are also priests, equipped and qualified to handle the things of God. Lest we be exalted over this magnificent privilege, we are a kingdom of priests to serve God, not to dominate men. The realization of all this leads us to worship, just as John recorded in the revelation!

Study 2: Revelation 1:7-14

1:7 *Look, he is coming with the clouds, and every eye will see him, even those who pierced him; and all the peoples of the earth will mourn because of him. So shall it be! Amen.*

What Jesus does only among His people at this time will be done in the future for the world to see. His appearance will be a source of mourning when people realize what humanity has done to Jesus. They will also mourn when they realize that any religious system that did not honor Him as God was the wrong system. At that point people will mourn over their wasted lives when they pursued empty gods. It is a historic fact that Jesus came, was executed, buried, and raised from the dead. The hope of the Church is His return. Come quickly, Lord Jesus!

All history will conclude with His return, whether nations or individuals accept this or not. We should not be lulled to a state of lethargy due to His delay. Are you ready for His return?

1:8 *"I am the Alpha and the Omega," says the Lord God, "who is, and who was, and who is to come, the Almighty."*

Alpha and *omega* are the first and last letters of the Greek alphabet. For anything to make sense, you need all the letters in between those two to compose words and sentences. Jesus is everything—He is all the letters and He arranges the letters to compose the messages He chooses.

He is also eternal. He was, is, and is to come. Therefore His message is eternal as well. He is Almighty. He has all might and power, which is why He can bestow revelation that can be trusted yesterday, today, and forever. What a powerful statement this is. The Lord God is everything for all time and beyond time. His proclamations are good forever, and He backs them up with His never-changing nature. Thus His authority and power are established so that you can receive the rest of the revelation with full confidence and pay attention to it with all diligence.

1:9 *I, John, your brother and companion in the suffering and kingdom and patient endurance that are ours in Jesus, was on the island of Patmos because of the word of God and the testimony of Jesus.*

Notice John used no title. He wasn't the Apostle John, Prophet John,

Bishop John, or Archbishop John. He was simply John, a brother and companion. Any revelation doesn't come from the man or woman delivering the revelation but comes from the One who reveals. The focus is or should always be on Jesus, not on Jesus' messengers.

What does John have in common with his readers? He shares three things: suffering, the kingdom of God, and patient endurance in Jesus. These aren't the three most attractive "selling points" of a relationship with Jesus, are they? Read on to see what I mean.

The Bible has much to say about suffering, and Jesus left us with an example of patient suffering that we are expected to follow. Suffering and the kingdom are related in this verse. When you suffer, you tend to rely on God more and call out for His help. In this life, suffering is something that every citizen of the kingdom encounters. When you suffer, you trust that the King of the kingdom is in control and call out to Him for help. In other words, you learn to patiently endure.

When Paul and Barnabas revisited a church they had planted, they "encouraged" the saints there with the words found in Acts 14:21-22: "They preached the good news in that city and won a large number of disciples. Then they returned to Lystra, Iconium and Antioch, strengthening the disciples and encouraging them to remain true to the faith. 'We must go through many hardships to enter the kingdom of God,' they said." That news may seem like unusual encouragement for some, although it is good to know that your suffering is not a result of something you did wrong but something you did right—follow Jesus.

John was in exile on Patmos for two reasons: the Word of God and John's testimony of Jesus. Those two things will get you into the kind of trouble that brings suffering and requires patient endurance to come through.

What does it mean to be "in Jesus"? Colossians 3:3 states, "For you died, and your life is now hidden with Christ in God." Think of that: your life is hidden in Christ, which means for something to get to you, it must get through Him first. That should change your perspective on suffering and tribulation. Jesus has preapproved it! Can you thank Him for it? What are you patiently enduring in your life right now? How do you know the difference between something you must fight to overcome and something you must patiently endure?

1:10 *On the Lord's Day I was in the Spirit, and I heard behind me a loud voice like a trumpet*

John was "in the Spirit." Note that he saw more clearly what was taking place in the seven churches than those who were physically present in those churches. When you are in the Spirit, you can see things more clearly than with your natural eyes. Ask God today to help you see some situation in your life in the Spirit.

God is a great communicator. He gets His message across with a loud voice. Yet we are told that Elisha heard a still, small voice. What a difference Jesus makes! Through Jesus, God speaks to mankind loud and clear. When His voice isn't heard, it's because people ignore it or something else has their attention. You will see that God and heaven speak with a loud voice throughout Revelation. Our goal is to walk in the Spirit so we can hear this voice as loudly as John did. There is no doubt that John received a clear revelation that was from God when he states it was loud.

1:11 *which said: "Write on a scroll what you see and send it to the seven churches: to Ephesus, Smyrna, Pergamum, Thyatira, Sardis, Philadelphia and Laodicea."*

John was ordered to write down what he saw. Yet he heard a loud voice like a trumpet. How did he receive the revelation—by hearing or seeing? When you hear the voice of God, it brings vision so that you see as well. You see with the eyes of your heart, however, not with natural eyes.

Writing down what you see is important. You need some system to record what the Lord is revealing to you. Then you need to share it with someone, just as John did. A faithful witness passes on what he or she sees and hears. Once you write things down, it helps to have a distribution network that can read and benefit from what you have written. With the Internet, sending something all over the world with little expense is easy.

John wrote to seven churches, and seven is the number of completion and perfection. Therefore, the message of Revelation was for the entire church both at that time and in the centuries to come. Remember, Revelation meant something both to the churches that received it and something to the churches today.

No denominations existed then, only city churches. There is a move today to reestablish one church in every city with city elders. I think that movement is doomed to failure. Denominations are here to stay, and the variety they offer is a good thing, not the evil that some consider it to be. How in the world could there be a city church in a city that has millions of people? I don't think it is possible, nor will I work to help make it happen.

1:12 *I turned around to see the voice that was speaking to me. And when I turned I saw seven golden lampstands*

The voice was behind John and made him turn to see where it was coming from. When we hear the voice of God, we must be in the active mode. This was a simple action that showed John was attentive and interested. You receive revelation by faith, and faith always requires some action (see James 2:17). What can you do to express your faith today?

John did not see what he thought he would see when he turned. Instead he saw seven golden lampstands. You need to be ready to act when God speaks because your action will help you see more than what you hear and see naturally.

The lampstands were made of gold, which is durable and strong—the metal of kings. It must go through a process, however, to become like that. The Church, represented by the lampstands, is also golden, symbolizing that it belongs to the King and has been purified and processed to be pure and valuable. The price for that purification was the blood of Jesus.

To a great extent, suffering is what purifies the "gold" in us. Can you thank God for your suffering today? "Be joyful always; pray continually; give thanks in all circumstances, for this is God's will for you in Christ Jesus" (1 Thessalonians 5:16-18).

1:13 *and among the lampstands was someone "like a son of man," dressed in a robe reaching down to his feet and with a golden sash around his chest.*

Jesus was seen walking among the churches, which is reminiscent of God walking in the garden in Genesis 3. If you are in church leadership, remember that you serve as an under-shepherd. It's not your church; it belongs to God. You serve not at your own pleasure but at God's pleasure. He walks through and conducts inspections from time to time, which is His right.

Notice in this verse that the "son of man" was dressed in the normal dress of the day. He didn't have on a business suit. God relates to man according to the culture of the day, including the language, dress, and customs. God makes Himself relevant in the context of each generation. Each generation has the tendency to try and force others to see God as they saw Him, using their cultural and generational music, customs, or language. That would be a mistake. Jesus reveals Himself in a fresh way to every generation with the timeless message of His love and sacrifice on the cross.

A lampstand is something that holds candles, which give off light. The church is to hold the candle of Christ and allow His light to illuminate the world around her. The lampstand doesn't own the candles; it just holds the candles. The church doesn't own Christ; it simply contains and showcases Him for the world to see.

1:14 *His head and hair were white like wool, as white as snow, and his eyes were like blazing fire.*

This is poetic language. The apostle John would have recognized Jesus the man, for he certainly spent enough time with Him. Yet this Jesus was different. Jesus never changes, but how you perceive Him can change. One time He can be warm and intimate; another time, He can be scary and unfamiliar. God has many facets, and no one comprehends them all. You must respond to Him however He reveals Himself to you.

That is a significant truth, for we often take our perspective of the revealed Christ and try to put it forth as the only perspective there is. Christ is more than what I see and know from my limited perspective. That is why I need your gift and perspective (and you need mine) if we are to see and know the whole Christ.

Study 3: Revelation 1:15–2:3

1:15 *His feet were like bronze glowing in a furnace, and his voice was like the sound of rushing waters.*

If you turned around and beheld the image of this Christ, it would definitely get your attention! I am sure John was describing Jesus as best he could, with analogies and metaphors that were most descriptive for him. Jesus allows Himself to be interpreted according to our experiences and vocabulary.

In spite of this poetic description, Jesus was and is a man, just like you and me, except that He was and is without sin. It is hard to imagine that our flesh sits at the right hand of God! Someone who understands us, even though He is exalted on high, is talking to God the Father about us. Praise the Lord!

1:16 *In his right hand he held seven stars, and out of his mouth came a sharp double-edged sword. His face was like the sun shining in all its brilliance.*

What do stars represent? They mostly come out at night, so they are light in the midst of darkness. It is never completely dark wherever Jesus is, which is wherever we take Him. Thank You, Lord. God used a star to guide the wise men to find the baby Jesus, so stars can also be a source of guidance.

I often want a word from the Lord, but it is double-edged—it cuts going in and coming out. A word from God will destroy everything that isn't from God in my life and that can cause pain and tribulation.

1:17 *When I saw him, I fell at his feet as though dead. Then he placed his right hand on me and said: "Do not be afraid. I am the First and the Last."*

Although John was old and had served the Lord for many years, he was still overcome by the presence of God. We should never grow accustomed to that presence. It should always inspire awe. Jesus appeared in such a manner to add emphasis to the message and revelation He was delivering.

John knew Jesus in the flesh, but when he saw Him as the revelator, he fell down as a dead man. When you say, "Lord, I want Your presence," do you really understand that God may not come in a form that is comfortable or intimate?

A pastor once said, "When God says to anyone 'Fear not,' it's generally too late!" Think of some of the instances in the Bible when the Lord said, "Fear not." At that point, something had already happened to make that person fearful! Saying, "Fear not," doesn't mean there's the absence of fear but rather the need to carry on in the midst of something fearful.

Jesus repeats what was stated in 1:8. He is the beginning and the end. Everything starts and ends with Him. Thus any pursuit that doesn't start or end with an awareness of Jesus and His will is an exercise in futility.

1:18 *"I am the Living One; I was dead, and behold I am alive for ever and ever! And I hold the keys of death and Hades."*

Whoever holds the keys is in charge. This individual opens and closes a door at will or at least as someone directs him. Jesus' resurrection gave Him this authority. If you have eternal life in Him, then any entity that doesn't is irrelevant and holds no meaning for you. In other words, don't exalt any wisdom or system above what God and His Word have to say to you about your life. (By the way, *Hades* is just a term for the realm of the dead and not for hell.)

Real power is to assign people to their eternal place. Imagine what this meant to the early church under persecution. Jesus had the real power. Even though temporal rulers could kill someone in the flesh, they could not kill anyone in spirit. Jesus rules supreme there; He holds the keys. If you believe that God raised Jesus from the dead, then your faith is strong! You can believe God for anything.

By Jesus' own testimony, He was dead. He did not just look like a dead man or exist in some comatose state. He was dead. Now also by His own testimony, He is alive forever.

1:19 *"Write, therefore, what you have seen, what is now and what will take place later."*

Because Jesus was in charge, He ordered John to write down what he saw about the past, present, and future. How is your journal (mentioned in the introduction) coming? Are you behind in your entries? Don't give up; keep writing! Nothing is too simple to record for your future reference.

1:20 *"The mystery of the seven stars that you saw in my right hand and of the seven golden lampstands is this: The seven stars are the angels of the seven churches, and the seven lampstands are the seven churches."*

Scripture interprets itself. Here we are informed that the seven stars represent the seven angels of the churches to which the revelation is addressed. Whenever possible, allow the Bible to interpret what it means. That is why the study of the entire Word is important.

It seems that each of these churches had an angel assigned to it. We can only speculate who these angels were. We cannot assume that they were guardian angels, nor can we assume that this referred to the church leaders, for the word *angel* there can simply be translated "messenger." Of course, the ultimate messenger was Jesus, so this could also be a reference to Him. (Let's establish at this point that there is much about this book of Revelation we don't understand and never will. It is best not to try and force an interpretation where there isn't one that is clear or convincing.)

The backdrop of Revelation was a church that in many locales was under pressure from persecution. What we have seen in Revelation thus far is the existence of another spiritual realm where Jesus rules supreme, having conquered death and hell. No mention is made of the existing world governments; they have no place in the spiritual focus of His Church.

Jesus' main concern isn't politics, commerce, economics, or even individuals. His concern is His Church and its condition, which for the most part wasn't healthy, as you will see in the coming verses. That is still Jesus' concern today and in some ways the condition of the Church hasn't improved.

2:1 *"To the angel of the church in Ephesus write: These are the words of him who holds the seven stars in his right hand and walks among the seven golden lampstands"*

The use of the word angel or messenger here implies that Jesus was addressing the church leadership. Even if He does it through a messenger, it is Jesus who is doing the talking, since angels are faithful messengers.

Ephesus was a great city in the ancient world. It had a population of around 250,000, one of the world's great libraries, an outdoor arena that seated 25,000 people (which still stands), and one of the seven wonders of the ancient world: the temple to Diana. This was no backwater town but a city that impacted the world.

I always assumed that the churches like the one in Ephesus had thousands of members. They probably did not, but instead had membership in the hundreds. These churches were beachheads in a corrupt world, and they had many struggles to survive in the midst of an evil world system. Yet the Lord was with them, and they not only survived but also thrived. Nonetheless, Jesus held them to a high standard. Excuses for sin or poor performance were not allowed. You may be going through tough times (or maybe your church is), but that is no excuse for bad, sloppy, or ungodly behavior.

Jesus is sovereign in the Church. He walks among the churches, so He is intimately acquainted with their condition. He holds the churches in His hand, so He cares for them. He also holds their purpose in His hands. We read how God walked through the Garden in the cool of the day in Genesis 3:8. It seems that Jesus walks through His Church world to check up on it regularly as well. What's more, no one can hide from His scrutiny.

Why didn't Jesus speak to these churches directly? He gave a message

Study 3: Revelation 1:15–2:3

for them to John either because they could not hear what He was saying or He chose to work through John's established leadership and relationship with these churches. Are you listening to what Jesus is trying to say to you, either directly or through His servants?

> **2:2** *"I know your deeds, your hard work and your perseverance. I know that you cannot tolerate wicked men, that you have tested those who claim to be apostles but are not, and have found them false."*

Figuratively speaking, Jesus has a big book and a sharp pencil and He records everything you do and say. He told the Ephesians that He knew their deeds but began by stating the positive things about the Ephesian church, the first one being that they tested those who claimed to be apostles.

How do you test someone who claims to be an apostle? Before you answer that, are there still apostles in the church today? Well, the word *apostle* means "sent forth one." Are messengers still being sent forth? I would have to answer yes. An apostle is not a formal church officer, but one who functions in a particular manner either to plant or oversee churches, or carry out other duties that can build up the local church. It seems too that the early church apostles had the miraculous working through their lives.

Some of my own consulting in churches is an apostolic ministry, for I am helping to oversee and build up the churches. I am not really sent forth by any ministry or agency, however, so I would not call myself an apostle. Yet I accomplish apostolic functions when I work closely with the established leadership of a church. So if Jesus sends me, does that make me an apostle?

In some sense, I suppose that Jesus sends me when I go, but that is subjective since many have engaged in crazy stunts and claimed that God sent them. So what title do I carry? None. You can call me John. I am not a bishop, apostle, prophet, or pastor. I am simply John. Those who call themselves apostles and bishops by putting those titles before their name intrigue me. I think they are misusing the terms. And if they call themselves apostles, are they planting churches or do they just pastor in one of these churches? I know one so-called "bishop" who has oversight for two churches, and one of them isn't doing so well! What right does he have to be called bishop?

Do these self-appointed apostles simply speak at conferences and on Christian television, a potentially lucrative profession, or do they help build churches by supporting local leaders and works? The latter is hard work. The former is much more financially rewarding!

Yet these men and women are not my enemy or problem, the devil is. So I don't want to be found fighting or opposing my brothers; I just want to be clear in my own mind of who I am and what the Lord has called me to do. I am God's servant; let's leave it at that.

2:3 *"You have persevered and have endured hardships for my name, and have not grown weary."*

This is a pretty impressive list of positives for this church. I think I would feel pretty good about my church if Jesus were able to tell us those things about our work!

Galatians warns us not to grow weary in doing good deeds (see Galatians 6:9). Why would it warn us not to grow weary unless we may have to endure much longer than we anticipated in doing the good we are doing? Are you tired of doing good and enduring?

Study 4: Revelation 2:4-8

2:4 *"Yet I hold this against you: You have forsaken your first love."*

It would make my knees buckle to think that Jesus would be holding something against me! I told you He has a big book and a sharp pencil, and He records it all—the good and the bad!

What is this first love mentioned? I knew of a church that made a list of what it was like to be in love for the first time with your life partner. I am not sure you can ever go back to how you were when you were young and in love. I don't think that is what Jesus is saying here. Love and relationships mature, so Jesus is not exhorting the church to be like they were when they first met Him. He wants more than that.

So what did Jesus mean here? I will share with you my educated opinion. He was not confronting the church because they had lost their feelings for Him nor because they were doing wrong things. The Ephesians had become professional church people. They knew the things to do, could do them well, and had a track record of success, but they forgot why they were doing it all.

I have often prayed, "Lord, don't let me be a professional clergyman!" I try to wake up in the morning and tell Jesus that I love Him. As I have grown in experience, I don't want to substitute experience for enthusiasm. I belong to Jesus, not a church. I will answer for my gifts and ministry not to the church but to Jesus. I do what I do because I owe Jesus my life, which makes my life His life. I belong to a church because that is what Jesus wants me to do (see Hebrews 10:25).

Jesus' followers did not receive this word or revelation from John unless they were attending a church since that is where it would be read. They could not watch it on television or read it on the Internet. They had to be there. Are you in a church and attending? If the answer is no, why not? No special exemptions from this requirement are allowed, regardless of how bad your experience may have been in a church setting.

When I have gone through tough times, I have had one prayer: "Lord, I'll do whatever You want me to do, wherever You want me to do it!" Since I have made five major moves to relocate my family to another state in my adult life, I think Jesus took me seriously.

I don't want to be what the world sees as responsible at the expense of being responsive to His promptings. When I first met Jesus, I gave all my money away. Will I now rely on a pension? When I first met Jesus, I read and learned about Him every chance I had. Will I now rely on college degrees instead of His decrees? When I first met Jesus, I abandoned everything, including relatives and career plans, to serve Him. Will I now try to be respectable instead of reliable? I want to respond to Him and not just do the right things out of habit, duty, or sense of responsibility.

How about you? Have you abandoned your first love? Are you still doing the things you once did passionately but in a more mature and meaningful manner?

2:5 *"Remember the height from which you have fallen! Repent and do the things you did at first. If you do not repent, I will come to you and remove your lampstand from its place."*

You are highest when you are lowest. The Bible exhorts you to humble yourself or you will be humbled. You either lower yourself from a high place or you are taken down. When you think you have accomplished something in the Lord, in a manner of speaking you have forgotten your first love and begun to trust in your own abilities. You are warned to humble yourself, lest you be humbled (see 1 Peter 5:6).

From my experience, pride is the one sin that God hates and deals with ruthlessly. Yet, repentance isn't a tearful session where you promise God everything and then produce little. Humility is acting out your total dependence on the Lord. You must repent and then do the things you did at first. Humility and repentance go hand in hand, and you cannot have one without the other.

God gives grace to the humble (see James 4:6). What can you do this week to humble yourself so you can get God's grace? Jesus establishes a church; He can take it down. Jesus is in charge of the church.

2:6 *"But you have this in your favor: You hate the practices of the Nicolaitans, which I also hate."*

Who were the Nicolaitans? No one knows for sure. The church has enemies in every generation, yet these enemies have the same patterns and teachings. Whoever the Nicolaitans were, you can be sure that they were confused in their understanding of who Jesus is and what He does. Almost all errors in the church relate to "Christology," an understanding of Jesus. It seems that those Nicolaitans were in the church. Often the Church's greatest enemies are within and not outside.

Their faulty Christology led them to practices that Jesus hated. Jesus hates some things! We would be wise to hate those things as well.

2:7 *"He who has an ear, let him hear what the Spirit says to the churches. To him who overcomes, I will give the right to eat from the tree of life, which is in the paradise of God."*

The message to each church in Revelation ends with the same formula: an exhortation to hear and a reward for those who overcome. What the Spirit is saying is not accessible to only a select few or the initiated but to all the people.

What is the Spirit saying to your church and therefore to you through your church? Individual revelation can be tricky and lead to deception. So balance what you are hearing personally with what you are hearing corporately.

That is why you need to be in a local church. No matter how many bad experiences you've had with a church, Jesus doesn't exempt you from being part of one. I had a negative experience in 2001, but my wife and I went through membership classes to join another church, and now I am on staff there. We could have decided not to attend church regularly or "church hop," but we know we need what a local church has to offer.

Jesus puts obstacles in your path so that you can overcome them with His help. Obstacles aren't an indication you've done something wrong, but something right. You also grow as you identify and overcome obstacles to your obedience.

Could this be another indication of how the Ephesians had abandoned their first love? They stopped listening to Jesus and started relying on their experience, on what they already knew. They overcame their obstacles in their own strength and not God's.

At any rate, their reward for listening and overcoming was to eat from the tree of life. This tree was made off limits in the garden of Eden. Someone once told me that what was lost in Genesis is restored by the time we reach Revelation. Because of Jesus, we can all now eat of the tree of life in Him.

Adam and Eve opted to eat from the tree of the knowledge of good and evil, and lost the life that the tree of life offered. Man is still making that choice. Instead of relying on God for life, we rely on our own abilities to make our way through life, and determine for ourselves what is good and bad. God promises to reverse that and make us eligible for the fruit of the tree of life, but only if we repent.

Jesus is my life and the life of the Church. Any other life or light is bogus. God lives with His people in their hearts! I will take the life of Jesus over any other kind of life!

2:8 *To the angel of the church in Smyrna write: These are the words of him who is the First and the Last, who died and came to life again.*

Jesus obviously identifies Himself with His death and resurrection. It seems to be His calling card and the credentials that both qualify Him to speak to the Church and that require the Church to pay attention.

It states in Acts 26:22-23,

And so, having obtained help from God, I stand to this day testifying both to small and great, stating nothing but what the Prophets and Moses said was going to take place; that the Christ was to suffer, and that by reason of His resurrection from the dead He should be the first to proclaim light both to the Jewish people and to the Gentiles (NAS).

We don't know anything about the church in Smyrna. This is its only mention in the New Testament. However, consider some important points about the resurrection:

1. Jesus was truly dead. He didn't appear to be dead or faint, as some throughout history have maintained. He died!

2. Jesus died in faith that the Father would raise Him up.

Brothers, I can tell you confidently that the patriarch David died and was buried, and his tomb is here to this day. But he was a prophet and knew that God had promised him on oath that he would place one of his descendants on his throne. Seeing what was ahead, he spoke of the resurrection of the Christ, that he was not abandoned to the grave, nor did his body see decay. God has raised this Jesus to life, and we are all witnesses of the fact (Acts 2:29-32).

3. Jesus' resurrection is proof that we too will attain to resurrection life. The Father did not raise Jesus because Jesus was God; He raised Him to prove that He could do it so that our faith would rest in Him. Jesus said, "I am the resurrection and the life. He who believes in me will live, even though he dies" (John 11:25)

4. The Holy Spirit has been given as a down payment that we will indeed be raised from the dead. "Exalted to the right hand of God, he has received from the Father the promised Holy Spirit and has poured out what you now see and hear" (Acts 2:33).

5. When Jesus was raised, He had a glorified body, but it was still flesh. He could eat, travel, pass through closed doors, and speak. He had memory of what had happened to Him prior to His death, and His body bore the scars of His crucifixion. That is an indication of what we will be like in the next age.

So will it be with the resurrection of the dead. The body that is sown is perishable, it is raised imperishable; it is sown in dishonor, it is raised in glory; it is sown in weakness, it is raised in power; it is sown a natural body, it is raised a spiritual body. If there is a natural body, there is also a spiritual body. So it is written: "The first man Adam became a living being"; the last Adam, a life-giving spirit. The spiritual did not come first, but the natural, and after that the spiritual (1 Corinthians 15:42-46).

6. When Jesus ascended to heaven, He went with this glorified flesh. Therefore heaven is a place that can contain not just human spirits but also resurrected bodies! That means that hell can house flesh as well.

Study 5: Revelation 2:9-12

2:9 *"I know your afflictions and your poverty—yet you are rich! I know the slander of those who say they are Jews and are not, but are a synagogue of Satan."*

Jesus knows what you are going through. I would rather be in trouble on earth than with Him who lives in heaven! The saints in 2:9 were poor, but Jesus considered them rich.

Jesus always kept His expectations in the Father and not in men. It was said of Him, "But Jesus would not entrust himself to them, for he knew all men. He did not need man's testimony about man, for he knew what was in a man (John 2:24-25).

Jesus knows what is being said about you. Just because people call themselves Jews or Christians doesn't mean they are in reality. They will be known and categorized by their fruit and so will you. You are tested so that your fruit can be evident to all, including principalities and powers. Are you being tested right now? If so, you can be glad, for God is at work in your life to prove that His presence in your life is real and will last forever!

A synagogue must have existed where these deceived people met. Imagine the reality of satanic churches and synagogues! These aren't only known by their doctrine but also by their fruit (or lack of it!).

2:10 *"Do not be afraid of what you are about to suffer. I tell you, the devil will put some of you in prison to test you, and you will suffer persecution for ten days. Be faithful, even to the point of death, and I will give you the crown of life."*

If Jesus tells you not to be afraid, then something is coming that is going to tempt you to fear. See how often the Lord gave that admonition to His people (see Is 35:4, Is 41:10, Is 41:13, Is 43:1, Luke 12:32, John 14:27, Rev 1:17). Jesus did not relieve their suffering, but warned them more was coming.

Paul wrote this prayer:

I want to know Christ and the power of his resurrection and the fellowship of sharing in his sufferings, becoming like him in his death, and so, somehow, to attain to the resurrection from the dead. Not that I have already obtained all this, or have already been made perfect, but I press on to take hold of that for which Christ Jesus took hold of me (Philippians 3:10-12).

This is a good prayer and goal for you and me as well. Help us, Lord, to press on!

The devil was active in Revelation and moves today in the Church. Do not underestimate his will or power. Even though those saints faithfully followed Jesus, they weren't immune from the persecution and even death that was part of following Jesus. We have a powerful enemy, but praise God, our Protector is stronger than the devil! Their persecution was for ten days. Every trial has its end. The more severe the trial, the greater the joy and benefit at its conclusion.

James wrote, "Blessed is the man who perseveres under trial, because when he has stood the test, he will receive the crown of life that God has promised to those who love him" (James 1:12).

The saints were going to be tested. Testing doesn't mean that they were given an exam, like in school. They were to be tested in the sense that metal is tested. It was submitted to fire and heat so its purity (or lack of it) could be revealed.

> *Then the Lord said to Moses, "I will rain down bread from heaven for you. The people are to go out each day and gather enough for that day. In this way I will test them and see whether they will follow my instructions"* (Exodus 16:4).

God will test you to see if you will follow His voice and instructions, to show where you stand in reality. God can even use a blessing to test you. When God tests you, He is often proving the reality and worth of what He has put in you. Think of it. There may be a trial you are going through now that would have overwhelmed you a few years ago. Now, however, you are patiently enduring and even experiencing victory over anxiety and fear. All those around you, including those in the unseen world, are able to see the good work of God in your heart and life.

In the end, God is trying to bless you through every test, as hard as that may be to receive. "He gave you manna to eat in the desert, something your fathers had never known, to humble and to test you so that in the end it might go well with you" (Deuteronomy 8:16). Has the Lord ever given you this kind of test? If so, how well did you do?

Jesus urged them to be faithful in the midst of trial, even if it meant death. He promised them a crown of life, however, if death was the result.

Study 5: Revelation 2:9-12

That requires faith, but it is the same faith that Jesus had when He died—faith that the Father would not allow His flesh to see corruption.

Remember that these words are coming from someone (Jesus) who understood death and resurrection, which is why He identified Himself as He did in 2:8. You can trust the words of someone who has been through what you are about to go through. Jesus has been through death, so you can trust what He says about it where you are concerned.

2:11 *"He who has an ear, let him hear what the Spirit says to the churches. He who overcomes will not be hurt at all by the second death."*

"He who has an ear." Well, we all have ears, but what does this mean? It means that it is possible to heed or ignore what Jesus is saying. What is Jesus "saying" to you? Jesus warned His disciples to listen carefully (see Mark 4:9 and 4:23; Luke 8:8 and 14:35). Also consider Luke 8:18, "Therefore consider carefully how you listen. Whoever has will be given more; whoever does not have, even what he thinks he has will be taken from him."

The first death is your physical death. The second death is the judgment of where you will spend eternity.

2:12 *"To the angel of the church in Pergamum write: These are the words of him who has the sharp, double-edged sword."*

Jesus went on to address the third church located in Pergamum. Not much is known about this church either.

The written Word in the power of the Spirit is a powerful weapon! That is why it is important to write. I am not equating your writings with the inspired Word of God; but at the same time, writing is a medium the Spirit has used through the centuries to direct, rebuke, and instruct the Church.

We know that His Word is a sword and can even judge our motives, as described in Hebrews 4 (see below). Someone who has a sword can either defend or attack. I want Jesus to defend me with His sword and not use it against me! We saw Jesus as One who has a sharp sword coming from His mouth in 1:16. Let's look at an important passage that describes how the Word acts in Hebrews 4:9-13.

> *There remains, then, a Sabbath-rest for the people of God; for anyone who enters God's rest also rests from his own work, just as God did from his. Let us, therefore, make every effort to enter that rest, so that no one will fall by following their example of disobedience. For the word of God is living and active. Sharper than any double-edged sword, it penetrates even to dividing soul and spirit, joints and marrow; it judges the thoughts and attitudes of the heart. Nothing in all creation is hidden from God's sight. Everything is uncovered and laid bare before the eyes of him to whom we must give account.*

Rest and the Word of God are related. We can put our trust in the Word of God and rest from our labors of trying to make things happen. The Bible, a book written thousands of years ago, is alive and active. You can read the Bible, and it judges whether or not you love your spouse, are generous, or love your neighbor. It can also judge and evaluate your thoughts. You can rest in the accuracy of the Bible not only in its doctrine but also in its ability to tell you what spiritual condition you are in now.

Nothing is hidden from God's sight, as you can see from these first verses in Revelation. Jesus knew exactly what was going on in each of the seven churches. He knew the good and the bad. Someone once advised not to ever read the Word of God but to allow the Word of God to read you!

Study 6: Revelation 2:13-17

2:13 *"I know where you live—where Satan has his throne. Yet you remain true to my name. You did not renounce your faith in me, even in the days of Antipas, my faithful witness, who was put to death in your city—where Satan lives."*

I think I would relocate if I lived where Satan lived. That would certainly be an evil place. Yet where would I move? There is no place in this life where I can escape evil or the Lord's presence! I should not fear the evil for the Lord is with me.

> *Where can I go from your Spirit? Where can I flee from your presence? If I go up to the heavens, you are there; if I make my bed in the depths, you are there. If I rise on the wings of the dawn, if I settle on the far side of the sea, even there your hand will guide me, your right hand will hold me fast* (Psalm 139:7-10).

Study 6: Revelation 2:13-17

Satan cannot be everywhere all the time. He is a created being and is limited in knowledge and scope. Few of us will ever deal directly with Satan but will most certainly deal with his kingdom and demons. Satan has some authority as indicated by the fact that he has a throne. I am never comfortable with people who mock or taunt Satan. I have faith in the Lord my God, but I have a healthy respect for our great adversary. I will let God deal with the devil and try to stay out of his way.

Spiritual warfare is part of our walk with God. Because I am a friend of God, I am an opponent of the kingdom of darkness. At times I must fight a spiritual battle with my spiritual enemy. You cannot choose not to participate in the battle that rages between good and evil.

What do we know about Satan? The Greek word for devil is *diabolos*, which means "an accuser, a slanderer." From it we derive the English word "devil." *Daimon*, "a demon," is frequently, but wrongly, translated "devil"; it should always be translated "demon."

There is one devil, but there are many demons. Being the malignant enemy of God and man, the devil accuses man to God, (see Job 1:6-11; 2:1-5; Revelation 12:9-10), and God to man (see Genesis 3). He afflicts men with physical sufferings (see Acts 10:38). Being himself sinful (see 1 John 3:8), he instigated man to sin (see Genesis 3), and tempts man to do evil (see Ephesians 4:27; 6:11), encouraging him also to embrace deception (see Ephesians 2:2).

Death was brought into the world by sin, therefore the devil had the power of death. Christ through His own death, however, has triumphed over him, and will bring him to nothing (see Hebrews 2:14).

His rank in heaven among the angels is indicated by his struggle with Michael over the body of Moses (see Jude 9). Judas, who gave himself over to the devil, was in such close partnership with him that Jesus described Judas as a devil (see John 6:70; 13:2).

As the devil raised himself in pride against God and was condemned, so believers are warned against a similar sin (see 1 Timothy 3:6). He lays snares seeking to devour believers as a roaring lion (see 1 Peter 5:8). If believers resist him, he will flee from them (see James 4:7). His fury will be especially exercised at the end of the present age (Revelation 12:12). His ultimate destination is the lake of fire (see Matthew 25:41; Revelation 20:10).[1]

2:14 *"Nevertheless, I have a few things against you: You have people there who hold to the teaching of Balaam, who taught Balak to entice* *the Israelites to sin by eating food sacrificed to idols and by committing sexual immorality."*

Jesus endorsed certain attitudes that existed at Pergamum as healthy, but He also had a few problems with them. One problem in particular was their acceptance of the teaching from a man named Balaam. We first see Balaam in Numbers 22 when Balak, king of a people who were enemies with the people of Israel, tried to hire him to curse Israel. Balaam rejected Balak's first overture; but when Balak offered more money, Balaam asked the servants carrying this revised offer to stay so that Balaam could ask God's permission to go one more time (see Numbers 22:1-20).

When he asked for permission to go a second time, God granted it to Balaam. When Balaam set out, however, God was angry and blocked his way, causing Balaam's donkey to stop when he saw the angel of the Lord in the road before him (see Numbers 22:35). Apparently God will allow you to go your own way if you disobey what He initially directs. God let Balaam go, but He was angry when he went because Balaam was disobedient.

Balaam spoke four blessings over Israel, and this angered Balak, his "employer." Balak's plan to have Balaam the prophet curse Israel failed (see Numbers 23–24) and actually backfired when Balaam proclaimed a blessing.

Eventually Israel's men fell into sexual immorality with the Moabite women. Balaam counseled Balak to so ensnare Israel with those foreign women, incurring God's wrath when they got involved. Thus, Balaam did not curse God's people verbally, but rather devised a scheme that would accomplish the same end (see Numbers 25:1-4).

When Joshua entered the land, he put Balaam to death (see Joshua 13:22). Peter told us that Balaam's sin was to sell his power to the highest bidder, for "he loved the wages of wickedness" (see 2 Peter 2:15).

Offering your spiritual gifts to the highest bidder is easy, but your gifts belong to God and should, at least in part, be used to bless God's people and build God's Church. How effectively are you using your gifts in that regard?

2:15 *"Likewise you also have those who hold to the teaching of the Nicolaitans."*

False teachings have always been in and around the Church. Paul wrote to Timothy,

Study 6: Revelation 2:13-17

> *The Spirit clearly says that in later times some will abandon the faith and follow deceiving spirits and things taught by demons. Such teachings come through hypocritical liars, whose consciences have been seared as with a hot iron. They forbid people to marry and order them to abstain from certain foods, which God created to be received with thanksgiving by those who believe and who know the truth. For everything God created is good, and nothing is to be rejected if it is received with thanksgiving, because it is consecrated by the word of God and prayer. If you point these things out to the brothers, you will be a good minister of Christ Jesus, brought up in the truths of the faith and of the good teaching that you have followed* (1 Timothy 4:1-6).

There are doctrines of demons, which explains their popularity. They are demonically and satanically inspired. Brothers and sisters, if a doctrine sounds strange, it probably is! Stay away from unusual interpretations and people who act as if they are wiser than most, with special insight on obscure topics. I toured Israel once with a man who claimed the Lord showed him where the garden of Eden had been. That is the kind of strange talk against which I am warning.

The Scriptures teach you two things: who Jesus is and how to live, work, and take care of your family once you are part of the family of God. Jesus came preaching the kingdom, which embodies God's government for everyday life. Don't worry about understanding all that the Bible teaches; that will come with time. Rather apply the clear teachings that you know and understand to every aspect of your life.

2:16 *"Repent therefore! Otherwise, I will soon come to you and will fight against them with the sword of my mouth."*

What Jesus says is powerful! His word alone can fight His battles, correct problems, tear down strongholds, and set people free. You and I are agents of His Word. You carry it with you and when you apply that Word, it has the same power.

Repentance is not just for the sinner before he or she knows Jesus. Anyone who is caught in a wrong attitude, practice, or behavior must repent, turn around, and go in another attitudinal or behavioral direction. Asking forgiveness for sin is often not enough. You must also repent or set off in another direction. Is there anything you need to repent of? You may also need to make restitution for your sin by asking forgiveness or actively correcting damage done by your sin. Proverbs 14:9 states, "Fools mock at making amends for sin, but goodwill is found among the upright."

2:17 *"He who has an ear, let him hear what the Spirit says to the churches. To him who overcomes, I will give some of the hidden manna. I will also give him a white stone with a new name written on it, known only to him who receives it."*

I use this verse when I talk to people about finding their life purpose. God is able to give you something that can feed you like He fed the Israelites on manna. Manna literally means, "What is it?" God can give you a statement that for you is a special summary of your life's purpose. Others can look at that same statement and not appreciate it, asking, "What is that?" You know, however, that it is hidden manna, something that nourishes you and you alone.

God can also give you a white stone that has a name written on it that only you can see. Others can look at that stone and declare, "It's blank!" You know otherwise, however, for God can give you a purpose statement that defines who you are and why you were born. It may not be special to anyone else, but it's special to you.

To get this purpose statement, you must overcome the temptation to quit before you find it; to settle for some religious, trite purpose statement; or to allow others to write what they think your purpose should be on your white stone. (I have many resources that can help you find your purpose. Those can be found on my website, www.purposequest.com or in several of my books, which are all listed on that site.)

Study 7: Revelation 2:18-22

2:18-19 *"To the angel of the church in Thyatira write: These are the words of the Son of God, whose eyes are like blazing fire and whose feet are like burnished bronze. I know your deeds, your love and faith, your service and perseverance, and that you are now doing more than you did at first."*

The imagery used to describe Jesus in Revelation does not promote intimacy. We cannot choose one aspect of God's being at the expense of the others. God is love and full of mercy, but He is also powerful and terrifying!

Study 7: Revelation 2:18-22

The Israelites wanted to hear God for themselves. After He spoke, they said in effect, "Maybe that wasn't such a good idea! Moses, you talk to God and let us know what He said" (see Deuteronomy 5:23-27).

Jesus has eyes like blazing fire. In Hebrews 4:13 it says: "Nothing in all creation is hidden from God's sight. Everything is uncovered and laid bare before the eyes of him to whom we must give account." Jesus sees it all and can burn through any façade, mask, or charade. Trying to hide from God is something that our parents, Adam and Eve, tried to do by covering themselves with fig leaves while hiding in the garden. What a ludicrous picture—hiding from an all-knowing, all-seeing God using leaves that will wither and crumble (see Genesis 3:6-24).

That leads to the issue of honesty. If you are honest with God about your sin or difficulty, it is not for His benefit but for yours. God already knows what you are going to tell Him, so why hesitate? Speaking the truth will set you free, and God will forgive your sin!

John, the same man who received the Revelation, wrote in his first epistle:

> *If we claim to have fellowship with him yet walk in the darkness, we lie and do not live by the truth. But if we walk in the light, as he is in the light, we have fellowship with one another, and the blood of Jesus, his Son, purifies us from all sin. If we claim to be without sin, we deceive ourselves and the truth is not in us. If we confess our sins, he is faithful and just and will forgive us our sins and purify us from all unrighteousness. If we claim we have not sinned, we make him out to be a liar and his word has no place in our lives* (1 John 1:6-10).

What could the feet of burnished bronze symbolize? Perhaps it shows that no place is off limits to Jesus. He can go where He wants to go, and that place won't affect or change Him at all. Burnished bronze is tested by fire and durable. That is how Jesus is! He can go to the tough places with you and walk through unscathed. We have a tough God. He's not afraid of your sin and will walk there to confront you or walk into the fire to deliver you.

In my book the *Faith Files*, a study of faith in the New Testament, I wrote about how often faith and love are joined together in the New Testament (see 1 Corinthians 13:13; Colossians 1:5; 1 Thessalonians 3:6, 5-8; 1 Timothy 1:14; 2 Timothy 1:13). Why is this?

Faith without some action or works is dead, as James wrote in James 2:17. Talking about faith is not enough. You must do something with your faith. What you do, however, cannot simply be out of duty; it must be out of love. That means the focus of your faith and love cannot be selfish but should be on someone else, and ultimately focused on God. You do what you do for others because you love and trust Him. Too often my faith has been self-serving instead of God- or others-serving.

Jesus knew about the service and perseverance of the church in Thyatira and commended them for their sacrifice. When you serve others, it is a death process of sorts. You die to yourself and your own way of doing things and enter into another person's world. That attitude requires diligence so that you won't give up when the going gets tough. You can expect to be tested when you make a commitment to serve.

As you walk with God, it requires more and not less faith. When your children are young you need "diaper" faith; when they are older you need "university-tuition" faith. If faith requires action, then greater faith requires greater deeds. Jesus told this church they were doing more than at first, and He commended them for it.

2:20 *"Nevertheless, I have this against you: You tolerate that woman Jezebel, who calls herself a prophetess. By her teaching she misleads my servants into sexual immorality and the eating of food sacrificed to idols."*

So much for the good news because Jesus also had something against this church as well. They were tolerating a woman called Jezebel who was causing trouble. Seducing and beguiling forces are always at work to attack the Church. Jesus can identify with the Church's temptation, but He will not excuse sin.

When Jesus said that the gates of hell would not prevail against the Church, He didn't say the gates of hell would not try to prevail! The churches in Revelation were under intense attack from the Nicolaitans and Jezebel. The Church is still under attack from false doctrines and seducing spirits. Protect us, Lord Jesus! I often pray, "Lord, keep me from weirdness. Protect me from strange doctrines that don't help people but that appear spiritual."

2:21 *"I have given her time to repent of her immorality, but she is unwilling."*

What do we know about Jezebel? She was a daughter of Ethbaal, king of the Sidonians. Ahab, king of Israel, married her. As her father's name suggests, she was a worshiper of Baal. Baal literally means "lord," and he was the god of the sun. Baal was worshiped to secure his provision and to placate his destructive powers. Although the Baal cult had many dimensions, there were sexual overtones in much of the Baal worship that took place.

When Jezebel became queen, she began killing the Lord's prophets and replacing them with Baal's prophets, supported from the royal treasury. During her reign, Elijah the prophet appeared on the scene and had the famous confrontation with the prophets of Baal in 1 Kings 18. When Jezebel heard what Elijah had done and how many of her prophets he had killed, she promised to have him killed as well (see 1 Kings 19:2). Elijah, who had confronted hundreds of false prophets and won, ran for his life. This gives you an idea of how intimidating this woman was. Elijah ran when confronted with the possibility of facing this woman after he had confronted a host of false prophets!

Later Jezebel conspired with the elders of a town to steal the vineyard of a man named Naboth by having the man falsely accused and killed. This is why many say that a spirit of confiscation and theft is connected with the spirit of Jezebel.

Ahab, Jezebel's husband, was a wicked man of whom the Bible says, "There was never a man like Ahab, who sold himself to do evil in the eyes of the Lord, urged on by his wife Jezebel" (1 Kings 21:25).

When Jezebel was killed, she was thrown down from her tower, and before anyone could rescue the body, dogs had eaten it! (see 2 Kings 9). This end had been prophesied and predicted, but Jezebel had ignored those predictions and continued her adulterous liaison with the Baal god. In Revelation, God gave this Jezebel time to repent as well, but she refused.

The word *Jezebel* is used today to describe a controlling woman given to domination through any means of manipulation, which of course is a form of witchcraft (see 1 Samuel 15:23). When the Holy Spirit wanted to use a graphic metaphor for the religious idolatry in the church at Thyatira, He used the name Jezebel. That said it all. Later in Revelation He will use the name Babylon to portray the same sinful condition.

What does this mean for the church today? False prophets are in the world, and the church must distinguish between the authentic and the counterfeit. False prophets are known by their fruit. They use illegitimate sources of divine revelation and issue prophesies that don't come true. False prophets do not speak for God, although some sound as though they do.

All prophecy must be judged not only for what is said but according to who says it. In Acts a slave girl had a spirit of divination (see Acts 16:16-19). What she said was true, but Paul still cast the spirit out of the girl. It wasn't enough that she spoke the truth; Paul discerned from what spirit she spoke. The Church needs to do the same.

Prophecy needs to be judged, not received as the infallible voice of God. Paul wrote, "Do not quench the Spirit; do not despise prophetic utterances. But examine everything, carefully hold fast to that which is good; abstain from every form of evil" (1 Thessalonians 5:19-22 NAS). Why include a command not to despise prophecy unless there is a tendency to do so?

The modern church either despises or is enamored by prophecy. The biblical position is neither. A prophet can stir things up and that is not always bad. Historically that is what they have done. And the prophet is one of the five-fold ministries mentioned in Ephesians 4:11. A prophet can speak out of his or her own understanding, which is always limited. Therefore all prophecy needs to be judged.

There are some prophets who are more accurate and insightful than others. Just because God tolerates something doesn't mean He approves of it. He is slow to anger so that all may have a chance to repent.

2:22 *"So I will cast her on a bed of suffering, and I will make those who commit adultery with her suffer intensely, unless they repent of her ways."*

People can suffer both for a godly purpose and also as a result of evil. The followers of Jezebel suffer for their evil. Those who join with anyone or anything other than God are considered adulterers, becoming intimate with someone or something other than their rightful partner. Of course, your ultimate right partner is the Lord Himself.

Study 8: Revelation 2:23-3:4

2:23 *"I will strike her children dead. Then all the churches will know that I am he who searches hearts and minds, and I will repay each of you according to your deeds."*

What a strong a statement! God will strike someone dead for not heeding His warning and leading His people astray. He will do this to judge those given to such foolishness and to warn those who have a tendency to stray. God is always teaching through what He does. Jesus' ministry on earth was largely a teaching and preaching ministry. God repays good with good, and evil with judgment.

2:24 *"Now I say to the rest of you in Thyatira, to you who do not hold to her teaching and have not learned Satan's so-called deep secrets (I will not impose any other burden on you)"*

Those who did not hold to Jezebel's teaching were exempt from the Lord's judgment. This is reminiscent of Moses coming down from the mountain.

> *Then Moses said, "This is how you will know that the Lord has sent me to do all these things and that it was not my idea: If these men die a natural death and experience only what usually happens to men, then the Lord has not sent me. But if the Lord brings about something totally new, and the earth opens its mouth and swallows them, with everything that belongs to them, and they go down alive into the grave, then you will know that these men have treated the Lord with contempt."*
>
> *As soon as he finished saying all this, the ground under them split apart and the earth opened its mouth and swallowed them, with their households and all Korah's men and all their possessions. They went down alive into the grave, with everything they owned; the earth closed over them, and they perished and were gone from the community. At their cries, all the Israelites around them fled, shouting, "The earth is going to swallow us too!" And fire came out from the Lord and consumed the 250 men who were offering the incense* (Numbers 16:28-35).

Our God is an awesome God, full of love and mercy, awesome in power, and faultless in judgment.

2:25 *"Only hold on to what you have until I come."*

The gospel of Jesus is not complicated, but it is impossible for sinful man to obey with human effort or understanding. You can only obtain spirituality through spiritual means, not natural or carnal means.

Lord Jesus, we need Your help to stay obedient and free from distractions and deception. Teach us how to follow You in the power of the Spirit and not our own strength. We want to hold on to what You have given us until You come. Amen.

The early church believed that Jesus would return in their lifetime. Much of today's church believes the Lord will return in this lifetime. The early church was wrong, and we will see if the modern church is wrong too. Someone once said, "We must act like the Lord will return tomorrow, but work like He will return in the next generation."

2:26-27 *"To him who overcomes and does my will to the end, I will give authority over the nations—'He will rule them with an iron scepter; he will dash them to pieces like pottery'—just as I have received authority from my Father."*

This promise is from Psalm 2, which we will refer to and quote again and again in *The Revelation Project*:

Why do the nations conspire and the peoples plot in vain? The kings of the earth take their stand and the rulers gather together against the Lord and against his Anointed One. "Let us break their chains," they say, "and throw off their fetters." The One enthroned in heaven laughs; the Lord scoffs at them. Then he rebukes them in his anger and terrifies them in his wrath, saying, "I have installed my King on Zion, my holy hill." I will proclaim the decree of the Lord: He said to me, "You are my Son; today I have become your Father. Ask of me, and I will make the nations your inheritance, the ends of the earth your possession. You will rule them with an iron scepter; you will dash them to pieces like pottery. Therefore, you kings, be wise; be warned, you rulers of the earth. Serve the Lord with fear and rejoice with trembling. Kiss the Son, lest he be angry and you be destroyed in your way, for his wrath can flare up in a moment. Blessed are all who take refuge in him.

The Church and followers of God will rule the earth, if not in this life, then the next. The Revelation church was encouraged with the promise that this present life was "training for reigning" and "schooling for ruling." Notice that the theme in Revelation is not a new one. The theme of victory is found in Genesis. Above we have a passage from the Psalms. Everything that began earlier in the Bible is shown to be complete in Revelation. I personally do not believe that the Church will fully reign in this age but certainly will in the one to come.

2:28 *"I will also give him the morning star."*

The morning star shines brightly before the sun appears. It is a sign in the heavens that darkness may reign but light is coming. Jesus was a bright star in the midst of great darkness, which is also the legacy of the Church. We will not extinguish the darkness completely, but we are an indication that something better is available in and from the Lord. For those who overcome, God will give them encouragement that better days are ahead.

2:29 *"He who has an ear, let him hear what the Spirit says to the churches."*

Are you listening to what the Spirit is saying? That doesn't mean you become strange, but that you are listening and are sensitive to the Spirit. How is your journal coming along, by the way? Are you still recording the insights that God has given you while you read and study?

3:1 *"To the angel of the church in Sardis write: These are the words of him who holds the seven spirits of God and the seven stars. I know your deeds; you have a reputation of being alive, but you are dead."*

You can fool some people, but you can't fool God! Jesus knew the true condition of this church regardless of what they appeared to be. The Church is a large, complex organism encompassing many nations, languages, and customs. Yet Jesus holds the churches in His hand. Things may be big to us, but they aren't to the Lord. You may not like what is going on in your church, but quite frankly, it's not your church! It belongs to Jesus. The question is: Is Jesus happy with what is going on in your church?

If you are in a leadership position, you must keep in mind that it isn't your church. You are serving as God's representative and cannot simply lead according to your own tastes or preferences. You must lead and represent God and His interests. You must also work with His people, not just those with whom you have more in common or whose personalities are more to your liking. Remember what Peter wrote:

To the elders among you, I appeal as a fellow elder, a witness of Christ's sufferings and one who also will share in the glory to be revealed: Be shepherds of God's flock that is under your care, serving as overseers— not because you must, but because you are willing, as God wants you to be; not greedy for money, but eager to serve; not lording it over those en-

trusted to you, but being examples to the flock. And when the Chief Shepherd appears, you will receive the crown of glory that will never fade away (1 Peter 5:1-4).

The Church is not a club but a living entity for which Jesus gave His life. He is the Chief Shepherd. You should not withhold your gifts or time because you have been hurt in church situations. Jesus gave His life for the Church; He shed His blood on her behalf. Can you do any less?

Do you know your place in the body? What are your spiritual gifts? Consider the following verses from 1 Corinthians 12.

Now to each one the manifestation of the Spirit is given for the common good (v. 7). *But in fact God has arranged the parts in the body, every one of them, just as he wanted them to be* (v. 18). *Now you are the body of Christ, and each one of you is a part of it* (v. 27)

The writer of Hebrews wrote, "Let us not give up meeting together, as some are in the habit of doing, but let us encourage one another—and all the more as you see the Day approaching" (Hebrews 10:25).

Some people complain about their church hurts (and there are many real, painful stories). Think of the pain, however, that Jesus went through for the Church. I can certainly empathize with anyone who has been hurt in church, but you and I cannot go home and sulk in disillusionment. We must be an active part of Christ's body, and we can't do that sitting at home or watching a church service on television. You should not withhold your emotional or financial support because you don't like how the money is spent. Find another church where you agree but don't stop giving!

3:2 *"Wake up! Strengthen what remains and is about to die, for I have not found your deeds complete in the sight of my God."*

This church in 3:2 was asleep, and God sent it a wakeup call. We can be lulled to sleep thinking we have a better doctrine, programs, or staff than other churches. Being better than other churches, however, doesn't mean that Jesus is pleased. After all, to whom much is given, much is required. Jesus didn't seem to take issue with their holiness but rather their deeds. In my opinion, many "holy people" are irrelevant when it comes to spreading the gospel or accomplishing God's purposes.

Proverbs 20:11 states, "Even a child is known by his actions, by whether his conduct is pure and right." God is interested in actions, but this church wasn't chastised for its lack of holiness but for its lack of deeds.

3:3 *"Remember, therefore, what you have received and heard; obey it, and repent. But if you do not wake up, I will come like a thief, and you will not know at what time I will come to you."*

Here is the order of progression: 1) wake up; 2) remember; 3) obey; 4) repent. Do you follow that order in your life concerning any issue?

God is patient, but Peter wrote: "The Lord is not slow in keeping his promise, as some understand slowness. He is patient with you, not wanting anyone to perish, but everyone to come to repentance" (2 Peter 3:9). Don't mistake God's patience for His approval.

3:4 *"Yet you have a few people in Sardis who have not soiled their clothes. They will walk with me, dressed in white, for they are worthy."*

God is always able to save the few from among the disobedient many. God isn't into blanket judgment. He judges every individual according to his or her deeds. Can you think of any biblical examples of this? How about the Lord's discussion with Abraham in Genesis 18 concerning Sodom and Gomorrah? Another example is when Noah and his sons were saved while everyone else perished (see Genesis 6). God blessed the Israelites in Goshen while the plagues were afflicting Egypt (see Exodus 8:22). Joshua and Caleb entered the land while the rest of the spies, who brought a bad report, never did (see Numbers 14:21-24). Are there any others you can think of or find?

Study 9: Revelation 3:5-9

3:5 *"He who overcomes will, like them, be dressed in white. I will never blot out his name from the book of life, but will acknowledge his name before my Father and his angels."*

Clothing is an important symbol in the Bible. How you are dressed often symbolically represents your status in the sight of God. Outward garments can be used to hide what is in the heart. Those who overcome in Revelation will be dressed in white. Their garments will mirror their heart condition and their standing before God.

"All of us have become like one who is unclean, and all our righteous acts are like filthy rags; we all shrivel up like a leaf, and like the wind our sins sweep us away" (Isaiah 64:6). Here you see that the Lord described their spiritual condition by the clothes they wore. God responds to you in the same way that you respond to Him. In some manner of speaking, you control how God treats you. Consider this passage:

> *The Lord has rewarded me according to my righteousness, according to the cleanness of my hands in his sight. To the faithful you show yourself faithful, to the blameless you show yourself blameless, to the pure you show yourself pure, but to the crooked you show yourself shrewd* (Psalm 18:24-26).

Consider also the words of Jesus:

> *Whoever acknowledges me before men, I will also acknowledge him before my Father in heaven. But whoever disowns me before men, I will disown him before my Father in heaven* (Matthew 10:32-33).

If you aren't happy with how God is responding to you at this time, could the problem be how you are responding to Him? If He seems distant, are you? If He is cold toward you, are you cold toward Him? Perhaps you need to repent of your attitude. God is actually acting as a mirror for your own behavior!

3:6 *"He who has an ear, let him hear what the Spirit says to the churches."*

Jesus said this same thing while on earth: "He who has ears, let him hear" (Matthew 11:15). Consider these other verses about hearing:

> *"If anyone has ears to hear, let him hear. Consider carefully what you hear," he continued. "With the measure you use, it will be measured to you—and even more. Whoever has will be given more; whoever does not have, even what he has will be taken from him"* (Mark 4:23-25).

> *Those along the path are the ones who hear, and then the devil comes and takes away the word from their hearts, so that they may not believe and be saved. Those on the rock are the ones who receive the word with joy when they hear it, but they have no root. They believe for a while, but in the time of testing they fall away. The seed that fell among thorns stands for those who hear, but as they go on their way they are choked by*

life's worries, riches and pleasures, and they do not mature. But the seed on good soil stands for those with a noble and good heart, who hear the word, retain it, and by persevering produce a crop (Luke 8:12-15).

By the way, how is your journal coming? Are you recording what you believe (by faith) you are hearing from God? There can be "flesh around your ears" that prevents you from hearing correctly. The problem is not whether or not God is speaking but whether or not you can hear: "You stiff-necked people, with uncircumcised hearts and ears! You are just like your fathers: You always resist the Holy Spirit!" (Acts 7:51).

Ask God to circumcise your ears. Remember Proverbs 20:12: "Ears that hear and eyes that see—the Lord has made them both." God has made your ears to hear Him. He knows what is blocking your hearing and can heal your deafness! Often it isn't what you think, and you need His help to see the real problem.

Many people in the gospel accounts heard Jesus' voice and words but had no idea what He was saying. They had spiritual impediments to hearing effectively.

> *Then some Pharisees and teachers of the law came to Jesus from Jerusalem and asked, "Why do your disciples break the tradition of the elders? They don't wash their hands before they eat!" Jesus replied, "And why do you break the command of God for the sake of your tradition? For God said, 'Honor your father and mother' and 'Anyone who curses his father or mother must be put to death.' But you say that if a man says to his father or mother, 'Whatever help you might otherwise have received from me is a gift devoted to God,' he is not to 'honor his father' with it. Thus you nullify the word of God for the sake of your tradition. You hypocrites! Isaiah was right when he prophesied about you: "These people honor me with their lips, but their hearts are far from me. They worship me in vain; their teachings are but rules taught by men." Jesus called the crowd to him and said, "Listen and understand"* (Matthew 15:1-10).

3:7 *"To the angel of the church in Philadelphia write: These are the words of him who is holy and true, who holds the key of David. What he opens no one can shut, and what he shuts no one can open."*

What is this key of David mentioned in 3:7? Let's see if the context where it is used provides any clues or the actual interpretation. If the Bible does not explain what is meant by something obscure, then we must be careful not to impose our own interpretation. You are always on safe ground when the Bible interprets itself.

A key opens and locks doors, and that is what Jesus is talking about in this verse. He opens and shuts doors, and no one can close (or reverse) what He has used the key to open. For what was David best known? He was known for music and worship, warfare, government, and providing for the building of the temple. Can you think of anything else?

These are the aspects that Jesus controls in His church: He draws men to worship Him; He is the Victor who has vanquished sin and the devil; He rules in the affairs of the Church; He builds the new temple of His people and lives in their midst. So in every way, He truly does hold the key of David!

This is another reminder of Jesus' supremacy in the Church. The Church is not about men and women but always about Jesus. No leaders are mentioned by name, for leaders come and go, but Jesus abides forever as the head of His Church.

3:8 *"I know your deeds. See, I have placed before you an open door that no one can shut. I know that you have little strength, yet you have kept my word and have not denied my name."*

You are reminded again that Jesus is well aware of all your deeds. You cannot hide from Him or deny what you have done. You can ask His forgiveness, which cancels the sin in His sight. It doesn't necessarily cancel the affects of the sin, but He no longer holds it against you.

When Jesus opens a door, consider it open! Paul wrote to the Corinthians: "Because a great door for effective work has opened to me, and there are many who oppose me" (1 Corinthians 16:9). It seems that adversaries gather around open doors. In fact, the greater the opportunity for God, the more opposition you may incur. Opposition may actually serve as confirmation that you are doing the will of God.

This church had a little strength. Yet they had kept Jesus' word and had not denied His name. It is one of the churches toward which Jesus had nothing negative to say. Even though they had little strength, He was pleased with them. Often believers do not act because they are waiting for the strength to act. God will not give you the strength you need until you act. Look at the following verse and see that the saints only received strength when they went into battle, not before:

And what more shall I say? I do not have time to tell about Gideon, Barak, Samson, Jephthah, David, Samuel and the prophets, who through faith conquered kingdoms, administered justice, and gained what was promised; who shut the mouths of lions, quenched the fury of the flames, and escaped the edge of the sword; whose weakness was turned to strength; and who became powerful in battle and routed foreign armies (Hebrews 11:32-34).

3:9 *"I will make those who are of the synagogue of Satan, who claim to be Jews though they are not, but are liars—I will make them come and fall down at your feet and acknowledge that I have loved you."*

When will what is described in 3:9 happen, in this life or in the one to come? I think it is in the one to come. The more important lesson here, however, is that Jesus has control over your enemies. He says, "I will make them come and fall down." Jesus is in control not only of the Church but also of all things!

As stated earlier in Study 2, Colossians 3:3 has an interesting concept: "For you died, and your life is now hidden with Christ in God." Your life is now hidden in Christ. For something to get to you, it must first get through Him. Jesus is in charge of my life. He determines what honor or persecution I will receive. I trust Him, so that what gets to me must have His approval. The Lord is my shepherd. He watches over my life.

It seems that all who call themselves a church (or synagogue) may not be a church of God. This verse indicates that there are gatherings of the evil one. Not all who claim to be Christians (or Jews) are worthy of that label, which confuses so many people. To take on the name of the Lord is easier than to live in a manner consistent with the glory of that name.

Study 10: Revelation 3:10-13

3:10 *"Since you have kept my command to endure patiently, I will also keep you from the hour of trial that is going to come upon the whole world to test those who live on the earth."*

My flesh doesn't want to endure a bad situation. I want to be free from suffering and pain, and be in control of my reputation and circumstances.

Such conditions are not possible if I am a Christian. Christ rules in my life and brings what I need, whether I understand that I need it or not. Suffering adds much to your life as nothing else can. It teaches you faith in God, develops patience, and helps you identify with others who are in pain.

Let's look at all the verses in the New Testament that instruct us to endure:

> *We work hard with our own hands. When we are cursed, we bless; when we are persecuted, we endure it* (1 Corinthians 4:12).

> *We do not want you to be uninformed, brothers, about the hardships we suffered in the province of Asia. We were under great pressure, far beyond our ability to endure, so that we despaired even of life* (2 Corinthians 1:8).

> *Endure hardship with us like a good soldier of Christ Jesus* (2 Timothy 2:3).

> *Therefore I endure everything for the sake of the elect, that they too may obtain the salvation that is in Christ Jesus, with eternal glory* (2 Timothy 2:10).

> *If we endure, we will also reign with him. If we disown him, he will also disown us* (2 Timothy 2:12).

> *But you, keep your head in all situations, endure hardship, do the work of an evangelist, discharge all the duties of your ministry* (2 Timothy 4:5).

> *Endure hardship as discipline; God is treating you as sons. For what son is not disciplined by his father?* (Hebrews 12:7).

> *But how is it to your credit if you receive a beating for doing wrong and endure it? But if you suffer for doing good and you endure it, this is commendable before God* (1 Peter 2:20).

Jesus said, "You have obeyed my command" and then says to endure. He said this through Peter and Paul, who were writing the Word of God. So when they wrote the verses above, they were writing Jesus' commands. Jesus considers the New Testament His commands, whether He said them or inspired them to be written by men through the Holy Spirit.

Jesus referred to an hour of trial coming upon the whole earth. Jesus is

Study 10: Revelation 3:10-13

the God of history. There isn't a period of secular history in which God has not been involved. The Old Testament prophets did not just have a word for Israel; they often had a word for the other nations that weren't part of God's covenant Israel. They had a word for everyone because God rules over all.

We saw in Study 7 that God is able to preserve His people from the judgment that is around them. God may not save His people from tribulation but may rather save them in or through tribulation.

3:11 *"I am coming soon. Hold on to what you have, so that no one will take your crown."*

The word *soon* in 3:11 means "soon." It doesn't mean two thousand years from the time it was spoken. That isn't soon. What was Jesus saying in 3:11? Second Peter 3:8 tells us that God doesn't view time as we do, for a day can be as a thousand years. Yet that is small consolation for someone who, for instance, must endure persecution at the hands of members from the synagogue of Satan.

As I write, I am almost sixty years old. The days and weeks are moving quickly. Five years from now doesn't seem as long as it used to seem. I am also much closer to death than I was twenty years ago, and those years have gone by quickly. In other words, Jesus is coming to my world soon.

Tribulation causes you to press into God in such a way that you are delivered from the urgency and pain of the situation. God can become so close and real to you that He has in a sense delivered you without changing the circumstances. When we see that He is all in all, the pressure seems less difficult. He has transferred you in this life to a place where you see the reality that Paul wrote about to the Ephesian church:

> *As for you, you were dead in your transgressions and sins, in which you used to live when you followed the ways of this world and of the ruler of the kingdom of the air, the spirit who is now at work in those who are disobedient. All of us also lived among them at one time, gratifying the cravings of our sinful nature and following its desires and thoughts.*
>
> *Like the rest, we were by nature objects of wrath. But because of his great love for us, God, who is rich in mercy, made us alive with Christ even when we were dead in transgressions—it is by grace you have been saved. And God raised us up with Christ and seated us with him in the heavenly realms in Christ Jesus* (Ephesians 2:1-6).

You are seated in heavenly places. That means you are above the cares of life with Him where He dwells. Almost every generation has thought it is the last generation before the Lord returns. This one is no exception. Can God make Himself so close to us that we feel like His return is imminent? Yes He can and does. Therefore He does intervene soon and deliver us from the pressure of the day. He does so by His presence in the power of the Spirit.

One more thought: Paul wrote about his suffering at the hands of those who belong to Satan's synagogue, and this is what he wrote:

> *Therefore we do not lose heart. Though outwardly we are wasting away, yet inwardly we are being renewed day by day. For our light and momentary troubles are achieving for us an eternal glory that far outweighs them all. So we fix our eyes not on what is seen, but on what is unseen. For what is seen is temporary, but what is unseen is eternal* (2 Corinthians 4:16-19).

Doesn't Paul sound like someone who already has the help and deliverance he needed from a difficult situation? Does this describe help that has come already to relieve his distress? Is this what Jesus was promising those churches in Revelation?

3:12 *"Him who overcomes I will make a pillar in the temple of my God. Never again will he leave it. I will write on him the name of my God and the name of the city of my God, the new Jerusalem, which is coming down out of heaven from my God; and I will also write on him my new name."*

You can (and must) come to a place where God is all and all. Everything else pales by comparison. You yield yourself to Him, and He is with you in a new and lasting intimacy.

Consider Enoch in the book of Genesis: "Enoch walked with God; then he was no more, because God took him away (Genesis 5:24). I am not suggesting you will be taken like Enoch, but suffering and maturity can cause you to become so close to God that everything else pales by comparison. You walk with Him and He becomes your life. In that sense, you have a new identity and walk in this life as if you are already in the next one. Paul wrote to the Philippians, "For to me, to live is Christ and to die is gain" (Philippians 1:21). He also wrote to the Galatians:

I have been crucified with Christ and I no longer live, but Christ lives in me. The life I live in the body, I live by faith in the Son of God, who loved me and gave himself for me (Galatians 2:20).

You get the sense from Paul's words that he was not talking about something that may happen to him; it had already happened. He was living in it and saw it clearly. If and when I get to that kind of relationship with Christ, the things of this world cannot affect me like they once did. Christ has indeed delivered me in every situation, but the fullness of that deliverance may not yet be reality. Is this too mystical or otherworldly? I hope not, for I want to be joined to Christ in such a way that I live the truth that "For in him we live and move and have our being" (Acts 17:28).

When that happens, you are a pillar, unmovable and steadfast. You belong to God. You are His servant in His church and nothing can change that, not even the failure of His servants or the imperfections of His Church. When you overcome, it means that you have come over some obstacles. There is no other way to be an overcomer! You cannot earn this title without going through and over some difficulties.

3:13 *"He who has an ear, let him hear what the Spirit says to the churches."*

What is the Spirit saying to you? Are you honoring it by writing it down? You aren't sure if it is the Spirit saying it to you? You can never be sure; that is where faith comes in. You must trust that you have heard from the Lord without being weird about it. Some people say they've heard strange things and are not open to input that what they heard may not be from God. I may often say, "God spoke to me." Yet I would not be shocked if I was wrong, misheard or misinterpreted what I thought I heard. Yet that would not make God or His ability to speak to me any less real.

"For we know in part and we prophesy in part" (1 Corinthians 13:9). This verse doesn't indicate that you don't know anything. It's just that you don't know it all. That doesn't make you any less spiritual, and it doesn't excuse you from walking out what you think you know or what you know in part.

Study 11: Revelation 3:14-22

3:14 *"To the angel of the church in Laodicea write: These are the words of the Amen, the faithful and true witness, the ruler of God's creation."*

The titles and descriptions used for Jesus in this verse cause me to think of what He said just before His crucifixion:

As for the person who hears my words but does not keep them, I do not judge him. For I did not come to judge the world, but to save it. There is a judge for the one who rejects me and does not accept my words; that very word which I spoke will condemn him at the last day. For I did not speak of my own accord, but the Father who sent me commanded me what to say and how to say it. I know that his command leads to eternal life. So whatever I say is just what the Father has told me to say (John 12:47-50).

Jesus was so obedient that He only said those things that the Father told Him to say. In addition, He said them in the way that the Father told Him to say them. It is not only important what you say, but how you say them. "Let your conversation be always full of grace, seasoned with salt, so that you may know how to answer everyone" (Colossians 4:6).

How has your tongue been behaving lately? Are you saying the things you feel prompted by God to say? Are you saying them in a way that makes what you have to say more acceptable to the hearer? As a public speaker, I ask God for the grace to speak His words in the way Jesus would speak them if He were present. As a supervisor and pastor, I ask the Lord to help me speak gracious one-on-one words too. I am not always successful, as James warned:

Not many of you should presume to be teachers, my brothers, because you know that we who teach will be judged more strictly. We all stumble in many ways. If anyone is never at fault in what he says, he is a perfect man, able to keep his whole body in check (James 3:1-2).

The Bible has so much to say about your words. They don't need much explanation, but here are a few other passages on the tongue: "Instead, speaking the truth in love, we will in all things grow up into him who is the Head, that is, Christ" (Ephesians 4:15). This is what Jesus was doing to the

Study 11: Revelation 3:14-22

seven churches in Revelation. He was speaking the truth in love to each church. Jesus never asks us to do anything He hasn't done. I stopped trying to speak the truth in love as often as I once did because I realized that many times I did not have enough truth or love to fulfill the intent of this verse. That has caused me to exercise a lot more grace where people are concerned and also to do a lot more listening.

"From the fruit of his mouth a man's stomach is filled; with the harvest from his lips he is satisfied. The tongue has the power of life and death, and those who love it will eat its fruit" (Proverbs 18:20-21). Those are powerful verses. My words have the power to give life or to take life away. Unfortunately, I have used words that take the life out of people all too often. Forgive me, Lord.

3:15-16 *"I know your deeds, that you are neither cold nor hot. I wish you were either one or the other! Because you are lukewarm—neither hot nor cold—I am about to spit you out of my mouth."*

When I think of someone who was spiritually cold, I think of Saul before his conversion on the Damascus road. He was about as cold as a non-Christian can be! Yet the Lord chose him to preach the gospel to the Gentiles. Perhaps Saul wasn't cold but rather hot!

God is not turned off by sin. By that I mean He does not always shun people in sin. In Exodus, He revealed who the spies were to Rahab the harlot before she left her life of sin (see Joshua 2). She was not even a Jew. Hebrews 11 contains many accounts of imperfect people whom God used. Jesus' earthly ministry produced many stories of hot and cold sinners with whom Jesus got along very well. It was the lukewarm Pharisees that caused Him the most aggravation.

My point is that the Church often avoids those who are cold or in sin, but God doesn't. In fact, Jesus said in these verses that He prefers people who are at an extreme as opposed to those who are lukewarm, who are neither good saints nor effective sinners!

3:17 *"You say, 'I am rich; I have acquired wealth and do not need a thing.' But you do not realize that you are wretched, pitiful, poor, blind and naked."*

This verse describes perhaps the worst spiritual condition to be in: to think you are in a good place with God when you are not. That is the epitome of being lukewarm. Jesus expects you to assess your situation accurately and not hold onto a false sense of spiritual security or superiority. In fact, if you are honest, you will admit that you have no spiritual worth apart from Jesus and His righteousness.

John wrote in his epistle,

If we claim to be without sin, we deceive ourselves and the truth is not in us. If we confess our sins, he is faithful and just and will forgive us our sins and purify us from all unrighteousness. If we claim we have not sinned, we make him out to be a liar and his word has no place in our lives (1 John 1:8-10).

It is only those who realize their need for God's grace who receive it on a continual basis. Jesus told a parable to this affect in Luke:

Two men went up to the temple to pray, one a Pharisee and the other a tax collector. The Pharisee stood up and prayed about himself: "God, I thank you that I am not like other men—robbers, evildoers, adulterers— or even like this tax collector. I fast twice a week and give a tenth of all I get." But the tax collector stood at a distance. He would not even look up to heaven, but beat his breast and said, "God, have mercy on me, a sinner." I tell you that this man, rather than the other, went home justified before God. For everyone who exalts himself will be humbled, and he who humbles himself will be exalted (Luke 18:10-14).

I regularly spend time confessing my sins to God. Maybe that is just part of me from my Catholic upbringing. I do not wallow in my sins, but I try to be conscious that I am needy before God, needy of His grace and forgiveness. Do you do the same? Do you cultivate a healthy awareness of who you are before God? Is this what Jesus called being poor in spirit (see Matthew 5:3)?

3:18 *I counsel you to buy from me gold refined in the fire, so you can become rich; and white clothes to wear, so you can cover your shameful nakedness; and salve to put on your eyes, so you can see.*

Jesus is the perfect Counselor. He assesses your situation and gives you direction that helps you escape and overcome your own waywardness. As unhappy as He is with this church in 3:18, He offered them a way out. God is merciful! He is patient, desiring that none perish but that all come to a knowledge of the truth.

Study 11: Revelation 3:14-22

While God is full of grace, He requires that you pay some price for what you receive from Him. It may cost you your pride, dignity, way of thinking, or standing before people, but a price must be paid. What price are you willing to pay to be right with God? He urged them to buy three things:

• Gold, which represents that which is durable yet malleable. This may represent His divine nature, available through the power of the Holy Spirit as Christ is formed in you. You are not a god, but you become like Him, conformed to the image of the Son.

• White clothes, which represent a standard of righteousness that you can never attain in your own strength but only in the power of God. Only the Holy Spirit can convict you of sin and only the Spirit can clothe you in the righteousness of God.

• Eye salve, which helps you see yourself as you really are: in desperate need of God and His grace. When Ananias prayed for Saul in Acts 9, something like scales fell from Saul's eyes and Saul could see again. I cannot trust my own vision and insight; I need help from God to see.

3:19 *Those whom I love I rebuke and discipline. So be earnest, and repent.*

Jesus loved those seven churches of Revelation. That is why He sent His words to them, and disciplined and rebuked them where necessary. It is always a sign of God's love when He shows you the truth about yourself or a situation. If God ignores you, you are in serious trouble!

Let's look at these verses that speak of God's love and discipline. Do any apply to you at this time?

Blessed is the man whom God corrects; so do not despise the discipline of the Almighty (Job 5:17).

Lord, do not rebuke me in your anger or discipline me in your wrath. Be merciful to me, Lord, for I am faint; O Lord, heal me, for my bones are in agony (Psalm 6:1-2).

My son, do not despise the Lord's discipline and do not resent his rebuke, because the Lord disciplines those he loves, as a father the son he delights in (Proverbs 3:11-12).

For these commands are a lamp, this teaching is a light, and the corrections of discipline are the way to life (Proverbs 6:23).

And you have forgotten that word of encouragement that addresses you as sons: "My son, do not make light of the Lord's discipline, and do not lose heart when he rebukes you, because the Lord disciplines those he loves, and he punishes everyone he accepts as a son."

Endure hardship as discipline; God is treating you as sons. For what son is not disciplined by his father? If you are not disciplined (and everyone undergoes discipline), then you are illegitimate children and not true sons. Moreover, we have all had human fathers who disciplined us and we respected them for it. How much more should we submit to the Father of our spirits and live! Our fathers disciplined us for a little while as they thought best; but God disciplines us for our good, that we may share in his holiness.

No discipline seems pleasant at the time, but painful. Later on, however, it produces a harvest of righteousness and peace for those who have been trained by it. Therefore, strengthen your feeble arms and weak knees (Hebrews 12:5-12).

3:20 *"Here I am! I stand at the door and knock. If anyone hears my voice and opens the door, I will come in and eat with him, and he with me."*

He stands at the door and knocks. We have the choice to open the door or not. Jesus initiates fellowship and relationship with us by speaking to us through His Word or through others. Notice He says, "I knock" and then "if anyone hears my voice." We open the door when we listen.

God is always speaking. The question is are we listening and obeying? If God wants us to do His will, He must tell us what that will is. Therefore, in faith, we can count on God's desire to speak to us. God is an effective communicator. He speaks every language but can also get His message through to us using circumstances, His Word, or other people. How does God usually speak to you?

3:21 *"To him who overcomes, I will give the right to sit with me on my throne, just as I overcame and sat down with my Father on his throne."*

Jesus did not accomplish what He did on earth simply by being God. He was a human like you and me and overcame by relying on the power of the Holy Spirit. We will overcome as He did by following His example. We should never lose sight of the fact that Jesus was like us in every way except sin. He left us a legacy of how to please the Father and do His will. Consider these passages that relate to Jesus humanity and see how you can apply them to your walk of faith.

> *But we see Jesus, who was made a little lower than the angels, now crowned with glory and honor because he suffered death, so that by the grace of God he might taste death for everyone. In bringing many sons to glory, it was fitting that God, for whom and through whom everything exists, should make the author of their salvation perfect through suffering* (Hebrews 2:9-10).

> *During the days of Jesus' life on earth, he offered up prayers and petitions with loud cries and tears to the one who could save him from death, and he was heard because of his reverent submission. Although he was a son, he learned obedience from what he suffered and, once made perfect, he became the source of eternal salvation for all who obey him* (Hebrews 5:7-9).

> *Therefore, since we have a great high priest who has gone through the heavens, Jesus the Son of God, let us hold firmly to the faith we profess. For we do not have a high priest who is unable to sympathize with our weaknesses, but we have one who has been tempted in every way, just as we are—yet was without sin. Let us then approach the throne of grace with confidence, so that we may receive mercy and find grace to help us in our time of need* (Hebrews 4:14-16).

I especially appreciate the last passage. Because Jesus experienced my humanity, I come to His throne with confidence that I will receive grace when I need it most. Jesus' throne is not to be feared but embraced! When you sin, it is time to run to God and not away from God.

3:22 *"He who has an ear, let him hear what the Spirit says to the churches."*

What is the Spirit saying today? Ask God in faith to let you hear and then trust that He will speak to you. By the way, how is your journal coming along in which you record what you believe God is showing you? If you need help with being able to hear God, consider this passage from Isaiah, for God is able to open your ears to hear His Word:

> *The Sovereign Lord has given me an instructed tongue, to know the word that sustains the weary. He wakens me morning by morning, wakens my ear to listen like one being taught. The Sovereign Lord has opened my ears, and I have not been rebellious; I have not drawn back* (Isaiah 50:4-5).

If you are not rebellious and don't draw back from the Lord, then He will open your ears to hear what the Spirit is saying to the churches. Let it be, Lord.

Study 12: Revelation 4:1-7

4:1 *After this I looked, and there before me was a door standing open in heaven. And the voice I had first heard speaking to me like a trumpet said, "Come up here, and I will show you what must take place after this."*

When you see things from heaven's perspective, you are much better off. These churches were living in the midst of political turmoil and religious persecution. Yet the Lord did not take them to Rome or some other earthly place, He took them to heaven!

The voice talking to John was like a trumpet. A blown trumpet is hard to miss. Often God is speaking loudly and clearly, but you miss what He is saying due to disobedience, hardness of heart, or an expectation that God will say something other than what He is actually saying. Your problem hearing God is often the same that you encounter in communicating with other people. Even though they are talking to you face to face, you can miss or misunderstand what they are saying for a variety of reasons.

He ordered John to "come up here." That makes me think of what Paul wrote to the Ephesians:

> *And God raised us up with Christ and seated us with him in the heavenly realms in Christ Jesus, in order that in the coming ages he might show the incomparable riches of his grace, expressed in his kindness to us in Christ Jesus* (Ephesians 2:6-7).

Study 12: Revelation 4:1-7

You experience resurrection life, having been raised with Christ, and now you are seated where He is. You do not bring Christ down to where you are, but rather join Him where He is.

John saw an open door in heaven. When God calls you to Himself, it is an exciting thing! God opens His world to you and that is the thing upon which you need to focus; that is where you need to go. Is there an open window in heaven for you? What is God saying to you? What are you seeing?

You should get the idea after reading this verse that God has everything under control. The words "after this" are used twice in this verse. God orders your affairs. There is no need for anxiety when He knows all the "after this" situations in your life.

4:2 *At once I was in the Spirit, and there before me was a throne in heaven with someone sitting on it.*

John saw more of what was going on in the Church and in the world from Patmos because he was in the Spirit. The open door in heaven led him to a throne, a symbol of power and authority. It is not an empty throne, but someone is on it. Kings sit on thrones and rule people in their kingdom. Jesus does not sit on a literal throne, but this is a picture we can understand of His position in creation.

You are to pray in the Spirit (see Ephesians 6:18) and love in the Spirit (see Colossians 3:18). In essence, you are to live in the Spirit, seeing what the Spirit sees and living by the Spirit's directives. This is what's called a Spirit-led life. This is not the exception but the rule. Are you living a Spirit-led life?

4:3 *And the one who sat there had the appearance of jasper and carnelian. A rainbow, resembling an emerald, encircled the throne.*

How can you describe heaven and God? Finite words can never do justice describing an infinite God set in the magnificence of heaven. So the Bible provides metaphors and similes to help you understand some of what He is like.

Heaven must be a colorful place! You are taken from the problems and weakness of the seven churches in the first three chapters to the splendor of heaven. You and I can get so hung up on earthly things, but the Spirit is contrasting for us the two worlds of earth and heaven. Where should your focus be? Which one is more beautiful? The Spirit is directing your attention to where it should be—on heavenly things!

4:4 *Surrounding the throne were twenty-four other thrones, and seated on them were twenty-four elders. They were dressed in white and had crowns of gold on their heads.*

Heaven is not only a place of beauty, but it is also a place of government. Elders historically sat at the gates of the city and ruled the affairs of that city, sort of like a city council. One of Jesus' titles is King of Kings. Jesus does not rule alone in the kingdom of God, but He is supreme ruler. You and I share in that heavenly government when we rule the portions of the kingdom that God assigns to us. We are kings with a little *k*, but He is the King with the capital *K*.

Any authority you have as a believer comes from the ultimate authority, the throne of God. Your ruling is centered on His throne and your qualifications—along with your white robes and crown—come from Him. You are made worthy to rule by means of Jesus' sacrifice and also by the fact that King Jesus rules in heaven.

There seems to be a partnership in this picture between heaven and the Church. The government of God is often delegated to His servants. I wonder if this is what the elders represent? This also appears to indicate that the Church is a heavenly entity and is not just relegated to work on earth. There is a comingling and partnership between heaven and earth and this is best expressed in the life of the Church.

4:5 *From the throne came flashes of lightning, rumblings and peals of thunder. Before the throne, seven lamps were blazing. These are the seven spirits of God.*

Heaven can also be a terrifying place to those who do not know God or His voice. It is hard to think of heaven like this, but many are afraid of God's presence. If they have not had their sins forgiven and are not washed in the blood of the Lamb, a sinner would be terrified at God's presence, for God is indeed awesome. Consider the words of the writer of Hebrews:

> *You have not come to a mountain that can be touched and that is burning with fire; to darkness, gloom and storm; to a trumpet blast or to such a voice speaking words that those who heard it begged that no fur-*

ther word be spoken to them, because they could not bear what was commanded: "If even an animal touches the mountain, it must be stoned." The sight was so terrifying that Moses said, "I am trembling with fear."

But you have come to Mount Zion, to the heavenly Jerusalem, the city of the living God. You have come to thousands upon thousands of angels in joyful assembly, to the church of the firstborn, whose names are written in heaven. You have come to God, the judge of all men, to the spirits of righteous men made perfect (Hebrews 12:18-23).

The story involving Moses in the passage above is from Exodus 19:16-25. The people wanted to hear God for themselves, but when He spoke they were so terrified that they changed their minds and told Moses to report all that God said. They had a heavenly encounter with God on earth, and it was a fearful thing. They chose instead for Moses to be their mediator with and representative to God. We also need a Mediator with God and His name is Jesus. He took the fear out of approaching God through His death and resurrection.

The lightning and thunder from the throne are symbolic of God's voice that goes forth from His seat of government. Lightning and thunder can also evoke fear at the wonder of nature and its God-given power. Consider Psalm 29 and how it describes the voice of God:

Ascribe to the Lord, O mighty ones, ascribe to the Lord glory and strength. Ascribe to the Lord the glory due his name; worship the Lord in the splendor of his holiness. The voice of the Lord is over the waters; the God of glory thunders, the Lord thunders over the mighty waters. The voice of the Lord is powerful; the voice of the Lord is majestic. The voice of the Lord breaks the cedars; the Lord breaks in pieces the cedars of Lebanon.

He makes Lebanon skip like a calf, Sirion like a young wild ox. The voice of the Lord strikes with flashes of lightning. The voice of the Lord shakes the desert; the Lord shakes the Desert of Kadesh. The voice of the Lord twists the oaks and strips the forests bare. And in his temple all cry, "Glory!" The Lord sits enthroned over the flood; the Lord is enthroned as King forever. The Lord gives strength to his people; the Lord blesses his people with peace.

Seven lamps are placed before the throne. God's Word brings light to every situation. "Your word is a lamp to my feet and a light for my path"

(Psalm 119:105). As stated before, the number seven is generally considered the number of completion in the Bible. God's Word provides perfect and complete light to any and every situation with no shadows. It is pure light! You can trust its perspective and content; it is straightforward and sure.

The seven spirits have also equipped the Church with all good gifts and knowledge to rule and carry out the mission of God's people on earth. Heaven and earth enjoy a partnership as expressed by the relationship of the Church and the Spirit. The saints are seated in heaven yet carry out heaven's will here on earth. We are not alone!

4:6 *Also before the throne there was what looked like a sea of glass, clear as crystal. In the center, around the throne, were four living creatures, and they were covered with eyes, in front and in back.*

Heaven is a place of purity. The "sea of glass" can serve to reflect God's radiance and beauty, thus taking what is already magnificent and making it even more dazzling. God's beauty has no end! No matter how much of His glory we behold, there is still much more to see. Heaven is also a place of transparency. No hidden agendas or lack of pure integrity exist in heaven. As one hymn said, "No shadow of turning with Thee." Everything is clear and pure: the worship, God's Word, God's will, and God's people. The Church needs to apply those two principles as well in all its business: purity and transparency.

In 4:6 four creatures are described that were covered with eyes. The book of Revelation is of course a vision; however, so much of what is contained therein is symbolic. You must be careful not to insist that there is only one way of interpreting and applying these symbols. If the Bible does not directly interpret the symbols, then you must be careful not to insist that you have special and exclusive insight into what they mean.

Symbols are given for reflection and learning, discussion and insight into deeper truths, and our objective for *The Revelation Project* is to determine how the early church applied this book to their daily walk so we can do the same. The symbols had to have meaning then as they do now. You cannot be dogmatic about the book of Revelation and insist you have the answers to its secrets. It is a book of wonder but not meant to be interpreted rigidly or dogmatically.

The life of the creatures does not come from themselves but from their position around the throne. The Church receives its life from God Himself.

Heaven is the source of everything for the Church. Heaven is also the headquarters for the Church and its source of light, insight and direction. Yet the Church functions here on earth with heavenly orders.

4:7 *The first living creature was like a lion, the second was like an ox, the third had a face like a man, the fourth was like a flying eagle.*

Four living creatures are alive and watching. They represent the role of the Church on earth. The lion is a figure of strength and majesty; the ox is a figure of diligence and work; the man of course represents man in all his humanity, created by God in His own image; and the eagle is the Church's ability to soar into the heavens to carry out the will of God and to see things from God's perspective

Study 13: Revelation 4:8-5:4

4:8 *Each of the four living creatures had six wings and was covered with eyes all around, even under his wings. Day and night they never stop saying: "Holy, holy, holy is the Lord God Almighty, who was, and is, and is to come."*

The creatures had six wings, which gave them the ability to go anywhere at anytime. This made me think of the Great Commission, which states:

Then Jesus came to them and said, "All authority in heaven and on earth has been given to me. Therefore go and make disciples of all nations, baptizing them in the name of the Father and of the Son and of the Holy Spirit, and teaching them to obey everything I have commanded you. And surely I am with you always, to the very end of the age" (Matthew 28:18-20).

Do the characteristics of the four creatures—strength, diligence, humanity, and ability to soar over the earth—apply particularly to spreading the gospel? Aren't we to use every means and all our ability and strength to extend the kingdom of God through evangelism? No matter how much persecution or how difficult times are, we are to soar and with all vigilance to pursue every opportunity to evangelize.

The message to theses churches and to us was and is: "No matter what you're going through, God is with you. Preach the Word!" That is the essence of the mission given to God's people. And no matter what you are going through, you must worship and declare God's holiness in every situation and in every land.

We are not to evangelize to build big churches but to increase the worshipers of God. While these creatures are carrying out their work, they are worshiping God. You can get so bogged down in the work of the Church that you can forget what the essence of that work is!

4:9-11 *Whenever the living creatures give glory, honor and thanks to him who sits on the throne and who lives forever and ever, the twenty-four elders fall down before him who sits on the throne, and worship him who lives forever and ever. They lay their crowns before the throne and say: "You are worthy, our Lord and God, to receive glory and honor and power, for you created all things, and by your will they were created and have their being."*

By giving glory to God while you work, you keep the work from becoming your own. I am not building *my church*; I can't talk about *my staff*; I can't refer to *my vision*; I don't work with *my people*. Everything belongs to and is about God. All that you do was and is God's idea; in His church, they are His people, His staff, His vision and His gifts. It's all about Him and not about bishops, evangelists, builders, members, deacons, elders or televangelists. We don't know the names of the elders in these verses because it's all about God and not about the men and women who serve God.

We saw the imperfections of the churches in the first three chapters; now we are beholding the beauty and perfection of heaven and how heaven relates to these imperfect churches. Chapter 4 is not a picture of how things will be but rather of how things already are. We are partnering with heaven to do God's will, and that will is to be done with all energy, diligence and haste.

5:1 *Then I saw in the right hand of him who sat on the throne a scroll with writing on both sides and sealed with seven seals.*

I am impressed once again with the transition from the first three chapters, where the focus is on earth, to the rest of the book, where the focus is on heaven. Our main attention and energy should be given to a heavenly agenda, not an earthly one. Where is your focus these days, on earthly or heavenly things? Paul understood this and wrote:

Study 13: Revelation 4:8–5:4

Since, then, you have been raised with Christ, set your hearts on things above, where Christ is seated at the right hand of God. Set your minds on things above, not on earthly things. For you died, and your life is now hidden with Christ in God. When Christ, who is your life, appears, then you also will appear with him in glory. Put to death, therefore, whatever belongs to your earthly nature: sexual immorality, impurity, lust, evil desires and greed, which is idolatry. Because of these, the wrath of God is coming (Colossians 3:1-6).

We are to set our mind on heavenly things. That is the answer Revelation provides to the persecution and pressure the church was encountering.

I appreciate writing as a medium of communication. There wasn't a video, cassette tape, website, drama program, CD ROM or DVD in the hand of the One who sits on the throne. There was a book in His hands. Books are the time-tested medium of heaven to communicate God's will and Word. What are you reading these days? How you can read a bit more than you presently do?

There is an earthly reality and a heavenly one. The early church was under pressure of persecution, yet the scene in heaven is where the sovereignty of God is the ultimate reality of existence.

5:2 *And I saw a mighty angel proclaiming in a loud voice, "Who is worthy to break the seals and open the scroll?"*

That is the age-old question: Who is worthy to understand the secret things of God, to reveal the mind of God to mankind? The angel asked in a loud voice, for everyone in every generation to hear and answer. Many have heard that question resounding in their spirit. The problem is that they come to the wrong conclusion as to its answer. Science, education, sociology, politics and medicine have not been able to open the scroll. Man in all his intelligence, learning and expertise has not been able to open the book.

The problem for mankind is that no one was, is or will be worthy. No system of thought is worthy. No scheme of good deeds is worthy. No amount of wishing, hoping, trying or praying will make anyone worthy. Buddha and Mohammed were not worthy. They never were and never will be.

Almost every doctrinal dispute throughout Church history has centered on or around the supremacy of Jesus. The dilemma of modern man is whether or not there is any one or any thing that can speak with authority on divine things.

One important message of Revelation is that Jesus is worthy. It's all about Him all the time. It's not about the Church, doctrine, denominations, or deed. It's only about Him. No one is worthy to act on behalf of God in a manner that is acceptable to God. Only Jesus is worthy.

5:3 *But no one in heaven or on earth or under the earth could open the scroll or even look inside it.*

My words are inadequate at this point, so let's look at God's words:

The one who comes from above is above all; the one who is from the earth belongs to the earth, and speaks as one from the earth. The one who comes from heaven is above all. He testifies to what he has seen and heard, but no one accepts his testimony. The man who has accepted it has certified that God is truthful.

For the one whom God has sent speaks the words of God, for God gives the Spirit without limit. The Father loves the Son and has placed everything in his hands. Whoever believes in the Son has eternal life, but whoever rejects the Son will not see life, for God's wrath remains on him (John 3:31-36).

Therefore God exalted him to the highest place and gave him the name that is above every name, that at the name of Jesus every knee should bow, in heaven and on earth and under the earth, and every tongue confess that Jesus Christ is Lord, to the glory of God the Father (Philippians 2:9-11).

It saves you by the resurrection of Jesus Christ, who has gone into heaven and is at God's right hand—with angels, authorities and powers in submission to him (1 Peter 3:21-22).

Only Jesus could and can open the scroll that the Father has written.

5:4 *I wept and wept because no one was found who was worthy to open the scroll or look inside.*

Human history is fraught with futile attempts to open the seals and understand God. Each attempt apart from Christ has ended in failure and weeping. Every ideal system and ideology has turned to dust. Another important message of Revelation is that Jesus is the only way.

To what are you giving your life? Why pursue so many things and interests that are doomed to failure and futility? I just finished watching the most recent Olympic games. They were enjoyable to watch at times, but the Olympics represent a humanistic philosophy trying to bring peace and harmony to a sinful world. Each Olympics has examples of cheating, human error, and gross commercialism. This year's events cost $310 million just for security while the world's hungry suffer for another day. The world tries desperately to find something that can provide meaning and lasting peace. Only One can provide both, and He is Jesus. That is the message of the Bible and of Revelation.

Your culture presents options every day that promise prosperity, peace, and happiness. Yet you should be weeping as John did in Revelation, for they are all exercises in futility that will pass away. You serve God in His kingdom that will never pass away. That is where your allegiance belongs; that is where your best efforts and energies should be devoted.

The Bible provides some examples of those who tried to open the scroll. Cain, the builders of Babel's tower, the Pharisees, and the Roman government, to name a few, all tried to please God, receive His endorsement, or achieve immortality. All failed.

Study 14: Revelation 5:5-10

5:5 *Then one of the elders said to me, "Do not weep! See, the Lion of the tribe of Judah, the Root of David, has triumphed. He is able to open the scroll and its seven seals."*

The good news for man is that there is One who is worthy to open the things of God for men. His name is Jesus. The conclusion throughout Revelation is that Jesus is the One! He is God's answer to all man's problems. Peter preached this same truth on one occasion.

If we are being called to account today for an act of kindness shown to a cripple and are asked how he was healed, then know this, you and all the people of Israel: It is by the name of Jesus Christ of Nazareth, whom you crucified but whom God raised from the dead, that this man stands before you healed. He is "the stone you builders rejected, which has become the capstone.' Salvation is found in no one else, for there is no other name under heaven given to men by which we must be saved (Acts 4:9-12).

Jesus is a lion—brave, strong, loud, deliberate, and supreme; He is also a Root—deep, immovable, and sustaining. Notice the Lion's residence is in heaven, but His pedigree is human. Our human flesh, one of our own whose name is Jesus, sits at the right hand of God and is worthy to open the scroll. Jesus' strength wasn't simply human. It came from a righteous life of obedience. He is exalted to the right hand of the Father because of what Paul wrote to the Philippian church (see Philippians 2:9-11 on page 58).

5:6 *Then I saw a Lamb, looking as if it had been slain, standing in the center of the throne, encircled by the four living creatures and the elders. He had seven horns and seven eyes, which are the seven spirits of God sent out into all the earth.*

What a graphic metaphor this verse provides! Jesus, at the center of the throne, looks like a lamb. We have seen the seven spirits mentioned in previous studies, and these seven spirits are epitomized in Jesus yet separate from Him. What's more, the Spirit of God isn't just sent to the Church, but He is sent to all the earth.

Jesus is likened to a lion, but that metaphor is not superior to any other. We should never overemphasize one part of God's character at the expense of another. While He is strong like a lion, He is also gentle like a lamb. Some people only want to think of God as a gentle, loving lamb. Then others want to see God only as a conquering, powerful warrior. The truth is that He is both, and you can and will encounter Him in both capacities in your lifetime.

5:7 *He came and took the scroll from the right hand of him who sat on the throne.*

Study 14: Revelation 5:5-10

Jesus didn't have to seize the book, or obtain it by force or trickery. He just went up and took it. That means that God the Father who held the book, released it to Jesus, the Lamb. There is cooperation in heaven among the three persons of God. Shouldn't there be the same cooperation on earth among His Church? Sadly, there is not. Jesus was close enough to the throne that He could take the book. And the hand holding the book allowed Him to take it, so He must have been considered worthy.

5:8 *And when he had taken it, the four living creatures and the twenty-four elders fell down before the Lamb. Each one had a harp and they were holding golden bowls full of incense, which are the prayers of the saints.*

The Lamb is worthy of worship. Some religions say that Jesus was a good man, a prophet, and the "son of God." If that is all Jesus is, He is worthy of admiration but not worship. If Jesus receives worship and He isn't God, then He is guilty of breaking God's commandments against idolatry. The point here is this: He is worthy because He is God, and consequently worthy of worship and honor.

Notice that the Lamb is the One worshiped. This Lamb was the One who suffered, who was slaughtered for His people. It is not the lion that is worshiped, but the suffering Lamb that was slain. Jesus' sufferings qualified Him to take an exalted place. Do you think your sufferings will enable you to do the same—to rule with Christ?

This verse gives us a picture of the partnership between heaven and earth, the heavenly church, so to speak, and the earthly one. The prayers of the saints are mixed with heavenly worship focused on the Lamb. The four creatures represent the role of the church on earth, and the twenty-four elders represent the ruling nature of the church and heaven together (see Study 12, Revelation 4:7).

When Jesus takes the book from the hand of the Father, the Church falls down before Him. The fact that He is worthy to take the scroll and open it is cause for worship and prayer. We worship and pray because He is all-powerful. That is how we express His sovereignty on earth. We should be known as a worshiping and praying people. The Bible is full of so many verses on prayer and worship that I will not even attempt to highlight them. But this verse reminds me of one particular story:

> At Caesarea there was a man named Cornelius, a centurion in what was known as the Italian Regiment. He and all his family were devout and God-fearing; he gave generously to those in need and prayed to God regularly. One day at about three in the afternoon he had a vision. He distinctly saw an angel of God, who came to him and said, "Cornelius!" Cornelius stared at him in fear. "What is it, Lord?" he asked. The angel answered, "Your prayers and gifts to the poor have come up as a memorial offering before God" (Acts 10:1-4).

Cornelius' prayers and generosity had come before God. They were like incense, which is how the prayers of the saints are portrayed in Revelation 5:8. Incense has a pleasant aroma, so incense is chosen as a symbol of something that brings pleasure to God. It smells good. Are you doing enough to bring pleasure to God through giving and prayer? Perhaps I should ask whether or not you smell good to Him?

The prayers in 5:8 are contained in golden bowls. No prayer escapes God's notice, but they are held in bowls, symbolically of course. What happens to a bowl? It can become full and so it seems that there is an aspect of prayer that requires waiting on God, until the bowl is full, and it overflows to God's attention.

One of the worship postures in the Bible is to "fall down." I don't fall down enough when I worship, symbolic of my complete surrender and subservience to the sovereign God.

The elders and living creatures worshiped Jesus, the Lamb. If Jesus was only a prophet or a good man, as some religions state, and He receives and received worship, then He is taking the place of God and is a false prophet! Of course I am saying that He is worthy in every way to receive honor, praise, and worship. If He was not, however, and received it, it would be a serious issue and would disqualify Him from being the prophet that some sects claim Him to be. He is not just a prophet; He is the King, Priest, Son of Man, and Lord God.

Of course, I am not saying that Jesus is anything less than God. He is worthy of all worship and honor, but when religions say Jesus was a "holy man" (like Islam does) and then sidestep the fact that He was worshiped, they are deceived. When Jesus was on earth, He allowed Himself to be worshiped: "When they saw him, they worshiped him; but some doubted" (Matthew 28:17). So when someone tries to tell you that Jesus was only a prophet or holy man, ask them how He could have allowed Himself to be worshiped unless He was also God!

Study 14: Revelation 5:5-10

5:9 *And they sang a new song: "You are worthy to take the scroll and to open its seals, because you were slain, and with your blood you purchased men for God from every tribe and language and people and nation."*

Heaven sings a new song, a fresh expression of who God is and what He has done. I don't care for songs that talk about me, we and I. More of our worship songs need to sing about God. Many of our worship songs today are more like prayers that are put to music, not songs expressing the goodness and magnificence of God! I am not against singing prayers; I just don't think they should be considered "worship" as such.

Author and pastor John Piper has wrote:

> Missions exists because worship doesn't. Worship is ultimate, not missions, because God is ultimate, not man. When this age is over and the countless millions of the redeemed fall on their faces before the throne of God, missions will be no more. It is a temporary necessity. But worship abides forever.[2]

Think about that saying. We must go to the nations and people groups where worship does not exist so worship can spring forth from a people who at present do not know God. Notice in 4:9 that Jesus has already purchased the people from every nation; we must go find them, but God has already done the work.

What are you doing to help reach the nations for Jesus? Are you singing about it or are you participating in it? Are you praying for a particular people or nation? How much of your time and money goes toward missions? Remember Jesus' words:

> *Then Jesus came to them and said, "All authority in heaven and on earth has been given to me. Therefore go and make disciples of all nations, baptizing them in the name of the Father and of the Son and of the Holy Spirit, and teaching them to obey everything I have commanded you. And surely I am with you always, to the very end of the age"* (Matthew 28:18-20).

5:10 *"You have made them to be a kingdom and priests to serve our God, and they will reign on the earth."*

God's people from every nation, tongue, and tribe are a kingdom through the blood and death of Jesus. A kingdom has a King and our King is Jesus! Our kingdom is a heavenly one, but we are also to reign on earth. There is a "now" aspect to your reign as well as a future aspect. In some circles, it is referred to as the "already/not yet" concept of Scripture. There is an aspect of something that has already been accomplished but is not yet in the fullness of how it will be. For example, the kingdom of God is already here but not yet here. If that doesn't make sense, it will in time. Just keep reading.

Once again, put yourself in the place of the early churches who were receiving this letter. They were small, insignificant and under pressure from the culture in which they lived. This vision of heaven undoubtedly gave them tremendous hope now; hope to carry on the work to extend the kingdom of God and reach more people from every nation. God will settle all accounts and establish His King on the throne for all nations to see and serve.

God's people are also priests through the blood and death of Jesus. A priest ministers to God on behalf of people and to the people on behalf of God. As priests we intercede, evangelize and help release people from their sins. A priest exists for others; so do we. Are you selfishly protecting your world and relationship with God, or are you acting as a priest of God, serving God and people?

Study 15: Revelation 5:11-6:3

5:11 *Then I looked and heard the voice of many angels, numbering thousands upon thousands, and ten thousand times ten thousand. They encircled the throne and the living creatures and the elders.*

This is the second time John said he "looked and heard." When God opens your eyes, He allows you to hear what He is doing with your eyes. I think of Proverbs 20:12, which states, "Ears that hear and eyes that see—the Lord has made them both."

John looked and saw a host of angels, which is similar to an account found in 2 Kings:

> *Then he sent horses and chariots and a strong force there. They went by night and surrounded the city. When the servant of the man of God got up and went out early the next morning, an army with horses and char-*

Study 15: Revelation 5:11–6:3

iots had surrounded the city. "Oh, my lord, what shall we do?" the servant asked. "Don't be afraid," the prophet answered. "Those who are with us are more than those who are with them." And Elisha prayed, "O Lord, open his eyes so he may see." Then the Lord opened the servant's eyes, and he looked and saw the hills full of horses and chariots of fire all around Elisha (2 Kings 6:14-17).

We are not alone! The early, persecuted church also needed to be reminded of what Elisha's servant saw in the previous passage. He saw that the forces of God actually outnumbered the opposition. The early church needed that assurance as well. You and I need it, too.

What a powerful picture 5:11 contains of the church, represented by the elders and living creatures, and heaven, with myriads of angels, standing around the throne where the Lamb is being worshiped. Nothing can overcome, dim, or mar that picture. The truth of Romans 8 has been and is for every generation:

Who shall separate us from the love of Christ? Shall trouble or hardship or persecution or famine or nakedness or danger or sword? As it is written: "For your sake we face death all day long; we are considered as sheep to be slaughtered." No, in all these things we are more than conquerors through him who loved us. For I am convinced that neither death nor life, neither angels nor demons, neither the present nor the future, nor any powers, neither height nor depth, nor anything else in all creation, will be able to separate us from the love of God that is in Christ Jesus our Lord (Romans 8:35-39).

5:12 *In a loud voice they sang: "Worthy is the Lamb, who was slain, to receive power and wealth and wisdom and strength and honor and glory and praise!"*

Here is the second song of heaven that is found in this passage. Notice once again that it was a song about the Lamb and what He has done. Heaven sings about Jesus' death. It was a landmark event in history and in heaven. Mankind can try to dismiss the significance of Jesus' death and resurrection and even deny that they occurred. Heaven, however, focuses on Jesus' death because it established His supremacy in the Church. He is the focus of worship because of it. Without His death, there is no forgiveness of sins and no resurrection. Paul wrote:

> *Your attitude should be the same as that of Christ Jesus: Who, being in very nature God, did not consider equality with God something to be grasped, but made himself nothing, taking the very nature of a servant, being made in human likeness. And being found in appearance as a man, he humbled himself and became obedient to death—even death on a cross! Therefore God exalted him to the highest place and gave him the name that is above every name, that at the name of Jesus every knee should bow, in heaven and on earth and under the earth, and every tongue confess that Jesus Christ is Lord, to the glory of God the Father* (Philippians 2:5-11).

The message of Revelation is that Jesus is Lord! He is the focus of worship, He is the centerpiece of the Church; He is worthy. That should be the message of the Church, no matter what the situation or circumstances. That was the message Jesus delivered to His church in the first century, and nothing has changed since then.

5:13 *Then I heard every creature in heaven and on earth and under the earth and on the sea, and all that is in them, singing: "To him who sits on the throne and to the Lamb be praise and honor and glory and power, for ever and ever!"*

This is the third song in this short passage. Each song exalts the goodness of God and Jesus! Do you see a pattern here? It is interesting that every creature everywhere in this verse entered into this worship song. There is a heavenly song that is the backdrop for all earthly ministry activity.

5:14 *The four living creatures said, "Amen," and the elders fell down and worshiped.*

Not much more can be said than the creatures said in 5:14. This is not a future view of heaven but a present view of the joint venture and partnership between heaven and earth. The Church enters into a partnership with heaven to worship God and glorify the Lamb.

Are you part of this venture, or do you have another agenda? Are you giving your life and energy to serve Him, or do you simply acknowledge Him and then pursue your own interests? I urge you to join with the heavenly hosts that focus on the throne and worship Him with all their being!

Study 15: Revelation 5:11–6:3

6:1 *I watched as the Lamb opened the first of the seven seals. Then I heard one of the four living creatures say in a voice like thunder, "Come!"*

Heaven is a loud place! John heard voices like trumpets and thunder. When heaven speaks, it is impossible not to hear. Men can ignore, turn their back, say that the voice belonged to someone or something else, disobey, misinterpret, or twist what was said, but it is impossible not to hear. At one point, the Father was so pleased with Jesus that He interrupted history by interjecting His voice that sounded like thunder to some and was attributed to an angel by others. That voice, however, was the Father's!

> *"Father, glorify your name!" Then a voice came from heaven, "I have glorified it, and will glorify it again." The crowd that was there and heard it said it had thundered; others said an angel had spoken to him* (John 12:28-29).

The voice in 6:1, however, was from one of the four living creatures. If the four creatures are symbolic of the Church as we assumed in a previous study, then that means the voice of the Church is powerful and should also be heard in all the earth. The Church should be declaring the glories of God for all the world to hear!

The voice in 6:1 said, "Come!" That should be the message of the Church: come to God! Too often, I am afraid, our message has not been to come but to stay away! We have not always made it easy for people to come and see what God is doing, but rather required that people be clean and holy before they came. No one can get clean and holy unless he or she comes to Christ, so we should be working to bring people in, not run them off.

The Lamb opened the first seal. Let us see what that opening represents.

6:2 *I looked, and there before me was a white horse! Its rider held a bow, and he was given a crown, and he rode out as a conqueror bent on conquest.*

The first seal revealed another aspect of the Lamb's personality. This time the image is not of a docile little lamb, but of a rider with a bow on a white horse. This symbol of Jesus is used in other places, so we are safe in defining this symbol as Jesus. When the Bible interprets itself, you are always on solid ground in your interpretation. When it doesn't, you must be very careful not to stretch the interpretation to fit your own understanding.

The more Bible you know, the more restricted you are in interpreting and preaching. You cannot teach what you want the passage to say, what you think it says, or what the "Lord showed you." You must discipline yourself to produce a careful interpretation of both symbols and difficult, obscure passages. That requires some study and understanding of basic principles of interpretation, or hermeneutics as it is called in the seminary (principles of interpretation).

Jesus is riding a white horse. Normally, the battle leader may not wish to distinguish himself with such a horse, not wanting to attract undue attention to himself from the enemy. And often the generals or leaders do not actually take part in combat. Jesus rides in front of the Church as its leader, however, leading the main attack against the enemy on behalf of His troops. Jesus is the head of His church and will lead it to victory! Even in spiritual warfare, He is riding the lead horse to bring us to victory!

The rider of the horse in 6:2 is holding a bow. What does a bow represent? Strength is required to pull a bow and skill to use it effectively, especially while riding on a horse. Jesus is our strength and protection. He is accurate with His bow and it always achieves the effect that He chooses. No occasional misses happen when Jesus uses His bow! He is always on target!

Jesus was not given a battle helmet but a crown! He is the King and He rides out as a conqueror. Jesus vanquishes His enemies and wins the nations for His Father.

6:3 *When the Lamb opened the second seal, I heard the second living creature say, "Come!"*

Notice that the living creature does not speak on its own initiative. The creature speaks as the Lamb opens the seals. Jesus takes the lead and the Church interprets what He says and what He has done for the world to see and understand.

What can you do to spread the message that men must "Come"? Are you willing to spread the gospel by whatever means possible? Are you willing to support those who are doing missions and outreach work?

Study 16: Revelation 6:4-11

6:4 *Then another horse came out, a fiery red one. Its rider was given power to take peace from the earth and to make men slay each other. To him was given a large sword.*

At one time, I thought God was definitely involved in church history but not in secular history. That of course is a wrong perspective. God rules in the affairs of men, both in and outside the Church.

I cannot explain everything that God wants to do by releasing this fiery red horse. I know that the Lamb on the white horse is also released and men can either take refuge in the Lamb's protection or be exposed to the rider with a large sword on the red horse. I have chosen the white horse! Jesus is my protector, and I don't have to fear any other force or being.

The twentieth century was the most violent in history and more people lost their lives then than in any other century of war. We should hate war and need to do all we can to prevent it, but war is one of the consequences of man's fallen state. Man's sin released terrible consequences. Unfortunately, wars will always be a part of the human experience until the Lord returns. There is only one source of peace on earth. It is not cultural exchange or tolerance. It is the Lamb on the white horse who can make war while at the same time giving peace to those who are in His army and under His protection.

Sinful man sometimes blames God for his troubles when trouble comes. Do man's troubles come from God or are they the result of man's attempts to live apart from God? Of course, man is the source of his own trouble and the Lord is not man's problem. God is man's only hope and solution to the dilemma sin created. Jesus is the only answer for the ills of man. Jesus was also the protector of the churches to whom Revelation was addressed. Jesus judged and evaluated those churches, but He was also their provider and protector.

6:5 *When the Lamb opened the third seal, I heard the third living creature say, "Come!" I looked, and there before me was a black horse! Its rider was holding a pair of scales in his hand.*

The rider on the black horse was holding scales. Was he weighing out justice or weighing business transaction? The next verse informs us that it was an economic scale. The color black is obviously negative, so this is a horse that represents lack and famine. That would seem to go with the red horse of war, for where men war with each other, it generally leads to a food shortages and suffering, especially for women and children.

Revelation is a book of symbols. You cannot attempt to tie this horse to any particular famine or historical event. This black horse conjures up a powerful image in the mind of the reader, especially the reader of the first century who was more familiar with the horse as part of everyday life.

6:6 *Then I heard what sounded like a voice among the four living creatures, saying, "A quart of wheat for a day's wages, and three quarts of barley for a day's wages, and do not damage the oil and the wine!"*

God has released seasons of distress throughout history. God initiated the plagues in Egypt. He was the one who sent Nebuchadnezzar to conquer Jerusalem. We are told in Psalm 105,

He called down famine on the land and destroyed all their supplies of food; and he sent a man before them—Joseph, sold as a slave. They bruised his feet with shackles, his neck was put in irons, till what he foretold came to pass, till the word of the Lord proved him true (vv. 17-19).

Is this just an indication of how cruel God can be, as His enemies suggest? No, God uses even these difficult situations to have men turn to Him for salvation. I know in my own life that lack and tragedy have caused me to cry out to God in a deeper, more meaningful way.

A quart of wheat for a day's wages sounds like a high price. Inflationary rises in prices with no increase in income erode the buying power of individuals. This is part of the black rider's effect on humanity. I have worked in Zimbabwe, where the inflation rate was astronomical at one point. The black rider, so to speak, was released and riding free through that land for a long season. It was due to greed and bad government fiscal policies.

6:7 *When the Lamb opened the fourth seal, I heard the voice of the fourth living creature say, "Come!"*

All four creatures spoke in response to the four seals that were opened. The Church should speak from a complete perspective when it addresses every area of life and interprets the things of God. That perspective can

Study 16: Revelation 6:4-11

only come from the Word of God and the wisdom of men and women who know the Lord and how to apply His principles to all of life, including education, the military, business, commerce, and family.

Again, the voice of the fourth living creature said, "Come!" This voice was calling people to God but also calling forth the purpose of God in the earth. Jesus instructed His disciples to pray, "Your kingdom, Your will be done, on earth as it is in heaven" (see Matthew 6:5-15). Are you praying as Jesus directed—for His will to be done here and now?

The Church is the only institution that can interpret the acts and ways of God. You are part of His Church. Therefore, you should help interpret the things of God for others.

6:8 *I looked, and there before me was a pale horse! Its rider was named Death, and Hades was following close behind him. They were given power over a fourth of the earth to kill by sword, famine and plague, and by the wild beasts of the earth.*

This is a terrible judgment, for the rider of the pale horse was riding among those who don't know God and their death led to hell. The only protection from the pale horse was the rider on the white horse. The red, black, and pale horses all led to destruction that men cannot avoid or escape. It was sudden and swift.

Consider the terrorist attack in America on September 11, 2001. It was swift and those who lost their lives had no chance of escape. Those who relied on the Lamb, the rider of the white horse, however, had a sure salvation that overcame the results of the pale horse that came to the Twin Towers that fateful day.

Everyone in life will encounter one or more of these four horses. While this may seem cruel, we know that God desires all men to be saved and to come to knowledge of the truth (see 1 Timothy 2:4). He is merciful and just. Yet He works after the counsel of His own will and His ways are inscrutable. I cannot understand all God does or why He does it, but I accept is as right and just. I also accept that God is doing all this to draw men to Himself. The following is a prayer you might want to pray.

> Jesus, I trust You to be my champion on a white horse. I need and rely on You to do for me what I cannot do for myself. I am powerless to resist death and the dangers of a sinful world, but You are all powerful. Protect me and lead me to victory in the power of Your great name.

6:9 ***When he opened the fifth seal, I saw under the altar the souls of those who had been slain because of the word of God and the testimony they had maintained.***

Those who were in danger of losing their lives at the time Revelation was written could only be encouraged by this verse. They were not alone in what they were facing. Others had lost their lives because of God's Word and their testimony, and they were in the presence of God. They did not die in vain and their souls were in a special place in the presence of God.

God never overlooks any sacrifice you make for Him, especially when you give your life unto death for His cause. "Precious in the sight of the Lord is the death of his saints" (Psalm 116:15). I have been on several moderately dangerous missions assignments, but I refuse not to go because my life may be in danger. I surrendered my life to God on May 18, 1973. How He chooses to bring me into His presence is God's business, not mine.

On my first international missions trip, I made a last will and testament and met with my family to give them final instructions in case something happened. I am mortal. I will die one day and I need to face the inevitability that it may happen sooner than I would like! The old die; the young can die. That is a fact of life.

Paul always fled when his life was in danger. That is wisdom. If there is any way you can escape the danger you face, you should. If you cannot, however, then you should take courage from the previous verse and the three following ones:

Even though someone is pursuing you to take your life, the life of my master will be bound securely in the bundle of the living by the Lord your God. But the lives of your enemies he will hurl away as from the pocket of a sling (1 Samuel 25:29).

What a beautiful analogy that verse gives us! We are bound securely in the bundle of the living. If we are taken out of that bundle, it is with God's permission and assistance!

The wicked lie in wait for the righteous, seeking their very lives; but the Lord will not leave them in their power or let them be condemned when brought to trial (Psalm 37:32-33)

He will rescue them from oppression and violence, for precious is their blood in his sight (Psalm 72:14).

6:10 *They called out in a loud voice, "How long, Sovereign Lord, holy and true, until you judge the inhabitants of the earth and avenge our blood?"*

God uses the death of His followers to give added testimony to those who do not believe. We know that Saul was a witness at the stoning of Stephen. My theory is that Stephen's death played a role in Saul's conversion. When Saul saw how nobly and joyfully Stephen died, it had to make an impression on him.

The martyrs also help to seal the eternal doom of their killers. The Pharisees were fond of saying that if they had been alive, they would not have killed the prophets as their forefathers did. Jesus addressed this issue when He said:

> *And you say, "If we had lived in the days of our forefathers, we would not have taken part with them in shedding the blood of the prophets." So you testify against yourselves that you are the descendants of those who murdered the prophets. Fill up, then, the measure of the sin of your forefathers! You snakes! You brood of vipers! How will you escape being condemned to hell? Therefore I am sending you prophets and wise men and teachers. Some of them you will kill and crucify; others you will flog in your synagogues and pursue from town to town. And so upon you will come all the righteous blood that has been shed on earth, from the blood of righteous Abel to the blood of Zechariah son of Berekiah, whom you murdered between the temple and the altar* (Matthew 23:30-35).

6:11 *Then each of them was given a white robe, and they were told to wait a little longer, until the number of their fellow servants and brothers who were to be killed as they had been was completed.*

This verse seems to imply that a certain number of saints are assigned to martyrdom. Or perhaps it simply implies that the number of those to be killed will end when the current age expires. Either way, martyrdom is a fact of Christian life. God takes special notice of those who give their lives as a testimony to His work in them. He gives them "white robes," symbolic of their holiness and purity before Him. I once wondered what would happen if I was given an ultimatum, "Renounce the Lord or die!" I no longer worry about that scenario. If the Lord puts me in that situation, He will give me the grace to respond and endure.

Those yet to be martyred are referred to as "fellow servants and brothers." As God's servant, I am a fellow servant and brother of Martin Luther, John Calvin, and all the other great servants of God. They are my cousins and uncles in the faith. Perhaps that is what the writer of Hebrews had in mind when he wrote that a great cloud of witnesses surrounds us (see Hebrews 12:1).

Study 17: Revelation 6:12-7:3

6:12 *I watched as he opened the sixth seal. There was a great earthquake. The sun turned black like sackcloth made of goat hair, the whole moon turned blood red*

Sometimes we can only watch what God is doing. We have no role to play; we are simply spectators of God's fearful and awesome cosmic play.

The earthquake and blood-red moon in the above verse are not to be taken literally but represent apocalyptic language that describes cataclysmic but not actual events. When the Lord moves in your life and shakes things up, it can seem like an earthquake and as though your sky is falling. Consider this passage:

> *At that time his voice shook the earth, but now he has promised, "Once more I will shake not only the earth but also the heavens." The words "once more" indicate the removing of what can be shaken—that is, created things—so that what cannot be shaken may remain. Therefore, since we are receiving a kingdom that cannot be shaken, let us be thankful, and so worship God acceptably with reverence and awe, for our "God is a consuming fire"* (Hebrews 12:26-29).

Is God shaking your life to show you something about the permanence and importance of His kingdom and government in some aspect of your life?

I heard someone say that we all meet God as a consuming fire. Some are in this life as we submit to God burning away those things that are not of Him; others are in the next life, where there is a fire that cannot be extinguished. I want my fire now so I can enjoy God forever! Then consider this Old Testament passage:

> *God is our refuge and strength, an ever-present help in trouble.*

Study 17: Revelation 6:12–7:3

> *Therefore we will not fear, though the earth give way and the mountains fall into the heart of the sea, though its waters roar and foam and the mountains quake with their surging. Selah. There is a river whose streams make glad the city of God, the holy place where the Most High dwells.*
>
> *God is within her, she will not fall; God will help her at break of day. Nations are in uproar, kingdoms fall; he lifts his voice, the earth melts. The Lord Almighty is with us; the God of Jacob is our fortress. Selah Come and see the works of the Lord, the desolations he has brought on the earth. He makes wars cease to the ends of the earth; he breaks the bow and shatters the spear, he burns the shields with fire. "Be still, and know that I am God; I will be exalted among the nations, I will be exalted in the earth." The Lord Almighty is with us; the God of Jacob is our fortress. Selah* (Psalm 46:1-11).

Did the churches in Revelation feel like their world was crumbling around them? God gave John this revelation so that they would see God's hand in the fearful events taking place. God doesn't stop the cataclysmic events, but He does make Himself a refuge in such times. Are you going through massive upheaval? Don't wish to get out of it, take refuge in God!

What does it mean to take refuge in God? You've probably had people tell you to give something to God. What were they trying to say? How can you be still in times of change? How can you rest in God when all around you is in turmoil? It must be possible or God would not tell you to do it.

6:13-14 *and the stars in the sky fell to earth, as late figs drop from a fig tree when shaken by a strong wind. The sky receded like a scroll, rolling up, and every mountain and island was removed from its place.*

Revelation was not written to scare people, in spite of how people use it today to do just that. Revelation was written to encourage those who were going through traumatic times to let them know that God was and is in control and to let them know that the Lamb is opening the seals of history that have been ordained by God the Father.

When anyone tries to scare you and uses Revelation as a tool to do so, you can reject that person's fear tactics. Revelation is a source of encouragement. Anyone who claims that Revelation is a book of specific future historical events dos not understand what they are talking about!

Revelation is not a history book. It is the last chapter in a great story of God creating and redeeming mankind. Someone once said, "I read the last book and we win!" The sky and stars may fall, but God is in control! Is that the story of your life?

6:15 *Then the kings of the earth, the princes, the generals, the rich, the mighty, and every slave and every free man hid in caves and among the rocks of the mountains.*

No one can stand before God and what He is doing! The churches of Revelation were being told that Caesar was king, that the emperor was divine and almighty. The picture in Revelation presents a totally different story.

Man started out hiding in Genesis (Adam and Eve hid from the Lord when He walked through the garden) and is still hiding in Revelation. What a ludicrous thought: trying to hide from the presence of God. That isn't possible. All men, all politicians, the rich, the famous, and the powerful will try to hide when God reveals His purpose and plan. Yet they will be unsuccessful no matter how smart, powerful, or rich they are.

6:16 *They called to the mountains and the rocks, "Fall on us and hide us from the face of him who sits on the throne and from the wrath of the Lamb!"*

That doesn't seem quite appropriate: the wrath of the Lamb! This is no ordinary Lamb. This Lamb is also the Lion of Judah!

The rocks will fall on those who are hiding, but it won't be to conceal them; it will be to crush them! "He who falls on this stone will be broken to pieces, but he on whom it falls will be crushed" (Matthew 21:44). I would rather fall on the stone by choice and be broken than have the stone fall on me and be crushed to powder! When you are broken to pieces, on the one hand there still may be something to reassemble. On the other hand, powder just scatters in the wind! The choice is given to every person.

6:17 *"For the great day of their wrath has come, and who can stand?"*

The day of wrath may delay, but it will come. I have put my faith in God that this wrath will pass by me. The wicked may prevail for a day, but God will have His way and blow them away like dust. I trust you, Lord! I

Study 17: Revelation 6:12–7:3

trust that what comes is from You and that You will preserve and protect me in the day of trouble. Amen. Is that your prayer too?

7:1 *After this I saw four angels standing at the four corners of the earth, holding back the four winds of the earth to prevent any wind from blowing on the land or on the sea or on any tree.*

This should have been the point when the seventh seal is opened, but the flow of the seals being opened was interrupted. We see angels poised to do something. Angels are powerful beings if four of them can do something that will affect the whole earth. Angels have whatever power they need to carry out God's will and purpose.

Keep in mind, however, that Revelation is a dream and vision, and it uses symbolic and apocalyptic language to get a message across to the reader or listener.

The Holy Spirit's activity was compared to the wind (see John 3:8), and in the verses we see the wind being held back by four angels. Paul refers to the wind of doctrine in Ephesians 4. I wonder if this verse is referring to God restraining false doctrines from affecting the Church. Or perhaps it refers to a limited move of the Holy Spirit for a season according to God's purpose.

7:2-3 *Then I saw another angel coming up from the east, having the seal of the living God. He called out in a loud voice to the four angels who had been given power to harm the land and the sea: "Do not harm the land or the sea or the trees until we put a seal on the foreheads of the servants of our God."*

Here we see another angel with a loud voice. You may worry that you will miss God's voice or what He is doing. God reveals what He is doing so that those who want to know will know. Everything is done in Revelation in loud tones.

Many people are concerned about the 666 that will be put on the forehead of men and women (we will see this symbol later in Revelation). Before the 666 is assigned, however, the righteous servants of God are sealed with the seal of the living God! God interrupts His judgment on the earth to take care of His people. God always takes care of His people. Even in the midst of the Egyptian plagues, God took care of His people, for none of the plagues affected the land of Goshen where the Hebrews lived.

This is the message of Revelation: tough times will come, but God will protect and take care of His people, even if they lose their lives in His service

When was a message of fear attached to the book of Revelation? Why hasn't the message of these verses been trumpeted for all to hear and to be encouraged? This message doesn't sell as many books as those that deal in morbid fantasies of the end times. In the midst of horses bringing disaster and seals of calamity, God seals His own.

A seal designates something that belongs to the one who owns the seal. We belong to Jesus, no matter what the world does or what happens therein. What's more, the earth is the Lord's. Nothing will happen that He does not designate or desire. This is why I don't fear a nuclear holocaust or some other kind of calamity. The earth is the Lord's and He reigns in the affairs of men. Let's once again read the words of the apostle Paul to the Romans:

> *What, then, shall we say in response to this? If God is for us, who can be against us? He who did not spare his own Son, but gave him up for us all— how will he not also, along with him, graciously give us all things? Who will bring any charge against those whom God has chosen? It is God who justifies. Who is he that condemns? Christ Jesus, who died— more than that, who was raised to life— is at the right hand of God and is also interceding for us. Who shall separate us from the love of Christ? Shall trouble or hardship or persecution or famine or nakedness or danger or sword?*
>
> *As it is written: "For your sake we face death all day long; we are considered as sheep to be slaughtered." No, in all these things we are more than conquerors through him who loved us. For I am convinced that neither death nor life, neither angels nor demons, neither the present nor the future, nor any powers, neither height nor depth, nor anything else in all creation, will be able to separate us from the love of God that is in Christ Jesus our Lord* (Romans 8:31-39).

Read the above passage one more time. Let the message sink deep into your heart and mind. You need to settle once and for all that God is for you and that nothing shall separate you from the love of God, not even disaster or death.

The message of Revelation is one of victory, revealing God's power to protect His own and showing God's ability to rule in the seemingly tumultuous affairs of men. Any other meaning is one that is foreign to the text and is a teaching that emanates from the fearful, imaginative or sinful heart of man.

Any Revelation message that instills fear into the hearts of people is a teaching of man. And any Revelation message that tries to assign literal historical events to the symbolic pictures of Revelation is a teaching of man and pure fiction.

Remember, you must put yourself in the place of those who first received the book. The Lord was addressing their situation then, not two thousand years hence. There was a message for those who received the Revelation as well as for those who read it today. The message is one of hope and victory!

Study 18: Revelation 7:4-13

7:4 *Then I heard the number of those who were sealed: 144,000 from all the tribes of Israel.*

Some sects have taught that there would be exactly 144,000 people saved based on this verse. This is nonsense. Why would we begin applying a literal interpretation to this verse, when everything up to this point has been symbolic? The 144,000 must be symbolic of something and is not to be taken literally. It is a number obtained by multiplying 12 times 12 times 10 times 10 times 10. I have done a little study on the meaning of biblical numbers and 12 is the number of God's government or rule (12 tribes, 24 elders around the throne, 12 apostles) and 10 is a combination of 7 plus 3, both being perfect and complete numbers.

The number 144,000 represents the fact that all who are to be sealed will be sealed. God's sovereign rule and oversight will not miss or overlook one single person! He will not overlook anyone who has called on His name for salvation. No one knows what that exact number is, but God knows. And if you are His servant, you will be sealed, identified and preserved as God's own, no matter what happens in human history.

> *Do not let your hearts be troubled. Trust in God trust also in me. In my Father's house are many rooms; if it were not so, I would have told you. I am going there to prepare a place for you. And if I go and prepare a place for you, I will come back and take you to be with me that you also may be where I am. You know the way to the place where I am going* (John 14:1-4).

There is a seal on the forehead because it is hard to miss! There will be no mistaking God's protection and distinctive presence on His people. Usually nothing is worn on the forehead; something can be worn on the nose, cheeks, ears, lips and eyes. But usually nothing is worn on the forehead. When God marks His people, all creation will know that they are His! It won't be possible to overlook.

The forehead is the frontal protector of the brain. I wonder if the seal is a protection at the front of the brain to keep your mind focused on Him. This could relate to the four winds being deceiving doctrines that could seduce and affect the minds of believers. God will seal your mind so that fear cannot rule your thoughts.

> **7:5-8** *From the tribe of Judah 12,000 were sealed, from the tribe of Reuben 12,000, from the tribe of Gad 12,000, from the tribe of Asher 12,000, from the tribe of Naphtali 12,000, from the tribe of Manasseh 12,000, from the tribe of Simeon 12,000, from the tribe of Levi 12,000, from the tribe of Issachar 12,000, from the tribe of Zebulun 12,000, from the tribe of Joseph 12,000, from the tribe of Benjamin 12,000.*

The world may seem in chaos to us, but God proceeds about His work in an orderly fashion. What's more, God is ultimately in the people business. God is concerned for His people and watches out for them without fail. Nothing and no one escapes His loving care. Each tribe receives equal attention.

Historically some of the tribes served the Lord more faithfully than others. God, however, doesn't play favorites. No one's heritage counts more than anyone else's when it comes to God's seal. No tribe, country, or ethnic group has special standing before the Lord. The blood of the Lamb is what determines salvation, not earthly heritage. One tribe not mentioned is the tribe of Dan. Dan had a propensity to idolatry, and God cannot and will not seal idolaters. Ephraim also isn't mentioned; instead, his father's name of Joseph is listed.

I don't think that the mention of the twelve tribes pertains to natural Israel here. After all, Paul refers to the true Israel as those who have faith in God:

> *It is not as though God's word had failed. For not all who are descended from Israel are Israel. Nor because they are his descendants are they all*

Abraham's children. On the contrary, "It is through Isaac that your offspring will be reckoned." In other words, it is not the natural children who are God's children, but it is the children of the promise who are regarded as Abraham's offspring (Romans 9:6-8).

My name is written in the book of life! I am sealed as His. Nothing shall separate me from the love of God. If I die, I am with Him. If I live, I serve Him as Paul pointed out:

I eagerly expect and hope that I will in no way be ashamed, but will have sufficient courage so that now as always Christ will be exalted in my body, whether by life or by death. For to me, to live is Christ and to die is gain. If I am to go on living in the body, this will mean fruitful labor for me. Yet what shall I choose? I do not know! I am torn between the two: I desire to depart and be with Christ, which is better by far; but it is more necessary for you that I remain in the body. Convinced of this, I know that I will remain, and I will continue with all of you for your progress and joy in the faith, so that through my being with you again your joy in Christ Jesus will overflow on account of me (Philippians 1:20-26).

Can someone, anyone please tell me how Revelation became anything but a book of hope and joy?

7:9 *After this I looked and there before me was a great multitude that no one could count, from every nation, tribe, people and language, standing before the throne and in front of the Lamb. They were wearing white robes and were holding palm branches in their hands.*

This is another reason why the 144,000 figure of verse four in the previous study cannot be literal. Here John saw a multitude that no one could count, but 144,000 can be counted.

Many have said it before me, but it bears repeating: If heaven is made up of every nation, tribe, people and language, shouldn't the church reflect that now? Today there are people saved from many nations, but why don't they worship together on earth? Some have said that the Sunday morning hour of worship is the most segregated hour in the world.

As I write this, I finished a book by Howard Thurman entitled *Jesus and the Disinherited*. In it Thurman wrote:

> The experience of the common worship of God is such a moment. It is in this connection that American Christianity has betrayed the religion of Jesus almost beyond redemption. Churches have been established for the underprivileged, for the weak, for the poor, on the theory that they prefer to be among themselves. Churches have been established for the Chinese, the Japanese, the Korean, the Mexican, the Filipino, the Italian, and the Negro, with the same theory in mind. The result is that in the one place in which normal, free contacts might be most naturally established—in which the relations of the individual to his God should take priority over conditions of class, race, power, status, wealth, or the like—this place is one of the chief instruments for guaranteeing barriers.
>
> The enormity of this sin cannot be easily grasped. The situation is so tragic that men of good will in all the specious classifications within our society find more cause for hope in the secular relations of life than in religion.[3]

While Thurman was addressing American Christianity just after World War II, in some ways things haven't changed. What's more, it is pretty much the same the world over. Has this been your experience as well? Why is this? What can or should be done to remedy this situation? Is it beyond redemption as Thurman suggested, in your opinion? What can you do to reach out to and include in your church world someone who isn't like you or from your background or economic world?

I am not sure if I will wear a white robe in heaven. This seems to be symbolic. White is of course the color of purity and holiness. The good guys always wear white in shows and movies.

What is the significance of the palm branches? History shows that conquering armies and peoples cut and carried palm branches as a sign of victory. This certainly fits with this verse, for God's people are victorious in His presence and ultimately in history.

7:10 *And they cried out in a loud voice: "Salvation belongs to our God, who sits on the throne, and to the Lamb."*

Here is another instance of something being done in a "loud voice." Heaven is a noisy place. I think of the phrase in the great old hymn that says, "Hark how the heavenly anthem drowns all music but its own."

Study 18: Revelation 7:4-13

No matter how many noisy, clamorous and catastrophic circumstances vie for your attention, the sounds of heaven should drown out everything else. If you set your heart to hear the sounds of heaven, they will come through loud and clear! What are you listening to these days? What is heaven saying to you?

Salvation is in the hands of our God. It does not come from money, education, wisdom or strength. He gives it to all those who cry out to Him to receive it. He sits on a sovereign throne of power and oversees His salvation operation. No one under His care escapes His notice and the Lamb applies His saving grace to all who stand before this throne.

For I have come down from heaven not to do my will but to do the will of him who sent me. And this is the will of him who sent me, that I shall lose none of all that he has given me, but raise them up at the last day. For my Father's will is that everyone who looks to the Son and believes in him shall have eternal life, and I will raise him up at the last day (John 6:38-40).

Salvation is not obtained through a system of works but is a gift under the oversight of the Lamb. Again, think of the comfort this gave the early churches to whom it was first written. Think of the comfort that can be to you and me right now!

7:11 *All the angels were standing around the throne and around the elders and the four living creatures. They fell down on their faces before the throne and worshiped God*

I read this and think of the line from another hymn that says all creation worships Him. The angels joined in with the elders and living creatures to worship God.

Falling on your face is another mode of worship, like the lifting of hands, kneeling and dancing. I don't fall on my face enough. This is symbolic that we are but dust and God is far above all flesh and creation.

It is said that Lucifer was the angel who coordinated worship before his fall from heaven. Angels were created to worship but Lucifer wanted the worship for himself. Read Isaiah 14:12-15 and Ezekiel 28:1-10 to understand the pride that motivated his fall. He tried to place himself where only God can stand to receive what only God can receive.

7:12 saying: "Amen! Praise and glory and wisdom and thanks and honor and power and strength be to our God for ever and ever. Amen!"

Heaven must be a noisy place! There is always a multitude singing. I was in Washington DC for the Promise Keepers' gathering of a million men many years ago. Those men were loud when they sang, not because they were rowdy in worship but because there were so many. I can't even imagine what John heard in his vision!

Yet this isn't only a picture of heaven. The Church should also be a place where public worship of God is going on for the world to see and hear. The Church is not a club but a living entity that exists to glorify God on the earth. The Church is made up of people who will populate heaven, so why should they wait until heaven to worship the King? Worship should be an important part of the people of God now!

John did not receive a general vision. He saw and heard specific things. He heard the words to the songs and beheld the events in great detail. I don't think this was a short vision he had. I am not sure how the angel delivered the message, but John certainly saw all God wanted him to see and was able to record or dictate it as it came.

Tradition has it that John received Revelation in a cave on the isle of Patmos. I have been to Patmos three times and visited that cave. I bought an artist's rendition of John in the cave dictating the vision to an assistant. Tradition has it that he received it over a period of time; it wasn't in one session.

7:13 Then one of the elders asked me, "These in white robes—who are they, and where did they come from?"

Jesus asked a lot of questions when He was on earth. That was an important part of His teaching ministry. One pastor said that God isn't looking for information when He asks a question. He already knows the answer. The question is for your benefit so you can clearly understand what He is trying to communicate.

Paul also asked many questions in his epistles. As preachers and teachers, we need to ask more questions and hear the thought process of our pupils and disciples. They need to hear our voices less and their own voices more. This tendency has led to culture where leaders talk too much and people think and respond too little.

I have recently started an online program called *What Would Jesus Ask?* The questions He asked then are still relevant today. They also still require an answer. "Who do men say that I am?" "What were you talking about on the road?" "Woman, where are your accusers?"

Study 19: Revelation 7:14-8:2

7:14 *I answered, "Sir, you know." And he said, "These are they who have come out of the great tribulation; they have washed their robes and made them white in the blood of the Lamb."*

The great tribulation has been portrayed by some as a specific historic event, confined to a certain timeframe. Tell someone who was imprisoned for their faith in Siberia during the rule of the Soviet regime that the tribulation is yet to come. Tell the saints suffering in China or the Middle East that the tribulation is yet to come. They will probably tell you that the tribulation is a now event, not a future one. That is not to say that there won't be a great tribulation period, but this again can be a principle that has an already/not yet fulfillment. We read of Paul:

> *They preached the good news in that city and won a large number of disciples. Then they returned to Lystra, Iconium and Antioch, strengthening the disciples and encouraging them to remain true to the faith. "We must go through many hardships to enter the kingdom of God," they said* (Acts 14:21-22).

Telling people they must go through many hardships is an interesting way of strengthening and encouraging people. Yet that was what Paul did and what the angel was doing through John in Revelation. He was comforting the church in every generation that tribulation was not an indication that God had abandoned His people but that He was with His people. If you know tribulation isn't due to lack of faith or some failure on your part, you can endure it much more easily, knowing that God is using it as one aspect of His great plan for you and His Church.

I had a strange thought when I gave my life to the Lord. (I've had many more since then!) I assumed that since I was a Christian, I would never again have a flat tire! That's a bit unusual, but I really believed that once I was serving God, no more bad things would happen to me. Well, I've had my share of flat tires since then. Just because something happens that is bad to my way of thinking doesn't make it bad. God uses it for good. Is there any hardship in your life at this time? Then you are right where you need to be. Don't agonize over it or think it strange. Remember what James wrote:

> *Consider it pure joy, my brothers, whenever you face trials of many kinds, because you know that the testing of your faith develops perseverance. Perseverance must finish its work so that you may be mature and complete, not lacking anything. If any of you lacks wisdom, he should ask God, who gives generously to all without finding fault, and it will be given to him.*
>
> *But when he asks, he must believe and not doubt, because he who doubts is like a wave of the sea, blown and tossed by the wind. That man should not think he will receive anything from the Lord; he is a double-minded man, unstable in all he does. The brother in humble circumstances ought to take pride in his high position. But the one who is rich should take pride in his low position, because he will pass away like a wild flower.*
>
> *For the sun rises with scorching heat and withers the plant; its blossom falls and its beauty is destroyed. In the same way, the rich man will fade away even while he goes about his business. Blessed is the man who perseveres under trial, because when he has stood the test, he will receive the crown of life that God has promised to those who love him* (James 1:2-12).

It is of note that James included wisdom in the context of what he had to say about suffering. You need wisdom to know what God is doing in and with you when you encounter suffering.

James painted a similar picture to the one in Revelation. The person who perseveres will receive a crown of life! I want my crown, but I must endure to the end, even through the circumstances that I don't like and would tend to consider bad. Jesus warned of this in His own ministry as well when He said:

> *Brother will betray brother to death, and a father his child. Children will rebel against their parents and have them put to death. All men will hate you because of me, but he who stands firm to the end will be saved* (Mark 13:12-13).

7:15 *Therefore, "they are before the throne of God and serve him day and night in his temple; and he who sits on the throne will spread his tent over them."*

I want God to spread His tent over me, but He does that only when I serve Him day and night and patiently endure tribulation. A tent is a place of refuge and covering, a place of rest and protection. I must stay before the throne, before the place of God's government in my life, if I am to enjoy the benefits of the tent.

7:16 *"Never again will they hunger; never again will they thirst. The sun will not beat upon them, nor any scorching heat."*

God takes care of His own, both in the next age and the current one. The tent of God's covering will protect me from intense heat. The seven churches of Revelation were all located in the Middle East and it is hot there! Imagine how pleasant the thought of a tent was that would protect them from the scorching sun! Put yourself in their place, and then understand that God will do the same for you.

> *The Lord is my shepherd, I shall not be in want. He makes me lie down in green pastures, he leads me beside quiet waters, he restores my soul. He guides me in paths of righteousness for his name's sake. Even though I walk through the valley of the shadow of death, I will fear no evil, for you are with me; your rod and your staff, they comfort me. You prepare a table before me in the presence of my enemies. You anoint my head with oil; my cup overflows. Surely goodness and love will follow me all the days of my life, and I will dwell in the house of the Lord forever* (Psalm 23:1-6).

The book of Revelation should provide the same comfort as the twenty-third Psalm. When we walk with God, we walk in a whole new world! The things that once ruled us like food and the things of this life don't rule over us anymore. I am not saying we don't need them, but we don't follow the fleshly impulses any longer. We are led by the Spirit of God!

7:17 *"For the Lamb at the center of the throne will be their shepherd; he will lead them to springs of living water. And God will wipe away every tear from their eyes."*

The water is not literal water in 7:17 because the Lamb will take you to springs of living water. That sounds like the promise Jesus made:

Jesus answered her, "If you knew the gift of God and who it is that asks you for a drink, you would have asked him and he would have given you living water." "Sir," the woman said, "you have nothing to draw with and the well is deep. Where can you get this living water? Are you greater than our father Jacob, who gave us the well and drank from it himself, as did also his sons and his flocks and herds?" Jesus answered, "Everyone who drinks this water will be thirsty again, but whoever drinks the water I give him will never thirst. Indeed, the water I give him will become in him a spring of water welling up to eternal life." The woman said to him, "Sir, give me this water so that I won't get thirsty and have to keep coming here to draw water." (John 4:10-15)

"Whoever believes in me," as the Scripture has said, "streams of living water will flow from within him." By this he meant the Spirit, whom those who believed in him were later to receive. Up to that time the Spirit had not been given, since Jesus had not yet been glorified (John 7:38-39).

Remember, Revelation is a dream and a vision. The book was never meant to be a history book. In almost all cases, the images used are symbolic and most have been used in other parts of Scripture. So don't take it to be anything but a book that concludes with a victorious message for God's people to take to heart.

If you were being persecuted, wouldn't you want a document from John in "secret code" so that if the persecutor read it, he wouldn't understand what it meant? That is in part why Revelation contains so many images. Those images would speak volumes to the initiated, but would be meaningless to the outsider. I am not saying that the message of Revelation is only available to some special group, except to say that the special group is anyone who knows God and His Word.

8:1 *When he opened the seventh seal, there was silence in heaven for about half an hour.*

We now return to the seventh seal. The first six seals were opened in chapter six. A sense of solemnity was present as this seventh and final seal was opened, hence the silence.

It is good to worship and sing in a loud voice. It is also good to reflect in silence on what the Lord God is doing and who He is. Both silence and loudness have their place in worship.

You get the impression that this dream or vision was being given to John in real time. When you dream at night, your dreams may not last very long, although they can be quite vivid and detailed. This Revelation vision seemed to play out over a long period of time. This would keep with the tradition that John received the Revelation over a period of days. Otherwise, how would he have known that there was silence for half an hour?

8:2 *And I saw the seven angels who stand before God, and to them were given seven trumpets.*

God always provides the angels with what they need to proclaim and deliver the message on His behalf. The angels did not take their own trumpets; they were given trumpets. You and I should not take our own trumpets but rather the trumpet that the Lord gives us. It is not our message but His message that we are to faithfully deliver.

You have to work not to hear the Lord. An angel is blowing a trumpet is hard to miss! Consider the following passage:

> *Does not wisdom call out? Does not understanding raise her voice? n the heights along the way, where the paths meet, she takes her stand; beside the gates leading into the city, at the entrances, she cries aloud: "To you, O men, I call out; I raise my voice to all mankind. You who are simple, gain prudence; you who are foolish, gain understanding.*
>
> *Listen, for I have worthy things to say; I open my lips to speak what is right. My mouth speaks what is true, for my lips detest wickedness. All the words of my mouth are just; none of them is crooked or perverse. To the discerning all of them are right; they are faultless to those who have knowledge* (Proverbs 8:1-9).

Wisdom is stationed at a high place "along the way" and cries out! Hearing the voice of God isn't that difficult if you are committed to hear it before you hear it. That's right, once you have determined to hear God, He will speak, through His Word, through a still, small internal voice, other people, or circumstances. How can we do the will of God unless He tells us what that is? What is God saying to you at this point in your walk with Him?

Study 20: Revelation 8:3-7

8:3 *Another angel, who had a golden censer, came and stood at the altar. He was given much incense to offer, with the prayers of all the saints, on the golden altar before the throne.*

I wonder if this angel was the Lord Himself? Since He is seated at the right hand of the Father and makes intercession, I wonder if this is a picture of the Church's partnership in prayer with the great Intercessor Himself! The saints mix their prayers with the incense or prayers of Jesus.

I have always liked the picture described in Acts 10, as previously mentioned in Study 14:

At Caesarea there was a man named Cornelius, a centurion in what was known as the Italian Regiment. He and all his family were devout and God-fearing; he gave generously to those in need and prayed to God regularly. One day at about three in the afternoon he had a vision. He distinctly saw an angel of God, who came to him and said, "Cornelius!" Cornelius stared at him in fear. "What is it, Lord?" he asked. The angel answered, "Your prayers and gifts to the poor have come up as a memorial offering before God" Acts 10:1-4).

Cornelius' gifts to the poor and prayers went up as a memorial offering to God. When you pray and give, it is like incense that goes up to God. No one else may "smell" it, but He does. It is a pleasant aroma to Him. I want the Lord to say about me, "Wow, you smell good!"

8:4 *The smoke of the incense, together with the prayers of the saints, went up before God from the angel's hand.*

The concept of what you do giving off a smell is a popular concept in the Bible. Let's consider some instances:

Be imitators of God, therefore, as dearly loved children and live a life of love, just as Christ loved us and gave himself up for us as a fragrant offering and sacrifice to God (Ephesians 5:1-2).

What Jesus did was a fragrant offering to the Lord. The Old Testament is full of references to the burnt offering (which was totally and completely burned; it was not eaten by the high priest; therefore the entire

Study 20: Revelation 8:3-7

sacrifice was for God) as a pleasing or fragrant offering to the Lord. Thus, Jesus was the burnt offering, a soothing aroma in God's nostrils.

> *I have received full payment and even more; I am amply supplied, now that I have received from Epaphroditus the gifts you sent. They are a fragrant offering, an acceptable sacrifice, pleasing to God* (Philippians 4:18).

Once again, you see that your giving can be a fragrant offering. God must have an excellent sense of smell, for He notices every offering given to Him with a right heart. Can you imagine then what our flesh must smell like to God? Have you ever smelled the dead body of an animal after a few days? It stinks! That is what our flesh smells like to God. You cannot cover that smell with perfume. In the same way, you cannot cover your fleshly deeds with something like perfume either. God knows whether or not it is spirit or flesh.

> *For we are to God the aroma of Christ among those who are being saved and those who are perishing. To the one we are the smell of death; to the other, the fragrance of life. And who is equal to such a task?* (2 Corinthians 2:15-16)

You see that you do have an odor, but even when you smell good to God, you may smell bad to someone else who doesn't know the Lord. Pleasing God with your aroma is more important than pleasing anyone else.

8:5 *Then the angel took the censer, filled it with fire from the altar, and hurled it on the earth; and there came peals of thunder, rumblings, flashes of lightning and an earthquake.*

Your prayers affect the events on earth. The censer, fire and angel all play a part in bringing about some cataclysmic events on earth. But remember, this is apocalyptic language, representing earthshaking events, often with spiritual implications, without referring to specific activities.

This is another reason why this angel may be Jesus. This angel had power to affect the events on earth and doesn't seem to take his direction from God the Father. He acts independently, so to speak, yet we know He acts in perfect harmony with God's will.

8:6 ***Then the seven angels who had the seven trumpets prepared to sound them.***

There were seven seals and then there were seven trumpets. Trumpets usually announce something; they are loud, regal sounding instruments. They both had a specific order in which they were to be opened or sounded. God's will is done in sequential order. The first had to happen before the second and so forth. God has a plan for human history. It unfolds according to His will. Nothing is a mistake or happens out of order.

8:7 ***The first angel sounded his trumpet, and there came hail and fire mixed with blood, and it was hurled down upon the earth. A third of the earth was burned up, a third of the trees were burned up, and all the green grass was burned up.***

This is a strange mixture: hail, fire, and blood. Again, this cannot be taken literally. Over the centuries, many wars and calamities have had their origins in heaven, no doubt. The Old Testament shows clearly that God is involved in famines, droughts, and other acts of God through nature. This verse is meant to show that the Lord is in control, even when things seem out of control to us.

Some have felt this storm is a picture of nuclear weapons being launched at some point in the future, for a nuclear bomb could conceivably cause the kind of damage described in this verse. My answer to that is: nonsense! Revelation is not a book of future events but a picture of heaven working behind the scenes of human history to bring about God's will. To speculate about a nuclear holocaust and then write books that make money off such speculation is foolishness indeed.

If Revelation is a book of symbols so that the uninitiated would read and not understand, thus protecting the saints, then we must think symbolically, without insisting that our interpretations are the exact ones implied by the Bible. Unless the Bible explains itself, we must be careful not to impose meaning on what we read.

Let me tell you what I think of when I read verse seven. I think of two other verses that say:

I, even I, am he who comforts you. Who are you that you fear mortal men, the sons of men, who are but grass? (Isaiah 51:12)

The grass withers and the flowers fall, but the word of our God stands forever (Isaiah 40:8).

There have been events in human history when there was great loss of human life. While this verse is not pointing to any one event that brought that result, it is nonetheless a fact of human history that this has happened again and again. We are not to fear during those terrible times. God is in control. Other times the Word of the Lord has been rare or confused by human institutions. Once again, this verse is not pointing to any one time in history, but rather that this phenomenon of a lack of grass to feed on, so to speak, will regularly occur.

The interesting image of these verses is the role that prayer plays in bringing them about! It was the fire from the prayer altar that started the trumpets sounding and the other awesome events taking place!

Are there predictions in the Bible that have come true? Yes, but they came true in Bible times, so to speak. Most of the predictions were focused on the coming of Jesus, the Messiah, and His earthly life. To think that the Bible would then make predictions about historic events that would take place after the Bible was written is a mistake.

Thus, when some see Russia, Iran, the United States, or some other modern state in the book of Revelation, they are making a serious mistake of interpretation. The Bible is about history, but it is not a history book. It is a book exalting the name and work of God through Jesus Christ. If an interpretation does not contribute to that end, it is useless speculation that detracts from and does not build up the faith of the saints.

Study 21: Revelation 8:8-13

8:8-9 *The second angel sounded his trumpet, and something like a huge mountain, all ablaze, was thrown into the sea. A third of the sea turned into blood, a third of the living creatures in the sea died, and a third of the ships were destroyed.*

This second trumpet seems to bring economic hardship. Since the sea was one of the main ways for goods to pass from one country to another, a loss of one third of the ships (not to be taken literally) would bring about a drastic reduction in commerce. Plus the sea was a major source of defense and food for the people of the times.

God controls the economic affairs of men. Keep these points in mind:

• He owns all the wealth. "'The silver is mine and the gold is mine,' declares the Lord Almighty" (Haggai 2:8). There is no such thing as good or bad money, dirty or clean. It belongs to Him. Bad men may abuse and misuse wealth, and men may worship it; but it is ultimately God's wealth misappropriated by evil men.

- He decrees economic hardship in certain seasons.

He called down famine on the land and destroyed all their supplies of food; and he sent a man before them— Joseph, sold as a slave. They bruised his feet with shackles, his neck was put in irons, till what he foretold came to pass, till the word of the Lord proved him true (Psalm 105:16-19).

God uses hardship to prove His people, to show that His work in them is real. He also used it to direct history as He chooses. God does this so men will cry out to Him for help.

Others went out on the sea in ships; they were merchants on the mighty waters. They saw the works of the Lord, his wonderful deeds in the deep. For he spoke and stirred up a tempest that lifted high the waves. They mounted up to the heavens and went down to the depths; in their peril their courage melted away. They reeled and staggered like drunken men; they were at their wits' end. Then they cried out to the Lord in their trouble, and he brought them out of their distress (Psalm 107:23-28).

People may ask, "Why would God do that or allow this?" The answer is so that people will come to their senses and seek Him. Suffering has a way of helping people realize their need for God. To that end, economic hardship can be a very good thing.

8:10-11 *The third angel sounded his trumpet, and a great star, blazing like a torch, fell from the sky on a third of the rivers and on the springs of water—the name of the star is Wormwood. A third of the waters turned bitter, and many people died from the waters that had become bitter.*

This trumpet and the resulting calamity intrigue me. Revelation stated that a star fell from the sky. That causes me to think of the star that announced Jesus' birth. It appeared in the sky and led the Magi to the home of Joseph and Mary. Jesus' star was steady but not spectacular. The star in this verse is drawing attention to itself.

The Roman emperor at the time of John's Revelation was considered a god. He was worshiped. This cult polluted the spiritual climate on earth, symbolized at times by the waters of the seas. Consider this reference from Isaiah: "They will neither harm nor destroy on all my holy mountain, for the earth will be full of the knowledge of the Lord as the waters cover the sea" (Isaiah 11:9).

This second trumpet polluted those spiritual waters that were God's waters. Why would God allow this to happen? Perhaps the answer is found in Paul's words:

For the time will come when men will not put up with sound doctrine. Instead, to suit their own desires, they will gather around them a great number of teachers to say what their itching ears want to hear. They will turn their ears away from the truth and turn aside to myths (2 Timothy 4:3-4).

If men reject the truth, God will send them teachers who will tell them what they want to hear. Heresy has been in every generation because men are sinful and don't want the truth. They prefer darkness. At times, God gives them over to their darkness and even helps them find the error they were seeking!

The disciples came to him and asked, "Why do you speak to the people in parables?" He replied, "The knowledge of the secrets of the kingdom of heaven has been given to you, but not to them. Whoever has will be given more, and he will have an abundance. Whoever does not have, even what he has will be taken from him. This is why I speak to them in parables: 'Though seeing, they do not see though hearing, they do not hear or understand.'

"In them is fulfilled the prophecy of Isaiah: 'You will be ever hearing but never understanding; you will be ever seeing but never perceiving. For this people's heart has become calloused; they hardly hear with their ears, and they have closed their eyes. Otherwise they might see with their eyes, hear with their ears, understand with their hearts and turn, and I would heal them.' But blessed are your eyes because they see, and your ears because they hear" (Matthew 13:10-16).

Doctrinal error should not surprise you when you find it. It should only encourage you to be faithful to seek and obey the truth.

8:12 *The fourth angel sounded his trumpet, and a third of the sun was struck, a third of the moon, and a third of the stars, so that a third of them turned dark. A third of the day was without light, and also a third of the night.*

What an eerie scene! I once encountered a solar eclipse and the darkness was very strange. It gave everything a green tint and covered everything in a spooky noon darkness. Jesus is the light of the world by His own declaration. The report in this verse seems to mean that His light and presence will not be felt for a while and the Church—His body and agent—will be rendered ineffective to the world at certain times.

I don't think this pertains to any one era or historical context, but it is a general phenomenon. For instance, during World War II, there was a great darkness over the earth. The Church seemed impotent to make much of a difference. People were praying for sure, but the world went crazy. At the end of the war, the climate changed, and light seemed to be restored. There have been many other dark times since Revelation was penned, and there will be others should the Lord tarry.

8:13 *As I watched, I heard an eagle that was flying in midair call out in a loud voice: "Woe! Woe! Woe to the inhabitants of the earth, because of the trumpet blasts about to be sounded by the other three angels!"*

As if things were not bad enough, an eagle appeared to warn of the next three trumpet blasts.

The Church should be aware of what God is doing on the earth. He wants to tell the Church (symbolized by the high-flying eagle that soars with the help of the Spirit's wind) so the Church can tell the unchurched and unsaved. "Surely the Sovereign Lord does nothing without revealing his plan to his servants the prophets" (Amos 3:7).

The prophetic today is an interesting phenomenon in the modern church. Some Christians are infatuated with prophets who can tell you what you had for breakfast. Why do I need to be told that? I already know what I ate for breakfast. I need to hear what God is saying without the fanfare and hoopla.

I believe in the prophetic, but it must always be judged without exception! In my opinion not enough prophets are taking responsibility for sloppy and incorrect prophetic utterances. The prophets must be released to speak, however, no matter how messy it can get. Paul addressed the need to do this:

Do not put out the Spirit's fire; do not treat prophecies with contempt. Test everything. Hold on to the good (1Thessalonians 5:19-21).

Two or three prophets should speak, and the others should weigh carefully what is said. And if a revelation comes to someone who is sitting down, the first speaker should stop. For you can all prophesy in turn so that everyone may be instructed and encouraged. The spirits of prophets are subject to the control of prophets (1 Corinthians 14:29-32).

I am in favor of prophets and prophecy. (Of course, it doesn't really matter what I favor. It's God's church and He can and will use whomever He wants, whenever He wants, to do whatever He wants.) Prophets are fallible, however, and if they deliver in public, what they say should be judged in public and not just on the day they deliver the word. Their word should be tracked to prove its validity or lack thereof.

Some prophets are what I call "upchuck" prophets. They have some "word" on their stomach and feel they have to spit it out and make a mess with no regard to the place or situation. They do not feel led, however, to help clean up the mess that their ministry may create in the life of the church! Some churches give prophets a free rein and others avoid them like the plague. In my opinion, both are wrong.

Study 22: Revelation 9:1-9

9:1 *The fifth angel sounded his trumpet, and I saw a star that had fallen from the sky to the earth. The star was given the key to the shaft of the Abyss.*

There is an unseen spiritual world where things are constantly in motion. We cannot see this world but it is as real as anything in the physical world. What happens in that world (the unseen) often determines what happens in the seen. That is why your eyes need to be opened to see the spiritual reality behind the natural reality. Paul wrote,

For though we live in the world, we do not wage war as the world does. The weapons we fight with are not the weapons of the world. On the contrary, they have divine power to demolish strongholds. We demolish

arguments and every pretension that sets itself up against the knowledge of God, and we take captive every thought to make it obedient to Christ (2 Corinthians 10:3-5).

He also wrote,

So we fix our eyes not on what is seen, but on what is unseen. For what is seen is temporary, but what is unseen is eternal (2 Corinthians 4:18).

You need to take your directions and instructions from the unseen world. That is why faith is so important. It opens your eyes to a whole new world. Often your problem or enemy is not in this world; it is in the spiritual world.

The star in this verse appears to have been a living being. This star fell from the sky to earth at the sounding of the fifth trumpet. This seems like a reference to the devil. He also was given a key, so God gave the devil any authority he has. The devil is God's devil, so to speak, and is under His authority.

What problem are you facing that you were treating as a natural problem that may be a spiritual problem? What are you going to do about it this week? Perhaps you can pray more. Maybe you can stop treating some of the people in your life as if they are the real problem, which they are not.

9:2 *When he opened the Abyss, smoke rose from it like the smoke from a gigantic furnace. The sun and sky were darkened by the smoke from the Abyss.*

Once again John employed apocalyptic language, using words of graphic exaggeration. When he wrote that the smoke of the Abyss darkened the sun and sky, he was describing his vision, but that is not to be taken literally. The language was used to make a point and to paint a vivid picture.

The opening of the Abyss, obviously a place of darkness and wickedness, will have tremendous impact on the earth and its inhabitants. Hell is a terrible place and it has the power to impact the earth because it is also the spiritual reality behind the natural.

9:3 *And out of the smoke locusts came down upon the earth and were given power like that of scorpions of the earth.*

Study 22: Revelation 9:1-9

The locusts are a reference to demonic powers that harass and trouble the people on earth, even the saints. Locusts devour what is alive and the sting of a scorpion may be deadly or at least bothersome. When I see a reference to scorpions, I think of two other passages:

And you, son of man, do not be afraid of them or their words. Do not be afraid, though briers and thorns are all around you and you live among scorpions. Do not be afraid of what they say or terrified by them, though they are a rebellious house. You must speak my words to them, whether they listen or fail to listen, for they are rebellious (Ezekiel 2:6-7).

In Ezekiel, the reference to scorpions is really a reference to the rebellious house of Israel, to which Ezekiel was sent with a prophetic message. The demonic influence released in 9:3 can overpower and then utilize people, who then become like scorpions. These people are to be avoided when possible, for their sting is troublesome and even fatal. "I have given you authority to trample on snakes and scorpions and to overcome all the power of the enemy; nothing will harm you" (Luke 10:19).

In Luke 10:19, Jesus announced that he had given believers authority to trample scorpions. This is a promise not just that the scorpions won't sting us (a defensive posture), but that we will actually hurt them (an offensive posture). You can once again see that these images would only frighten those who don't know their God and His power to protect and sustain His people. For the believer, this is actually an encouraging picture!

9:4 *They were told not to harm the grass of the earth or any plant or tree, but only those people who did not have the seal of God on their foreheads.*

Here again we see the first mention of the seal of God on the foreheads of the people. Is this a literal branding of some kind? I doubt it. In the Old Testament, Moses and the Jews put blood on their doorposts the night the avenging angel moved through Egypt to kill the firstborn males (see Exodus 12). That was a type or shadow of the blood of Jesus that would be shed to protect God's people from eternal death. In a sense, God sealed those who were His in that first Passover story and protected them from all harm. He seals His people today and forever through the blood of Jesus.

There is no external marking on my house or me, but God protects and watches over me nonetheless. God knows those who are His. He has marked them, so to speak. I would imagine that the angels and demons see something when they behold a believer so they know who they are dealing with and to whom he or she belongs. This would be a good place to insert Psalm 91 in its entirety:

> *He who dwells in the shelter of the Most High will rest in the shadow of the Almighty. I will say of the Lord, "He is my refuge and my fortress, my God, in whom I trust." Surely he will save you from the fowler's snare and from the deadly pestilence. He will cover you with his feathers, and under his wings you will find refuge; his faithfulness will be your shield and rampart.*
>
> *You will not fear the terror of night, nor the arrow that flies by day, nor the pestilence that stalks in the darkness, nor the plague that destroys at midday. A thousand may fall at your side, ten thousand at your right hand, but it will not come near you. You will only observe with your eyes and see the punishment of the wicked*
>
> *If you make the Most High your dwelling—even the Lord, who is my refuge—then no harm will befall you, no disaster will come near your tent. For he will command his angels concerning you to guard you in all your ways; they will lift you up in their hands, so that you will not strike your foot against a stone. You will tread upon the lion and the cobra; you will trample the great lion and the serpent.*
>
> *"Because he loves me," says the Lord, "I will rescue him; I will protect him, for he acknowledges my name. He will call upon me, and I will answer him; I will be with him in trouble, I will deliver him and honor him. With long life will I satisfy him and show him my salvation."*
> (Psalm 91:1-16).

You need to remember these promises while you are reading the terrible events outlined in Revelation. Do you believe what the Lord has said concerning His protection for you? If so, do you have any reason to be afraid?

9:5 *They were not given power to kill them, but only to torture them for five months. And the agony they suffered was like that of the sting of a scorpion when it strikes a man.*

God is in control, even during times of trouble. These evil forces mentioned in this verse weren't free to do whatever they wanted for as long as they chose. They were on a leash, so to speak, and God was holding the leash. They could only go as far as He would let them.

Study 22: Revelation 9:1-9

God allows trouble in the lives of those who don't know Him so they will realize their need for Him. He allows trouble in the lives of those who do know Him so they can increase their faith in His promises and eternal, unchanging faithful nature. Are you in trouble? Then rejoice for God is with you, and He will deliver you in His own way and time.

9:6 *During those days men will seek death, but will not find it; they will long to die, but death will elude them.*

Some men will try anything except God to relieve their time of distress. Death is in God's hands, and cannot and should not be chosen as an option by any man or woman. The best time to seek the Lord is when you are not in such distress. If you know Him, the distress is manageable by His grace once it comes.

9:7 *The locusts looked like horses prepared for battle. On their heads they wore something like crowns of gold, and their faces resembled human faces.*

These cannot be literal locusts, for they are too "human" in appearance. They were on horses (If Revelation were written today, they would be riding tanks and motorcycles. My point is that Revelation was given in the culture of the day, with images to which the people at that time could relate.) God deployed locusts several times in the Old Testament as instruments of His judgment. God's judgment was likened to a swarm of locusts on several other occasions. A few include:
- Locusts were one of the plagues on Egypt—see Exodus 10.
- Locusts were promised if Israel disobeyed—see Deuteronomy 28:38.
- The Lord took credit for swarms of locusts—see Amos 8:9.

So these locusts with human features were consistent with the rest of Scripture—people used by God for His own purposes, even judgment.

9:8 *Their hair was like women's hair, and their teeth were like lions' teeth.*

These other locusts were natural looking, but they could be fierce. They will do whatever it takes to overcome the people against which they are sent. There certainly is a human resemblance to these so-called locusts. A locust with teeth like a lion would be able to devour a lot of flesh or vegetation! These locusts were destructive.

9:9 *They had breastplates like breastplates of iron, and the sound of their wings was like the thundering of many horses and chariots rushing into battle.*

When you read graphic, unusual descriptions such as the one above, it certainly activates your imagination. What did all these locusts look like in their totality? What did they sound like? What did they smell like? I don't know, but I'm glad I don't have to deal with them directly. I have the seal of my God and therefore they don't attack me. That is the power of this apocalyptic language; it stirs you to see things that are out of the ordinary. Furthermore, such language stirs all your senses to meditate on the picture at hand and then to rest in God's protective love.

You may think you have problems, but just think of how much worse things could be. Think about having problems and not knowing how to cry out to God for help. That would be terrible! Yet that is the plight of those who aren't sealed with the mark of God. They have no hope and little help. They can only "ride out the storm" until it passes, only to face another storm at some point in time. And one of those storms will lead to death and an eternity apart from God!

These locusts were able to make a lot of noise. I knew a pastor once who used to say, "Error is halfway around the world before truth ever gets off the mark!" False doctrines have a way of appealing to the unregenerate mind and become the latest spiritual fad. In my lifetime, I have seen transcendental meditation, new age philosophies, Scientology, and Sun Yung Moon come on the world scene in a powerful way. Then they seem to subside and give way to another fad.

The angels made a loud noise and so did the locusts. Many sounds try to drown out the sounds of heaven, distracting people and keeping them from the truth. That is why Jesus was so emphatic that His sheep know His voice. He will not allow them to be distracted.

> *I am the good shepherd; I know my sheep and my sheep know me—just as the Father knows me and I know the Father—and I lay down my life for the sheep. I have other sheep that are not of this sheep pen. I must bring them also. They too will listen to my voice, and there shall be one flock and one shepherd* (John 10:14-16).

Study 23: Revelation 9:10-17

9:10 *They had tails and stings like scorpions, and in their tails they had power to torment people for five months.*

For some reason, this aspect of a five-month limit to their effectiveness is reasserted after we had already seen it in 9:5.

A scorpion injects poison into its victims. These locusts and scorpions had the ability to inject poison into the hearts and souls of mankind. Their effectiveness was limited, however, to certain seasons and time frames.

9:11 *They had as king over them the angel of the Abyss, whose name in Hebrew is Abaddon, and in Greek, Apollyon.*

There is a hierarchy in the spirit world. These locusts had a king (and they themselves wore crowns as described in 9:7 earlier). This world at times seems to be ruling, but it is a false crown that cannot last.

Abaddon and Apollyon refer to the word *destroyer*. That is what the kingdom of darkness does so effectively. It seeks to kill and destroy. "The thief comes only to steal and kill and destroy; I have come that they may have life, and have it to the full" (John 10:10).

Wickedness must exist for men to see the goodness God offers and for them to have a choice between good and evil. The remarkable thing isn't that God allows evil; the remarkable thing is that men continue to choose evil over good and blame God for the consequences.

> *The light shines in the darkness, but the darkness has not understood it. There came a man who was sent from God; his name was John. He came as a witness to testify concerning that light, so that through him all men might believe. He himself was not the light; he came only as a witness to the light. The true light that gives light to every man was coming into the world. He was in the world, and though the world was made through him, the world did not recognize him. He came to that which was his own, but his own did not receive him* (John 1:5-11).

Given a chance to choose light, men continue to choose darkness and its ramifications.

9:12 *The first woe is past; two other woes are yet to come.*

There were two woes yet to come. The early church, to whom this was addressed, must have been living in quite an onslaught of wickedness, but they survived. If you and I have to go through something similar, we will too! That is the message of Revelation. They made it because God is in control and we will make it too! Amen. Thank You, Lord.

9:13 *The sixth angel sounded his trumpet, and I heard a voice coming from the horns of the golden altar that is before God.*

The first trumpet sounded in Revelation 8. It has taken a while for us to reach the sixth trumpet. Seven seals were also opened and then seven trumpets were to be sounded. Remember how the number seven figures prominently in Revelation. There were also seven churches, seven angels of the churches, seven stars, and seven lamp stands. I had a Bible teacher tell me once that when he found seven points in his teaching lesson, he stopped looking for any more.

This is the first and only reference in Revelation to a golden altar before God. The altar in the Old Testament was a place of sacrifice, atonement for sin, and mercy or judgment. The altar could be a place of mercy for anyone who unintentionally sinned and took hold of the horns of the altar. That person's case would then be evaluated to see what his or her punishment would be. If that person killed somebody willfully, the altar could not provide mercy. The man or woman was condemned to death. If that person killed someone by accident, he or she could receive mercy. Even in the Old Testament, God judged the thoughts and intentions of the heart as indicated in Hebrews 4:12-13:

> *For the word of God is living and active. Sharper than any double-edged sword, it penetrates even to dividing soul and spirit, joints and marrow; it judges the thoughts and attitudes of the heart. Nothing in all creation is hidden from God's sight. Everything is uncovered and laid bare before the eyes of him to whom we must give account.*

The Old Testament altar was a shadow of this heavenly altar mentioned in 9:17. This altar had a voice and it spoke to mankind. This altar spoke of the sacrifice for sin that Jesus made once and for all. Those who do not appropriate that sacrifice are condemned to eternal suffering. Those who apply that blood to their lives find forgiveness for sins and eternal life.

Study 23: Revelation 9:10-17

The writer of Hebrews told us that the earthly tabernacle was a shadow or type of the heavenly one:

> *It was necessary, then, for the copies of the heavenly things to be purified with these sacrifices, but the heavenly things themselves with better sacrifices than these. For Christ did not enter a man-made sanctuary that was only a copy of the true one; he entered heaven itself, now to appear for us in God's presence.*
>
> *Nor did he enter heaven to offer himself again and again, the way the high priest enters the Most Holy Place every year with blood that is not his own. Then Christ would have had to suffer many times since the creation of the world. But now he has appeared once for all at the end of the ages to do away with sin by the sacrifice of himself.*
>
> *Just as man is destined to die once, and after that to face judgment, so Christ was sacrificed once to take away the sins of many people; and he will appear a second time, not to bear sin, but to bring salvation to those who are waiting for him* (Hebrews 9:23-28).

9:14 *It said to the sixth angel who had the trumpet, "Release the four angels who are bound at the great river Euphrates."*

Revelation was written to the churches located in what is modern-day Turkey. The river Euphrates was a good distance away from these churches. Very often God releases an answer to prayer or a judgment on a nation, but both take time to arrive. Remember what the angel told Daniel, who had been praying for two weeks when the angel appeared:

> *At that time I, Daniel, mourned for three weeks. I ate no choice food; no meat or wine touched my lips; and I used no lotions at all until the three weeks were over. On the twenty-fourth day of the first month, as I was standing on the bank of the great river, the Tigris, I looked up and there before me was a man dressed in linen, with a belt of the finest gold around his waist.*
>
> *His body was like chrysolite, his face like lightning, his eyes like flaming torches, his arms and legs like the gleam of burnished bronze, and his voice like the sound of a multitude. I, Daniel, was the only one who saw the vision; the men with me did not see it, but such terror overwhelmed them that they fled and hid themselves. So I was left*

alone, gazing at this great vision; I had no strength left, my face turned deathly pale and I was helpless.

Then I heard him speaking, and as I listened to him, I fell into a deep sleep, my face to the ground. A hand touched me and set me trembling on my hands and knees. He said, "Daniel, you who are highly esteemed, consider carefully the words I am about to speak to you, and stand up, for I have now been sent to you." And when he said this to me, I stood up trembling.

Then he continued, "Do not be afraid, Daniel. Since the first day that you set your mind to gain understanding and to humble yourself before your God, your words were heard, and I have come in response to them. But the prince of the Persian kingdom resisted me twenty-one days. Then Michael, one of the chief princes, came to help me, because I was detained there with the king of Persia (Daniel 10:2-13).

If you are praying for something, don't assume the answer isn't coming just because it delays. Assume that it is on the way and thank God for the answer in advance. Jesus said, "Therefore I tell you, whatever you ask for in prayer, believe that you have received it, and it will be yours" (Mark 11:24).

9:15 *And the four angels who had been kept ready for this very hour and day and month and year were released to kill a third of mankind.*

God has a plan and He carries it out to perfection. He is never late or early. And God does release judgment on the earth. As we have mentioned in previous studies, God does this in part so that men will cry out to Him for salvation and mercy. But too often, the hard heart of man resists to his destruction.

Is this a literal third of all mankind to be killed? I doubt it, but rather language that communicates great tragedy and loss of life without trying to predict a specific number of deaths.

9:16 *The number of the mounted troops was two hundred million. I heard their number.*

John heard the noise of a lot of troops! There is no way for men or nations to resist the judgment of God. As powerful as the Roman legions were at the time of Revelation, a heavenly host could easily overwhelm the might of Rome. That is another message or theme of Revelation. God is in control, not Caesar. God is more powerful than Caesar. Caesar is to be feared, but God even more! And God's power can be used for salvation or judgment, depending on the decisions of men.

God is mindful of numbers—there is even a book of the Bible called Numbers. God is both administrative and creative. When He functions in one aspect of His being, it does not take away from the other. God created the universe, yet we know what time the sun will rise tomorrow. He is a God of both order and creativity.

9:17 *The horses and riders I saw in my vision looked like this: Their breastplates were fiery red, dark blue, and yellow as sulfur. The heads of the horses resembled the heads of lions, and out of their mouths came fire, smoke and sulfur.*

Apocalyptic literature stirs the human imagination. Do you find yourself trying to picture what these creatures looked like? These creatures and their horses stir fear and awe in the heart of anyone who would visualize them. They looked fierce and smelled bad, like sulfur.

This is once again an imagery with which the receiving churches could identify. If John had seen a tank or a missile, he would not have had any cultural context to understand the warlike nature of what was being described. He could not have described it to the churches to which he was writing. So the Spirit chose something that the Revelation churches could identify with, horses and riders, and future generations were left to draw their own conclusions.

Some commentators have seen specific wars, weapons, and battles in these verses. I do not. That would be too subjective, with no one to say whether or not anyone is right or wrong. Don't use the Bible in that manner. These verses are an image of the fearful and terrible nature of God's wrath, which has been released on mankind from time to time, and will on some again at the final judgment.

Study 24: Revelation 9:18-10:7

9:18 *A third of mankind was killed by the three plagues of fire, smoke and sulfur that came out of their mouths.*

This verse points to the power of the heavenly army to achieve earthly results. Does this verse predict an actual time when a third of mankind will perish? Probably not. The thought of a third of mankind dying, however, is evidence of some cataclysmic event produced by spiritual forces, under God's control and with His knowledge.

9:19 *The power of the horses was in their mouths and in their tails; for their tails were like snakes, having heads with which they inflict injury.*

If God can think and communicate with such visual richness, the Church should encourage the artistic gifts and abilities of its members as well. There is power in art to communicate the message and words of God. What's more, one's creativity is actually an expression from God. He is the Creator and everyone is created to be creative in His image.

That is why *The Chronicles of Narnia* along with *The Space Trilogy* by C. S. Lewis are still so popular today. He used graphic images and wonderful storytelling to communicate spiritual truth. *The Lord of the Rings* by J. R. R. Tolkien is another example of tremendous creativity that came from a believer and touched the world. Are you fully expressing your God-given creativity?

Symbols as found in 9:18 are not to be interpreted literally down to their details, saying that the tail means this and the mouth means that. The image is to be considered as a whole. These creatures represent powerful spiritual forces, under God's control, that will do some kind of damage on the earth. The Church simply needs to know whenever they are loosed that God is in control and that the Church can be protected, just as God protected the Jews in Egypt when the plagues came.

9:20 *The rest of mankind that were not killed by these plagues still did not repent of the work of their hands; they did not stop worshiping demons, and idols of gold, silver, bronze, stone and wood—idols that cannot see or hear or walk.*

How far man fell when Adam and Eve sinned! We lost our ability to see God, and now we actually blame God for our problems when it is our sin that has caused the problems. So we should not be surprised that people do not repent or change when calamity strikes. The hardness of man's heart does not allow him to turn to God. Human history is full of examples of men redoubling their efforts to avoid God when God has revealed His power and judgment.

Study 24: Revelation 9:18–10:7

9:21 *Nor did they repent of their murders, their magic arts, their sexual immorality or their thefts.*

The Church must continue to preach to a world that has not only ignored God but has also rejected Him outright. It took me some time to get accustomed to the idea that some people don't ignore God, they hate Him! They despise what He stands for and actively work against His purposes and consequently hate His people.

The fact that these verses report that men did not repent leads me to believe that the fearful events described were allowed for that to happen: that men would repent and turn to God when they saw His awesome judgments. Paul wrote: "This is good, and pleases God our Savior, who wants all men to be saved and to come to a knowledge of the truth" (1 Timothy 2:3-4).

While judgment is released from time to time, God wants all men to know Him. Therefore what He does happens to bring men to a saving knowledge of His grace. The Church must avoid rhetoric that portrays God as someone who is angry all the time. Yes, we must tell the world that His patience has an end, but we must continue to point to God's love and appeal for men and women everywhere to repent and accept God's loving salvation in Christ.

10:1 *Then I saw another mighty angel coming down from heaven. He was robed in a cloud, with a rainbow above his head; his face was like the sun, and his legs were like fiery pillars.*

This "messenger" was so impressive in his appearance that it causes me to wonder whether or not it is the Lord Jesus Himself! Angels are usually depicted as cute, chubby little creatures that look like children. That picture could not be further from reality. The angel in this verse was overwhelming. No wonder those who had angels appear to them in the Bible were usually overcome with fear. Angels are ministering spirits. They do God's bidding, so we know that God sent this angel on a mission.

A popular notion says that everyone has a guardian angel. The Bible does not verify this belief, although angels have intervened and do intervene on behalf of God's people. There is no biblical evidence, however, that one particular angel has been assigned to every person or Christian.

The rainbow is of course a symbol of the covenant between God and man that was made with Noah (see Genesis 9:13). The rainbow is a sign of peace; the sun is a source of heat and light; and the fiery pillars for legs indicated that this angel can move anywhere without any hindrance, overcoming every obstacle. When it moves, however, it moves in the spirit of God's covenant with man.

10:2 *He was holding a little scroll, which lay open in his hand. He planted his right foot on the sea and his left foot on the land*

Angels are impressively large beings as symbolized by this angel having one foot on the water and the other on dry land. If this is the Lord Jesus, He is indeed Lord over all the earth, dry land and sea together. What's more, Jesus showed His supremacy over nature when He walked on the water. While He established the forces and principles that hold the universe together, He Himself is not subject to those principles.

John saw the first scroll in chapter five. It had seven seals. This particular scroll was open in the angel's hand.

10:3 *and he gave a loud shout like the roar of a lion. When he shouted, the voices of the seven thunders spoke.*

This angel was mighty in every way, including his voice. Since the angel roared like a lion, it would indicate to me that this was no ordinary angel but rather Jesus. Remember what we already read in Revelation 5:5: "Then one of the elders said to me, 'Do not weep! See, the Lion of the tribe of Judah, the Root of David, has triumphed. He is able to open the scroll and its seven seals.'"

Revelation is rich in symbols, metaphors and unusual word pictures. Here we see that the seven thunders "spoke." In theology, there is what is called general revelation. General revelation is the term that describes how all nature and creation point to the existence of God. Creation "speaks" to mankind, telling him that there is a God, an intelligent being behind all that is.

This general revelation, however, does not speak to man's need for salvation or how this salvation can be obtained. That lies in what is called special revelation, and that can only be secured through God's Word. Yet creation itself does in fact give testimony to God's existence and might.

In this verse, the thunders spoke in response to the roar of the angel. Creation responds to the Word of God! God rules not only in the affairs of men, but also through all the activities of creation, including the weather. It

Study 24: Revelation 9:18–10:7

seems there can be demonic activity that affects the weather as well. Consider the following report:

> *Then he got into the boat and his disciples followed him. Without warning, a furious storm came up on the lake, so that the waves swept over the boat. But Jesus was sleeping. The disciples went and woke him, saying, "Lord, save us! We're going to drown!" He replied, "You of little faith, why are you so afraid?" Then he got up and rebuked the winds and the waves, and it was completely calm. The men were amazed and asked, "What kind of man is this? Even the winds and the waves obey him!"* (Matthew 8:23-27).

Jesus getting into the boat seemed to instigate the storm. Furthermore, it would seem that He spoke to some intelligent force behind the storm to calm it. Even if there was no demonic activity in this story, it still shows Jesus' control over the forces of nature.

10:4 *And when the seven thunders spoke, I was about to write; but I heard a voice from heaven say, "Seal up what the seven thunders have said and do not write it down."*

God can show you things that are personal and are not to be shared with other people. John was recording what he saw and heard, but he was ordered not to record what the seven thunders spoke. Timing is an important factor in reporting what God is doing. Not everyone is ready to hear what you have to say or what you have seen. On several occasions, for example, Jesus ordered His disciples not to report what they had seen and heard. Can you keep God's secrets until the time is right to share them?

10:5 *Then the angel I had seen standing on the sea and on the land raised his right hand to heaven.*

This would be unusual behavior for an angel, for this angel was either initiating or endorsing certain activity. Since angels don't initiate on their own, this would seem to be another indication that this angel was Jesus.

10:6-7 *And he swore by him who lives for ever and ever, who created the heavens and all that is in them, the earth and all that is in it, and the sea and all that is in it, and said, "There will be no more delay!*

> *But in the days when the seventh angel is about to sound his trumpet, the mystery of God will be accomplished, just as he announced to his servants the prophets."*

The angel announced that there should be no more delay. If something happened two thousand years after this, it would represent a significant delay. My point is that the angel was announcing something that was taking place at that time, not something that would take place in the future. And we have seen that there is a possibility that it would occur over and over again.

What is the mystery in 10:7? The biblical context for a mystery is something that was once hidden but now is revealed. Paul wrote,

> *Surely you have heard about the administration of God's grace that was given to me for you, that is, the mystery made known to me by revelation, as I have already written briefly. In reading this, then, you will be able to understand my insight into the mystery of Christ, which was not made known to men in other generations as it has now been revealed by the Spirit to God's holy apostles and prophets.*
>
> *This mystery is that through the gospel the Gentiles are heirs together with Israel, members together of one body, and sharers together in the promise in Christ Jesus. I became a servant of this gospel by the gift of God's grace given me through the working of his power* (Ephesians 3:2-7).

Paul explained that the mystery was the Gentiles were now included in the administration of the grace of the gospel! The cataclysmic events, the turmoil in heaven, and the terrible events on earth described in these verses in Revelation were all about salvation. God was and is saving the Gentiles. The Lord of the land and sea, who has firm footing standing on either one, was declaring in this verse that God's purpose will be accomplished! All the in habitants of the world, not just Israel, have access to the salvation of God. One of the Old Testament prophets wrote,

> *Surely the Sovereign Lord does nothing without revealing his plan to his servants the prophets. The lion has roared—who will not fear? The Sovereign Lord has spoken—who can but prophesy?* (Amos 3:7-8).

The Lord announced His plan to bless all nations, not just Israel, over and over again in the Old Testament. Jesus came and tried to direct God's people toward the nations so that this mystery could be revealed and the promise fulfilled. Of course, many of the Jews rejected and resisted His efforts. In Revelation, we see our sovereign Lord speaking to John, a Jewish apostle and prophet, with a message for the Gentile churches. The focus of Revelation is on the good news of the gospel, which is for every man in every nation!

Study 25: Revelation 10:8-11:4

10:8-9 *Then the voice that I had heard from heaven spoke to me once more: "Go, take the scroll that lies open in the hand of the angel who is standing on the sea and on the land." So I went to the angel and asked him to give me the little scroll. He said to me, "Take it and eat it. It will turn your stomach sour, but in your mouth it will be as sweet as honey."*

Another prophet named Ezekiel was given a similar command to eat a scroll:

> *And he said to me, "Son of man, eat what is before you, eat this scroll; then go and speak to the house of Israel." So I opened my mouth, and he gave me the scroll to eat. Then he said to me, "Son of man, eat this scroll I am giving you and fill your stomach with it." So I ate it, and it tasted as sweet as honey in my mouth.*
>
> *He then said to me: "Son of man, go now to the house of Israel and speak my words to them. You are not being sent to a people of obscure speech and difficult language, but to the house of Israel—not to many peoples of obscure speech and difficult language, whose words you cannot understand. Surely if I had sent you to them, they would have listened to you. But the house of Israel is not willing to listen to you because they are not willing to listen to me, for the whole house of Israel is hardened and obstinate* (Ezekiel 3:1-7).

The scroll tasted sweet but it upset John's stomach. That is how the Word of God is: it tastes good but it works on the inside, the heart, and that can definitely upset your bodily systems. The Word of God works in you to have its way and to shape you into the person that God wants you to be.

10:10 *I took the little scroll from the angel's hand and ate it. It tasted as sweet as honey in my mouth, but when I had eaten it, my stomach turned sour.*

The will of God is pleasant and good, but often it causes you internal problems as it works out God's purpose in your heart and mind. The Word works in you as Paul wrote to the Thessalonians:

And we also thank God continually because, when you received the word of God, which you heard from us, you accepted it not as the word of men, but as it actually is, the word of God, which is at work in you who believe (1 Thessalonians 2:13).

10:11 *Then I was told, "You must prophesy again about many peoples, nations, languages and kings."*

This is the mystery of God, which is a mystery no longer. God wants to address all the nations, not just Israel or the Church. We must declare to the nations the message of God. We don't carry the message of a particular church or denomination, or our own agenda for that matter. We must deliver the message of God to the nations. This is why we have missions work and outreach, not just to do social work but also to declare the gospel. We can and should do social work, but that is not the main focus of who we are as the people of God. John ate the scroll, it did its work in his heart, and then he had to prophesy to the peoples of the earth.

Are you working among the nations to spread God's Word, or are you sitting in the comfort of your own culture, reading Revelation, and trying to figure out what the symbols mean? If you are doing the latter, you are missing the point. The message of Revelation is that God is spreading the good news to all people in the midst of spiritual warfare and cataclysmic events on earth. What's more, the implication is that you have a role to play in spreading God's message and mystery. What are you doing to play your role as the great cosmic drama described in Revelation is played out in your generation as it has in every generation since it was written?

11:1 *I was given a reed like a measuring rod and was told, "Go and measure the temple of God and the altar, and count the worshipers there."*

The prophet Ezekiel was also instructed to measure the temple as described in Ezekiel 40-42. In that passage, the Lord was restoring the temple after Israel had profaned it through idolatry.

The Lord may judge and punish His people, yet it is always with a view toward restoration. He is always mindful of the Church and is aware of all His people. The Church can never be too big for God not to be able to "measure it and count the worshipers."

I had a seminary professor who said, "No matter how severe God's judgment throughout history, there are always signs of His mercy. And His judgment, though at times severe, is never as severe as it could be." I agree.

Below is what the Lord told Ezekiel after the temple had been measured and described:

> *While the man was standing beside me, I heard someone speaking to me from inside the temple. He said: "Son of man, this is the place of my throne and the place for the soles of my feet. This is where I will live among the Israelites forever. The house of Israel will never again defile my holy name—neither they nor their kings—by their prostitution and the lifeless idols of their kings at their high places.*
>
> *When they placed their threshold next to my threshold and their doorposts beside my doorposts, with only a wall between me and them, they defiled my holy name by their detestable practices. So I destroyed them in my anger. Now let them put away from me their prostitution and the lifeless idols of their kings, and I will live among them forever.*
>
> *"Son of man, describe the temple to the people of Israel, that they may be ashamed of their sins. Let them consider the plan, and if they are ashamed of all they have done, make known to them the design of the temple—its arrangement, its exits and entrances—its whole design and all its regulations and laws. Write these down before them so that they may be faithful to its design and follow all its regulations* (Ezekiel 43:6-11).

If the people of God repent and follow God's commands, He is always willing to restore them. God wants to live in the midst of His people forever. That is His objective. Yet He will not live in a people who are not obedient to His will and purpose, so He must work to purify and cleanse His "temple."

11:2 *But exclude the outer court; do not measure it, because it has been given to the Gentiles. They will trample on the holy city for 42 months.*

At times the world and the Gentiles oppress the people of God and the Church, but God chooses and controls these seasons. God was not concerned for those who were not His people in this context, thus they weren't measured. God uses the Gentiles to chastise His people and then chastises the Gentiles for being such willing instruments!

Then I looked up—and there before me were four horns! I asked the angel who was speaking to me, "What are these?" He answered me, "These are the horns that scattered Judah, Israel and Jerusalem." Then the Lord showed me four craftsmen. I asked, "What are these coming to do?" He answered, "These are the horns that scattered Judah so that no one could raise his head, but the craftsmen have come to terrify them and throw down these horns of the nations who lifted up their horns against the land of Judah to scatter its people" (Zechariah 1:18-21).

Ultimately, the Lord's concern is for His people. That is why at times judgment begins with the household of God. Yet afterwards, God becomes her protector and avenger!

For it is time for judgment to begin with the family of God; and if it begins with us, what will the outcome be for those who do not obey the gospel of God? (1 Peter 4:17).

11:3 *"And I will give power to my two witnesses, and they will prophesy for 1,260 days, clothed in sackcloth."*

Should we search for two witnesses who can be identified someplace and time in history that fit this description? Is Revelation referring to Martin Luther and Bishop Athanasius, for example? Probably not. Why would Revelation get literal at this point when everything up to this point has been symbolic?

The Lord's cause at times seems to be overwhelmed by His enemies. Only two witnesses for the Lord were mentioned in this verse, but the Lord gives His true witnesses power. That empowers those witnesses to withstand all the power of the kingdom of darkness. The Church will always be able to withstand superior numbers and survive, due not to its own power but the power of God, which sustains His people.

Study 25: Revelation 10:8–11:4

You may seem to be overwhelmed at times, but the Lord will empower you if you humble yourself (clothe yourself in sackcloth). Great spiritual power is housed in humility, as seen in the verses below:

He mocks proud mockers but gives grace to the humble (Proverbs 3:34).

But he gives us more grace. That is why Scripture says: "God opposes the proud but gives grace to the humble" (James 4:6).

Young men, in the same way be submissive to those who are older. All of you, clothe yourselves with humility toward one another, because, "God opposes the proud but gives grace to the humble" (1 Peter 5:5).

God is seldom without a witness in society whom He empowers to speak or prophesy on His behalf.

Is there any significance to the 1260 days, which equal three and half years? It is not necessarily to be taken literally but represents a beginning and an end to every ministry that is from God. Think of John the Baptist. He had a definite period of effective ministry and then it was over. It is interesting that Jesus had a public ministry of about three and a half years. Even Jesus' ministry had a beginning and end (as far as His physical presence on earth; obviously He is still ministering!). No ministry of man lasts for long, yet God perpetuates His witness in every generation by raising up new prophets and spokespersons for His cause.

11:4 *These are the two olive trees and the two lampstands that stand before the Lord of the earth.*

In Zechariah, we read:

Then I asked the angel, "What are these two olive trees on the right and the left of the lampstand?" Again I asked him, "What are these two olive branches beside the two gold pipes that pour out golden oil?" He replied, "Do you not know what these are?" "No, my lord," I said. So he said, "These are the two who are anointed to serve the Lord of all the earth" (Zechariah 4:11-14).

An olive tree is long-lasting and provides an abundance of oil from an olive crop. That oil is rich and has many uses, including being consumed by humans. The symbolism here is obviously that the Lord anoints His witnesses with an unending supply of spiritual anointing and that "oil" helps sustain the people of God. The oil can also serve to keep the flame burning on the lampstand. The anointing on God's servants gives off light to the world, although darkness does not want to submit to this light.

Have you noticed how many Old Testament images and themes reappear in Revelation? God was connecting what He did in ancient times to what He was doing in the Church at the time Revelation was written. Of course, those connections continue today. The Scriptures are unified with one theme, and that is the work of God to redeem His people through Christ.

Study 26: Revelation 11:5-11

11:5 *If anyone tries to harm them, fire comes from their mouths and devours their enemies. This is how anyone who wants to harm them must die.*

It may seem like God's witnesses are outnumbered so that their opposition has the upper hand. God is watching, however, and will eventually destroy those who oppose them and Him. It may seem like God isn't watching or acting on our behalf, but He is and will continue to do so.

It is interesting that the words that came from the witnesses' mouths have the power to destroy their enemies. It is important that you continue to speak the Word of God in times of opposition and trouble. It has the power to deliver you and destroy the opposition.

Therefore this is what the Lord God Almighty says: "Because the people have spoken these words, I will make my words in your mouth a fire and these people the wood it consumes" (Jeremiah 5:14).

Once again, put yourself in the place of the churches that were receiving this Revelation letter. They weren't examples of power or perfected ministry. They had their problems and would seem to have been insignificant. Yet they read this and were encouraged to stand and speak even though their numbers were small and their power limited.

That is the same message for the Church today. Your numbers may be small; but if God is with you, it doesn't matter. Stand in the power of your testimony and in the light that you have. God will do the rest!

Study 26: Revelation 11:5-11

11:6 *These men have power to shut up the sky so that it will not rain during the time they are prophesying; and they have power to turn the waters into blood and to strike the earth with every kind of plague as often as they want.*

Both these references are from actual prophetic actions in the Old Testament. Elijah declared that there would be no rain in Israel during Ahab's reign (see 1 Kings 17-18), and Moses decreed the ten plagues on Egypt (see Exodus 7-11). The Spirit was reminding the churches that the prophetic messengers of God have tremendous power, more power than the Roman armies that ruled the world at that time.

Those who read this, if they had any familiarity at all with the Old Testament scriptures, would know exactly what John was referring to with stories of Elijah and Moses. Yet the ignorant would read them and think it foolish and have no comprehension whatsoever. Revelation was a book written in code so that those on the inside (church members) would know what was meant.

Today's prophets continue a long tradition of men and women chosen by God to speak on His behalf. Today's prophets are connected in the prophetic family tree to Moses, Elijah, Daniel and Amos. What God is doing today He has been doing for millennia, and that is to communicate to His people to instruct them and to the world to cause them to repent and turn to Him. Today's prophets are not adding to God's Word; Revelation was and is the last book. Yet prophets help God's people interpret the Word and apply it to modern times.

Some strenuously object to the concept of the prophetic being active in modern times. You can think of it like this: A prophet speaks the words of and for God. When a pastor preaches, he speaks the words of God. Therefore when a pastor preaches, he is prophesying the word of the Lord to the people. It is safe to say that the prophetic is alive and well in the pulpits of God's churches on a regular basis.

11:7 *Now when they have finished their testimony, the beast that comes up from the Abyss will attack them, and overpower and kill them.*

Every testimony, ministry or human institution, no matter how noble or spiritual, has an end. Only God is never ending. This verse would seem to indicate that these two witnesses lost their lives to the superior power of the evil one. While that may have happened, that is not the full picture.

God is in control of all things. Your life is hidden in Christ (see Colossians 3:3). For something to get to you it has to get through Him first. These witnesses died because they had finished the work God had for them to do. He brought them home to be with Him. For example, Herod executed John the Baptist, yet God's purpose was accomplished through Herod. John himself had predicted that it was time for him to decrease so Jesus' ministry could increase (see John 3:30).

At times, it seems like God's enemies have the upper hand. They do not. The Church is to walk in faith at all times. God is the victor! He will get the glory!

11:8 *Their bodies will lie in the street of the great city, which is figuratively called Sodom and Egypt, where also their Lord was crucified.*

At times, God allows His enemies to publicly triumph over His people and His cause. Their victories never last.

What is the great city mentioned in this verse? It sounds like Jerusalem since that is where the Lord was crucified. If it is, what a negative connotation for a city that was once the headquarters for God's work in the earth. Jerusalem had been a spiritual center but now had sunk to a spiritual Sodom and Gomorrah. God is not interested in real estate; He is interested in the city of God, made up of His people who have Jesus as their light and salvation.

11:9 *For three and a half days men from every people, tribe, language and nation will gaze on their bodies and refuse them burial.*

Not only were God's witnesses killed but they were subjected to public humiliation. This may be a reminder to the churches of what happened to Jesus when He was subjected to the most cruel and shameful torture and death. The nations of the world at Jerusalem beheld it. What's more, Pilate (Rome's representative) and Herod (the part Jew, part Gentile Jewish king appointed by Rome) became friends after Jesus' death (see Luke 23:12). The world rejoiced over its seeming victory over Jesus, the King of the Jews. Should we, God's servants, expect any different treatment than our Lord received?

When humiliating things happen to God's servants, it is not an indication that they have done something wrong or that God has withdrawn His favor. It is just another means by which God accomplishes His will.

11:10 *The inhabitants of the earth will gloat over them and will celebrate by sending each other gifts, because these two prophets had tormented those who live on the earth.*

God allows the enemies of His Church to gloat and think they are prevailing. That is what happened to the Egyptians. They thought they had Israel trapped at the Red Sea and acted accordingly. Their confidence was misplaced, however, and they all lost their lives.

Israel and Rome thought they had finished off Jesus and His followers. They probably congratulated themselves on a job well done. Jesus had tormented them, just like John the Baptist tormented Herod because he had taken his brother's wife. Herod had John killed and the religious leaders had Jesus killed. Killing those witnesses did not bring relief, however, for it only strengthened the power of their message. The world and the demons thought they were victorious. They were not. Jesus was and always will be the Victor.

11:11 *But after the three and a half days a breath of life from God entered them, and they stood on their feet, and terror struck those who saw them.*

Let us review one of the rules to help interpret Revelation. This book was being addressed to God's people who were under pressure and persecution. It is delivered using symbols and stories that were not familiar to the unsaved, so that it was written in a sort of secret code. Those in the Church reading this book would understand but were in no danger of someone outside the Church reading it and actually understanding what was meant. The message of the book is: God is in control. Trust Him for everything is going according to His plan. Even if you lose your life in the battle, you will win.

This verse is a veiled reference to Jesus and the power of His resurrection. Only we would see that as people because we know the Lord and His Word. Someone unsaved reading this would think it is a reference to some future event.

Yet the principle of God vindicating His servants is seen in 11:11, as it was in what Paul wrote:

> *Therefore, since through God's mercy we have this ministry, we do not lose heart. Rather, we have renounced secret and shameful ways; we do not use deception, nor do we distort the word of God. On the con-*

trary, by setting forth the truth plainly we commend ourselves to every man's conscience in the sight of God. And even if our gospel is veiled, it is veiled to those who are perishing.

The god of this age has blinded the minds of unbelievers, so that they cannot see the light of the gospel of the glory of Christ, who is the image of God. For we do not preach ourselves, but Jesus Christ as Lord, and ourselves as your servants for Jesus' sake. For God, who said, "Let light shine out of darkness," made his light shine in our hearts to give us the light of the knowledge of the glory of God in the face of Christ.

But we have this treasure in jars of clay to show that this all-surpassing power is from God and not from us. We are hard pressed on every side, but not crushed; perplexed, but not in despair persecuted, but not abandoned; struck down, but not destroyed. We always carry around in our body the death of Jesus, so that the life of Jesus may also be revealed in our body. For we who are alive are always being given over to death for Jesus' sake, so that his life may be revealed in our mortal body. So then, death is at work in us, but life is at work in you (2 Corinthians 4:1-12).

Why would God allow this or work in this manner? He would do so because He wants all men to come to the knowledge of the truth. When the Sanhedrin, for example, heard that the tomb was empty, it was so they could repent and come to the truth. They chose not to do so. They maintained their hard hearts and stubborn minds and continued to resist the work of God. They will have no excuse when they stand before God.

It is the same for everyone who beholds God's works and closes his or her heart to the message of His love.

Study 27: Revelation 11:12-19

11:12 *Then they heard a loud voice from heaven saying to them, "Come up here." And they went up to heaven in a cloud, while their enemies looked on.*

This verse refers back to the two witnesses introduced in chapter 11. The beast that came from the abyss had killed them. Then they were revived by the breath of life and were alive again to the terror of their adversaries.

Study 27: Revelation 11:12-19

Once again, we have a veiled reference to Jesus' death, resurrection, and, ascension. Jesus ascended to heaven while His enemies plotted how they were going to explain His missing body and discredit the faith of His disciples. The work and will of God go on while men conspire and plot against God. All their planning is futile.

As stated throughout *The Revelation Project*, Revelation is written with veiled images so that those who understand could avoid further persecution and trouble. This story of the two witnesses reminds the reader of Jesus' victory over sin and death. The message of Revelation continues to be one of God's triumphant power.

Heaven speaks with a loud voice. There is no way that heaven's will won't be accomplished. Nothing can stand in the way of God achieving His purpose. What's more, there is no way that those who want to know God's will won't know it.

Jesus wasn't on earth any longer than the Father willed. When His time was finished, the order was issued for Him to come home. It is the same for you and me. We will be called to heaven one day and there will be no resisting the call. Our times are in His hands.

11:13 *At that very hour there was a severe earthquake and a tenth of the city collapsed. Seven thousand people were killed in the earthquake, and the survivors were terrified and gave glory to the God of heaven.*

When God moves in heaven, creation can express the ramifications of His will. The earthquake in this verse reminds me of Jesus' death.

> *And when Jesus had cried out again in a loud voice, he gave up his spirit. At that moment the curtain of the temple was torn in two from top to bottom. The earth shook and the rocks split. The tombs broke open and the bodies of many holy people who had died were raised to life.*
>
> *They came out of the tombs, and after Jesus' resurrection they went into the holy city and appeared to many people. When the centurion and those with him who were guarding Jesus saw the earthquake and all that had happened, they were terrified, and exclaimed, "Surely he was the Son of God!"* (Matthew 27:50-54).

Anyone familiar with the events surrounding Jesus death would have recognized this reference to an earthquake in 11:13. Jesus' resurrection was also accompanied by an earthquake.

After the Sabbath, at dawn on the first day of the week, Mary Magdalene and the other Mary went to look at the tomb. There was a violent earthquake, for an angel of the Lord came down from heaven and, going to the tomb, rolled back the stone and sat on it (Matthew 28:1-2).

There is a connection between the spirit world and nature, between heaven and earth. Storms, earthquakes and other natural phenomena can be triggered by spiritual activity. That is why Jesus could speak to the wind and waves and they calmed down. If God has such control over the forces of nature and creation, then why are we so afraid? What are you afraid of and why?

Revelation is not the only book that shows you how turbulent it can be as you serve the Lord and live in this world. Consider what David wrote:

God is our refuge and strength, an ever-present help in trouble. Therefore we will not fear, though the earth give way and the mountains fall into the heart of the sea, though its waters roar and foam and the mountains quake with their surging. Selah. There is a river whose streams make glad the city of God, the holy place where the Most High dwells. God is within her, she will not fall; God will help her at break of day. Nations are in uproar, kingdoms fall; he lifts his voice, the earth melts. The Lord Almighty is with us; the God of Jacob is our fortress. Selah (Psalm 46:1-7).

The message throughout the Bible is that upheaval and unexpected turmoil will occur, but God is with us! God is our fortress, refuge and strength. The fear and confusion generated by Revelation and the interpretations that focus on its cataclysmic, apocalyptic symbolism are unwarranted. The message is one of victory in the midst of any situation, opposition and attack.

11:14 *The second woe has passed; the third woe is coming soon.*

It seems that God has ordered and even numbered our woes and sorrows. None will occur that he hasn't ordained and that He doesn't oversee by His might and power.

11:15 *The seventh angel sounded his trumpet, and there were loud voices in heaven, which said: "The kingdom of the world has become* *the kingdom of our Lord and of his Christ, and he will reign for ever and ever."*

Finally, we come to the seventh angel sounding its trumpet. The result again is a lot of noise produced by voices in heaven. It is impossible to escape what heaven is saying and doing. You may grow deaf to its sounds, but that doesn't mean heaven has stopped broadcasting!

This trumpet, unlike the others we have seen in Revelation, ushered in a triumphant expression of God's rule. Notice that heaven announces not that God rules in heaven, but rather that He rules on the earth! Through the death of Jesus, the kingdoms of this world are now the kingdoms of our Lord and Christ.

Then Jehoshaphat stood up in the assembly of Judah and Jerusalem at the temple of the Lord in the front of the new courtyard and said: "O Lord, God of our fathers, are you not the God who is in heaven? You rule over all the kingdoms of the nations. Power and might are in your hand, and no one can withstand you" (2 Chronicles 20:5-6).

One of the things necessary to change a kingdom is to bring in a new king. That new King is Jesus! This is another message of Revelation. The focus was not and should not be the Antichrist, plagues, or imperfect churches. The message is Jesus! He reigns!

11:16 *And the twenty-four elders, who were seated on their thrones before God, fell on their faces and worshiped God.*

If heaven worships because of the truth that is proclaimed, how much more should we worship? We are the recipients of this glorious kingdom. All authority comes from God's authority. These elders sit on thrones, but they recognize the source of their power and exalted position. It is the Lamb of God, so they worship. What's more, the elders and church on earth worship. You and I don't have to wait until heaven to worship the King. We will worship Him then, but we also worship Him now!

Are you worshiping as a response to heaven's "noise," which is the message of the good news of the gospel?

11:17 *saying: "We give thanks to you, Lord God Almighty, the One who is and who was, because you have taken your great power and have begun to reign.*

The elders gave thanks to their God who ruled and reigned. I too am thankful that One so merciful, kind and gracious controls everything! Reading Revelation should result in praise and thanks, not gloom and doom!

11:18 *"The nations were angry; and your wrath has come. The time has come for judging the dead, and for rewarding your servants the prophets and your saints and those who reverence your name, both small and great—and for destroying those who destroy the earth."*

The earth is the focus of God's attention and action. In this verse, we see the nations, God's servants, and those who destroy the earth all mentioned. While we constantly see pictures of heaven, our attention is always brought back to where it is all worked out, and that is here on earth.

As the verse above says, some servants of God are great and some are "small," yet God will reward them all. God is concerned for the earth, its inhabitants, and all created things. He will reward His servants who reverence Him but punish those who destroy His creation and oppose His people on earth.

The above verse also says that the nations were angry. I refer again to the psalmist's words:

> *Why do the nations conspire and the peoples plot in vain? The kings of the earth take their stand and the rulers gather together against the Lord and against his Anointed One. "Let us break their chains," they say, "and throw off their fetters."*
>
> *The One enthroned in heaven laughs; the Lord scoffs at them. Then he rebukes them in his anger and terrifies them in his wrath, saying, "I have installed my King on Zion, my holy hill." I will proclaim the decree of the Lord: He said to me, "You are my Son; today I have become your Father. Ask of me, and I will make the nations your inheritance, the ends of the earth your possession. You will rule them with an iron scepter; you will dash them to pieces like pottery."*
>
> *Therefore, you kings, be wise; be warned, you rulers of the earth. Serve the Lord with fear and rejoice with trembling. Kiss the Son, lest he be angry and you be destroyed in your way, for his wrath can flare up in a moment. Blessed are all who take refuge in him* (Psalm 2:1-12).

Themes that are introduced throughout the Bible are repeated in Revelation, which serves as a kind of summary and concluding point for

Study 27: Revelation 11:12-19   127

these major themes. God's reign is a consistent theme that runs throughout the Bible and is one of the most important lessons in the book of Revelation. He ruled in the churches is the message in the first four chapters. He rules all the earth is the message after that.

God is moving the earth toward ultimate judgment. Those so-called kings who do not see their authority and position as from God resist God and His righteous demands. They will be swallowed up if they do not repent and turn to Him.

"Blessed are all who take refuge in him" (Psalm 2:12). That is also the message of Revelation.

11:19 *Then God's temple in heaven was opened, and within his temple was seen the ark of his covenant. And there came flashes of lightning, rumblings, peals of thunder, an earthquake and a great hailstorm.*

We know that much of the Old Testament world of worship was a shadow or type of what exists in heaven.

> *It was necessary, then, for the copies of the heavenly things to be purified with these sacrifices, but the heavenly things themselves with better sacrifices than these. For Christ did not enter a man-made sanctuary that was only a copy of the true one; he entered heaven itself, now to appear for us in God's presence. Nor did he enter heaven to offer himself again and again, the way the high priest enters the Most Holy Place every year with blood that is not his own. Then Christ would have had to suffer many times since the creation of the world.*
>
> *But now he has appeared once for all at the end of the ages to do away with sin by the sacrifice of himself. Just as man is destined to die once, and after that to face judgment, so Christ was sacrificed once to take away the sins of many people; and he will appear a second time, not to bear sin, but to bring salvation to those who are waiting for him* (Hebrews 9:23-28).

Is there an actual ark of the covenant in heaven? No, but that symbol is repeated because we are familiar with it and what it stands for. Remember, Revelation is a book of symbols and metaphors, and symbols are a means of communicating a story or lessons. These metaphors are for our benefit and education.

I must always seek the presence of God, but His presence can be a frightening experience as symbolized by the lightning, thunder, and earthquakes mentioned in 11:19. That reminds me of another passage:

> *On the morning of the third day there was thunder and lightning, with a thick cloud over the mountain, and a very loud trumpet blast. Everyone in the camp trembled. Then Moses led the people out of the camp to meet with God, and they stood at the foot of the mountain.*
>
> *Mount Sinai was covered with smoke, because the Lord descended on it in fire. The smoke billowed up from it like smoke from a furnace, the whole mountain trembled violently, and the sound of the trumpet grew louder and louder. Then Moses spoke and the voice of God answered him* (Exodus 19:16-19).

One more related passage can be found in Hebrews:

> *You have not come to a mountain that can be touched and that is burning with fire; to darkness, gloom and storm; to a trumpet blast or to such a voice speaking words that those who heard it begged that no further word be spoken to them, because they could not bear what was commanded: "If even an animal touches the mountain, it must be stoned." The sight was so terrifying that Moses said, "I am trembling with fear."*
>
> *But you have come to Mount Zion, to the heavenly Jerusalem, the city of the living God. You have come to thousands upon thousands of angels in joyful assembly, to the church of the firstborn, whose names are written in heaven. You have come to God, the judge of all men, to the spirits of righteous men made perfect, to Jesus the mediator of a new covenant, and to the sprinkled blood that speaks a better word than the blood of Abel.*
>
> *See to it that you do not refuse him who speaks. If they did not escape when they refused him who warned them on earth, how much less will we, if we turn away from him who warns us from heaven? At that time his voice shook the earth, but now he has promised, "Once more I will shake not only the earth but also the heavens."*
>
> *The words "once more" indicate the removing of what can be shaken—that is, created things—so that what cannot be shaken may remain. Therefore, since we are receiving a kingdom that cannot be shaken, let us be thankful, and so worship God acceptably with reverence and awe, for our "God is a consuming fire"* (Hebrews 12:18-29).

What is God shaking in your life? Whatever it is, you can trust Him.

that He will prove to be the stability in your life throughout the duration of the shaking.

Study 28: Revelation 12:1-9

12:1 *A great and wondrous sign appeared in heaven: a woman clothed with the sun, with the moon under her feet and a crown of twelve stars on her head.*

In Genesis, the promise was given that there would be enmity between the serpent and the offspring of woman (see Genesis 3:15). Here we see that promise repeated. This woman in 12:1 stands for the Church. Anyone reading this who is outside the Church would have no idea what was being described here. Believers would be able to understand this symbolism, however.

Remember, Revelation was written to churches under threat of persecution from Rome. Any direct correspondence that portrayed Rome or Caesar in an inferior position to God or His people could have been used to increase the pressure against the Church. If you are going to understand Revelation, you must in part understand what it meant to the churches to which it was written.

The message to those early churches was that the opposition they were encountering was real and powerful. God was with them, however, and would preserve them. Rome was not supreme; God was supreme. The church and their leaders needed to remember that truth and act accordingly.

The same message applies today for anyone or any church encountering any system, philosophy, or government trying to establish its rule or law above God's. They may succeed for a season, but ultimately, they will fail and God will emerge victorious.

The woman was adorned in symbols. She was human, but she was also heavenly. She stood on creation but was above it. She had the stars of the gospel and the Church in her hair, for she is the bride of Christ. The Church is born in heaven but revealed on earth. And what the Church does on earth impacts heaven:

I will give you the keys of the kingdom of heaven; whatever you bind on earth will be bound in heaven, and whatever you loose on earth will be loosed in heaven (Matthew 16:19).

The Revelation Project 130

12:2 *She was pregnant and cried out in pain as she was about to give birth.*

The Church is always in labor to bring forth sons and daughters of God. The Church's job is to preach the gospel; angels cannot do it. The task is not easy because there is great opposition to thwart God's desire that all men come to the knowledge of the truth. "This is good, and pleases God our Savior, who wants all men to be saved and to come to a knowledge of the truth" (1 Timothy 2:3-4).

Satan, the enemy of the Church, does not want this to occur and uses all his power to oppose the birthing of spiritual children. He does not want the Church to be successful and tries with all his might and cunning to prevent the mission from being accomplished.

12:3 *Then another sign appeared in heaven: an enormous red dragon with seven heads and ten horns and seven crowns on his heads.*

Satan and his kingdom of darkness are pictured as a red dragon. The numbers attributed to his heads, horns, and crowns are references to Rome (founded on seven hills, with ten provinces, and seven leaders who persecuted the church). Or maybe the numbers just added to the fierce portrayal of the Church's opponents. The numbers really aren't important. What is important is the picture portrayed of the intense spiritual opposition that the Church encounters in every generation.

Notice that a dragon is a serpent of sorts, but much more fierce and foreboding than the serpent pictured in Genesis who tempted Adam and Eve. The serpent has grown in strength and power since then.

12:4 *His tail swept a third of the stars out of the sky and flung them to the earth. The dragon stood in front of the woman who was about to give birth, so that he might devour her child the moment it was born.*

The dragon has waged war against the offspring of God. He has the assistance of numerous rebellious angels who were cast out of heaven with him. God promised Abraham that his descendents would be more numerous than the stars of heaven. Could these stars be a reference to those fallen angels that were cast from heaven because of Satan's rebellion?

Study 28: Revelation 12:1-9

The dragon stood vigilant, ready to oppose any of the woman's offspring. He desires to destroy those who would turn from his kingdom to God's. The dragon was using the current world government to achieve his ends, but the Church was not to mistake whom she was fighting. Paul wrote,

> *For though we live in the world, we do not wage war as the world does. The weapons we fight with are not the weapons of the world. On the contrary, they have divine power to demolish strongholds. We demolish arguments and every pretension that sets itself up against the knowledge of God, and we take captive every thought to make it obedient to Christ* (2 Corinthians 10:3-5).
>
> *Finally, be strong in the Lord and in his mighty power. Put on the full armor of God so that you can take your stand against the devil's schemes. For our struggle is not against flesh and blood, but against the rulers, against the authorities, against the powers of this dark world and against the spiritual forces of evil in the heavenly realms.*
>
> *Therefore put on the full armor of God, so that when the day of evil comes, you may be able to stand your ground, and after you have done everything, to stand. Stand firm then, with the belt of truth buckled around your waist, with the breastplate of righteousness in place, and with your feet fitted with the readiness that comes from the gospel of peace.*
>
> *In addition to all this, take up the shield of faith, with which you can extinguish all the flaming arrows of the evil one. Take the helmet of salvation and the sword of the Spirit, which is the word of God. And pray in the Spirit on all occasions with all kinds of prayers and requests. With this in mind, be alert and always keep on praying for all the saints* (Ephesians 6:10-18).

Some of what you are now experiencing in your family, on your job or in other relationships is spiritual warfare. You must approach it as such or be found fighting the wrong enemy with the wrong weapons. You are never ultimately fighting people, but rather you are fighting the evil one. Don't make people your focus, although they are the ones most visible, standing right in front of you.

12:5 *She gave birth to a son, a male child, who will rule all the nations with an iron scepter. And her child was snatched up to God and to his throne.*

The Church in conjunction with Christ will rule the nations. Note that Christ, who shares in the humanity of the Church, came into the world the same way: through the birth of a woman. This would not have escaped the notice of the readers in the early church. We are all in training to rule with Christ.

12:6 *The woman fled into the desert to a place prepared for her by God, where she might be taken care of for 1,260 days.*

God protects the Church. The woman in 12:7 was under attack from the dragon, but the Lord hid her for a season. He had prepared a place for her while He prepared her for war.

Praise be to the Lord my Rock, who trains my hands for war, my fingers for battle (Psalm 144:1).

So they brought the five kings out of the cave—the kings of Jerusalem, Hebron, Jarmuth, Lachish and Eglon. When they had brought these kings to Joshua, he summoned all the men of Israel and said to the army commanders who had come with him, "Come here and put your feet on the necks of these kings." So they came forward and placed their feet on their necks. Joshua said to them, "Do not be afraid; do not be discouraged. Be strong and courageous. This is what the Lord will do to all the enemies you are going to fight (Joshua 10:23-25).

At times the Lord will hide you, but He is always training you to do battle against the enemy so you can participate as the Lord extends His kingdom. What season of life are you in—in hiding or in the battle?

12:7 *And there was war in heaven. Michael and his angels fought against the dragon, and the dragon and his angels fought back.*

How do the angels fight? Do they have spirit swords, or do they fight hand to hand? However they fight, they do indeed battle. The Church doesn't do the fighting; the angels do the fighting, yet the people of God are definitely involved. It is a spiritual battle, assisted by the prayers of the saints.

Study 28: Revelation 12:1-9

12:8 *But he was not strong enough, and they lost their place in heaven.*

Satan loses. It's as simple as that. Every "ism"—such as communism, humanism, Buddhism—has become a "wasm" because God is victorious and protects the Church. He has already been cast from heaven, yet now Satan tried to establish His supremacy on earth. He is already a defeated foe.

12:9 *The great dragon was hurled down—that ancient serpent called the devil, or Satan, who leads the whole world astray. He was hurled to the earth, and his angels with him.*

The devil is a formidable opponent and has some power and permission to create havoc on the earth. By the way, Satan is only one created being. He cannot be everywhere all the time. He is not omnipresent or omniscient. He cannot read your mind. When people say the devil did it, or when they rebuke Satan, seldom are the directly dealing with him. They are dealing with his angels or demons.

The Church has outlived and survived despots, armies, and ideological opponents. It will continue to do so. The Church needs to act as if it is invincible spiritually but not allow that to translate into arrogance. The Church is victorious through Christ. That is the message of Revelation. The Church has withstood her own mistakes, the attempts by governments to wipe her out, and the onslaught of the devil to stand victorious, but only victorious in Christ.

The truth that Paul wrote was true for the Revelation church, and it is still true today. Take hope in his words. Walk in their truth and power.

> *And we know that in all things God works for the good of those who love him, who have been called according to his purpose. For those God foreknew he also predestined to be conformed to the likeness of his Son, that he might be the firstborn among many brothers. And those he predestined, he also called; those he called, he also justified; those he justified, he also glorified.*
>
> *What, then, shall we say in response to this? If God is for us, who can be against us? He who did not spare his own Son, but gave him up for us all— how will he not also, along with him, graciously give us all things? Who will bring any charge against those whom God has chosen? It is God who justifies. Who is he that condemns? Christ Jesus, who*

died—more than that, who was raised to life—is at the right hand of God and is also interceding for us.

Who shall separate us from the love of Christ? Shall trouble or hardship or persecution or famine or nakedness or danger or sword? As it is written: "For your sake we face death all day long; we are considered as sheep to be slaughtered." No, in all these things we are more than conquerors through him who loved us. For I am convinced that neither death nor life, neither angels nor demons, neither the present nor the future, nor any powers, neither height nor depth, nor anything else in all creation, will be able to separate us from the love of God that is in Christ Jesus our Lord (Romans 8:28-39).

We walk in the tension between persecution and hatred from the world system where we live and the reality of the protection of heaven. Jesus warned us that we would be in the world but not of the world.

I have given them your word and the world has hated them, for they are not of the world any more than I am of the world. My prayer is not that you take them out of the world but that you protect them from the evil one. They are not of the world, even as I am not of it. Sanctify them by the truth; your word is truth. As you sent me into the world, I have sent them into the world (John 17:14-18).

Study 29: Revelation 12:10-17

12:10 *Then I heard a loud voice in heaven say: "Now have come the salvation and the power and the kingdom of our God, and the authority of his Christ. For the accuser of our brothers, who accuses them before our God day and night, has been hurled down.*

There is another instance when John heard a loud voice in heaven. It is difficult to miss what heaven is saying. One must actively work to ignore what someone is saying in a loud voice. In several instances when the Father spoke to Jesus, those around mistook the voice for something else. There are also a few exhortations to heed the voice from heaven:

While he was still speaking, a bright cloud enveloped them, and a voice from the cloud said, "This is my Son, whom I love; with him I am well pleased. Listen to him!" When the disciples heard this, they fell facedown to the ground, terrified (Matthew 17:5-6).

And the Holy Spirit descended on him in bodily form like a dove. And a voice came from heaven: "You are my Son, whom I love; with you I am well pleased" (Luke 3:22).

"Father, glorify your name!" Then a voice came from heaven, "I have glorified it, and will glorify it again." The crowd that was there and heard it said it had thundered; others said an angel had spoken to him. Jesus said, "This voice was for your benefit, not mine (John 12:28-30).

He fell to the ground and heard a voice say to him, "Saul, Saul, why do you persecute me?" "Who are you, Lord?" Saul asked. "I am Jesus, whom you are persecuting," he replied. "Now get up and go into the city, and you will be told what you must do." The men traveling with Saul stood there speechless; they heard the sound but did not see anyone (Acts 9:4-7).

As has just been said: "Today, if you hear his voice, do not harden your hearts as you did in the rebellion" (Hebrews 3:15).

At that time his voice shook the earth, but now he has promised, "Once more I will shake not only the earth but also the heavens" (Hebrews 12:26).

God can and does shake the earth and heavens with His voice.

> *The voice of the Lord is over the waters; the God of glory thunders, the Lord thunders over the mighty waters. The voice of the Lord is powerful; the voice of the Lord is majestic. The voice of the Lord breaks the cedars; the Lord breaks in pieces the cedars of Lebanon.*
>
> *He makes Lebanon skip like a calf, Sirion like a young wild ox. The voice of the Lord strikes with flashes of lightning. The voice of the Lord shakes the desert; the Lord shakes the Desert of Kadesh. The voice of the Lord twists the oaks and strips the forests bare. And in his temple all cry, "Glory!"* (Psalm 29:3-9)

What is heaven saying to you? Listen carefully; His voice is all around, sometimes in circumstances or through other people, sometimes through His Word or His still, small voice. I trust you are writing what you hear in your Revelation journal. Someone once said that the problem with taking mental notes is that the ink fades so quickly.

What is God shaking in your life? As you read the above verses, His voice will shake created things and that means that some of the relationships or circumstances in your life may be shaken when God speaks. What do you think He is trying to tell you in the midst of that shaking?

12:11 *They overcame him by the blood of the Lamb and by the word of their testimony; they did not love their lives so much as to shrink from death.*

Satan accuses the people of God to God. You can overcome his accusations with three things. First is the blood of Jesus. I heard someone say once that there is more power in one drop of Jesus' blood than in all the powers of darkness. You must learn to stand in the power and authority of what Jesus accomplished on the cross.

Second is the word of your testimony. You must always declare God's goodness and what He has done for you. Are you giving enough testimony to the grace of God in your life? Are you writing about it and posting it somewhere for others to read?

Third is to allow no fear of death. The worst person to be in a fight with is one who isn't worried about the outcome or personal injury. That person is trying to win the fight, instead of trying not to lose. You can fight the evil one without fear, for even if you lose your life, you will be with Jesus in the next life. You cannot lose, for even if you lose this life, you have another. That makes you a dangerous person and us a dangerous people to the evil one. Paul wrote:

> *I eagerly expect and hope that I will in no way be ashamed, but will have sufficient courage so that now as always Christ will be exalted in my body, whether by life or by death. For to me, to live is Christ and to die is gain. If I am to go on living in the body, this will mean fruitful labor for me. Yet what shall I choose? I do not know! I am torn between the two: I desire to depart and be with Christ, which is better by far; but it is more necessary for you that I remain in the body* (Philippians 1:20-24).

How do you view death? Are you afraid? If so, why? What else are you afraid of? How can the Spirit of God help alleviate your fears? You can only be victorious if you don't count your life worth too much.

When the perishable has been clothed with the imperishable, and the

Study 29: Revelation 12:10-17

> *mortal with immortality, then the saying that is written will come true: "Death has been swallowed up in victory. Where, O death, is your victory? Where, O death, is your sting?" The sting of death is sin, and the power of sin is the law. But thanks be to God! He gives us the victory through our Lord Jesus Christ. Therefore, my dear brothers, stand firm. Let nothing move you. Always give yourselves fully to the work of the Lord, because you know that your labor in the Lord is not in vain* (1 Corinthians 15:54-58).

Please do not misunderstand. On the one hand, you should always protect your life and not be reckless. On the other hand, however, you should not try to protect your life if God puts you in a dangerous or precarious situation. At that point, if you cannot flee, you should stand without fear.

12:12 *Therefore rejoice, you heavens and you who dwell in them! But woe to the earth and the sea, because the devil has gone down to you! He is filled with fury, because he knows that his time is short."*

Since you are seated in heavenly places with Christ (see Ephesians 2:6), you should rejoice. The devil's power over you has been broken. Those who don't know your God or have the power of the Spirit in their lives are subject to the devil's fury. I trust that is not the case with you.

Are you rejoicing? The command to rejoice is found throughout the New Testament. Joy is not a feeling but a decision that you are commanded to make: "Rejoice in the Lord always. I will say it again: Rejoice!" (Philippians 4:4).

12:13 *When the dragon saw that he had been hurled to the earth, he pursued the woman who had given birth to the male child.*

Because the devil is so angry, he makes war against the Church of God. You are his target. We began to discuss spiritual warfare in the previous Study. In Revelation 12:7, however, the war was in heaven. Now in 12:13, it was on the earth.

12:14 *The woman was given the two wings of a great eagle, so that she might fly to the place prepared for her in the desert, where she would be taken care of for a time, times and half a time, out of the serpent's reach.*

As stated in 12:6, God protects the Church. The Church cannot protect herself without God's divine and supernatural help. Jesus prayed for this protection:

> *"I pray for them. I am not praying for the world, but for those you have given me, for they are yours. All I have is yours, and all you have is mine. And glory has come to me through them. I will remain in the world no longer, but they are still in the world, and I am coming to you. Holy Father, protect them by the power of your name—the name you gave me—so that they may be one as we are one. While I was with them, I protected them and kept them safe by that name you gave me. None has been lost except the one doomed to destruction so that Scripture would be fulfilled.*
>
> *"I am coming to you now, but I say these things while I am still in the world, so that they may have the full measure of my joy within them. I have given them your word and the world has hated them, for they are not of the world any more than I am of the world. My prayer is not that you take them out of the world but that you protect them from the evil one"* (John 17:9-15).

He prayed this not only for those who were with Him during His earthly ministry, but also for all those who would come after them. Therefore, God still protects His Church! That is the message of Revelation. God is victorious and the Church is also, but only through Him.

12:15 ***Then from his mouth the serpent spewed water like a river, to overtake the woman and sweep her away with the torrent.***

When I read this verse, I think of Ephesians 5, which states:

Husbands, love your wives, just as Christ loved the church and gave himself up for her to make her holy, cleansing her by the washing with water through the word (Ephesians 5:25-26).

What has that verse from Ephesians got to do with 12:15? There were many heresies and false interpretations of Jesus and His work that plagued the early church. The Word is likened to the work of water in Ephesians 5:26. In 12:15 we see the devil trying to overwhelm the Church with false doctrines. In a manner of speaking he tried to drown the Church in its own

Study 29: Revelation 12:10-17

water. He tried to destroy her by ruining the doctrine concerning Jesus and His work.

On the one hand, Christ washes the Church with the water of the Word. On the other hand, Satan tries to drown the Church with the water of his perverted doctrine and words.

Remember, the devil proved that he knows the Word well when he tempted Jesus (see Matthew 4). His use of the Word was twisted and perverse, however, and not quite accurate. When he failed to trap Jesus using the Word, he has tried to deceive the Church using the same techniques.

> *Bear in mind that our Lord's patience means salvation, just as our dear brother Paul also wrote you with the wisdom that God gave him. He writes the same way in all his letters, speaking in them of these matters. His letters contain some things that are hard to understand, which ignorant and unstable people distort, as they do the other Scriptures, to their own destruction.*
>
> *Therefore, dear friends, since you already know this, be on your guard so that you may not be carried away by the error of lawless men and fall from your secure position. But grow in the grace and knowledge of our Lord and Savior Jesus Christ. To him be glory both now and forever! Amen* (2 Peter 3:15-18).

This has been true even for the book of Revelation, which has been used to make men rich as they interpret the events depicted through wild and mostly inaccurate interpretations.

Our study is through chapter 12, and at no point have we resorted to interpretations of historical or future events. We have rather applied the Word of God as revealed in Revelation to our everyday lives. We have seen the simplicity of the message: Jesus is Lord of all! Yet there is a concept in biblical interpretation that states "already/not yet." Some of the things in Revelation have been fulfilled or will continue to be fulfilled but are not yet fulfilled.

12:16 *But the earth helped the woman by opening its mouth and swallowing the river that the dragon had spewed out of his mouth.*

Throughout history, God has raised up champions who have helped bring clarity and accuracy to every doctrinal perversion of the devil. He also empowers you and me to handle the Word accurately, if we so choose. This can only happen as we study and grow in our knowledge of the Word.

We should not be alarmed when doctrinal counterfeits and false prophets arise. The reason there are counterfeits is that there are real ones. No one would make a three-dollar U.S. bill because there are no real ones. Yet there are plenty of counterfeit $100 bills. That is the same way with the spiritual world. Satan counterfeits the real.

In fact, God used every doctrinal war in history to help the true Church define the doctrines of the faith accurately for future generations. That is why it is important to walk in the historical or what is called the orthodox teachings of the Church. Remember the warning in 2 Peter 1:18-21:

> *We ourselves heard this voice that came from heaven when we were with him on the sacred mountain. And we have the word of the prophets made more certain, and you will do well to pay attention to it, as to a light shining in a dark place, until the day dawns and the morning star rises in your hearts.*
>
> *Above all, you must understand that no prophecy of Scripture came about by the prophet's own interpretation. For prophecy never had its origin in the will of man, but men spoke from God as they were carried along by the Holy Spirit.*

You are not free to interpret the Word as you see fit but only as the Spirit intended. The more Word you know, the less free you are to interpret it after your own bias or needs. The Word is only interpreted by the Word itself or through the Spirit's illumination.

12:17 *Then the dragon was enraged at the woman and went off to make war against the rest of her offspring—those who obey God's commandments and hold to the testimony of Jesus.*

The devil's attacks against the Church have always failed, although they do reap short-term results. This has only enraged him more, and he will not stop attacking the Church until the return of the Lord. We, however, are always victorious in Christ and he will continue to fail. Thanks be to God for the victory we have in Christ Jesus!

Study 30: Revelation 13:1-10

13:1 *And the dragon stood on the shore of the sea. And I saw a beast coming out of the sea. He had ten horns and seven heads, with ten crowns on his horns, and on each head a blasphemous name.*

Whatever this beast represents, whether a specific government or an underlying philosophy of governments that set themselves up in opposition to the kingdom of God, it was blasphemous in nature. It set itself up against God and assumed roles and powers that only belong to God.

Ten horns, seven heads and ten crowns represented a powerful beast with great authority and many allies. The beast also had some authority to rule as represented by the kingly crowns. Yet it was a bizarre and unnatural picture, which is just how any illegitimate government is. No government has the right to rule apart from the rule and laws of the Lord.

The source of this beast is the depths of the sea, the unknown regions that men cannot see or comprehend. Many horror movies portray the unknown spiritual realm, which is terrifying to those who don't understand spiritual things. In horror movies, the evil usually runs rampant until one hero, whether through luck or sheer willpower, overcomes the "beast." There is an element of spiritual truth in this, except for the fact that Jesus, the true good hero, was neither lucky nor willful. He is the Son of God! Through the power of a righteous life, He overcame the evil that was running rampant on the earth.

A horror movie can be terrifying unless you know that all things will turn out well by knowing the end of the movie in advance. It is the same with Revelation. Once you read Revelation, you know the end of the movie, so to speak, so you can observe everything else that happens leading up to the end and not be fearful.

13:2 *The beast I saw resembled a leopard, but had feet like those of a bear and a mouth like that of a lion. The dragon gave the beast his power and his throne and great authority.*

There is always an element of devilish assistance with any evil empire or emperor. They are successful beyond their intelligence and resources. In modern times, the Soviet Union, Hitler and other totalitarian regimes had supernatural help of a demonic nature. The dragon gave the beast power and authority.

This beast had an aggressive nature with great strength as represented by the symbols of the bear, lion and leopard. Those three animals are naturally fierce predators. The nature of dictators is to expand their influence by force, just like these animals.

13:3 *One of the heads of the beast seemed to have had a fatal wound, but the fatal wound had been healed. The whole world was astonished and followed the beast.*

I recently read the book *Left Behind*, the fictional novel set in the end times as interpreted and predicted in many Christian circles. This novel depicted an antichrist that arose to take over the world through the United Nations. While I applaud the *Left Behind* series' evangelistic efforts, the authors' attempts to depict and predict actual events from a symbolic, apocalyptic book like Revelation are unfortunate. It represents a broad misunderstanding among Christians about the end times and the role of Revelation in describing them.

Consider this scenario. This beast is shot in the head but miraculously recovers. That does not pertain to a literal person. In recent times, think of how the world relaxed when the Soviet Union no longer represented the communist threat that it was. Now, however, greater, more ruthless threats have arisen and the world is astonished and fearful. People who once were enslaved by communism are now enslaved by a new world power and influence. It is a never ending pattern of history.

Just as you think one governmental or economic philosophy is dead, shot in the head so to speak, another arises to take its place and delude the world and its inhabitants. That's what it was like when Revelation was written, and that's what it's like today. The message of Revelation is that every beast, while ferocious and empowered by the dragon, is no match for the Lamb who sits on the throne at the right hand of God.

13:4 *Men worshiped the dragon because he had given authority to the beast, and they also worshiped the beast and asked, "Who is like the beast? Who can make war against him?"*

When it comes down to spiritual things, the key question is: Who or what will be worshiped? When the devil tempted Jesus, what did he want? He wanted Jesus to fall down and worship him! It's all about worship. The devil wants to be worshiped.

> *Again, the devil took him to a very high mountain and showed him all the kingdoms of the world and their splendor. "All this I will give you," he said, "if you will bow down and worship me." Jesus said to him, "Away from me, Satan! For it is written: 'Worship the Lord your God, and serve him only.'" Then the devil left him, and angels came and attended him* (Matthew 4:8-11).

13:5-6 ***The beast was given a mouth to utter proud words and blasphemies and to exercise his authority for forty-two months. He opened his mouth to blaspheme God, and to slander his name and his dwelling place and those who live in heaven.***

As I get older, I realize more than ever that God is in control. If something doesn't happen in my life, it is because God chooses not to have it happen. Period.

This beast only does what he does because God gives him the permission to do it. Note how he was given a mouth to utter blasphemies and how he had a fixed period in which to say those things. His authority to do these things came from outside himself. His authority came from God.

Why would God do such a thing? As mentioned in earlier studies, it is because God wants all men to come to knowledge of Him. When they refuse after repeated efforts on God's part to turn them to Him, God then gives them over to the desires of their hearts. If people continually reject the truth and choose a lie, then God will eventually send a lie for them to believe, since that is what they want. This is further explained by what Paul wrote to the Roman church:

> *The wrath of God is being revealed from heaven against all the godlessness and wickedness of men who suppress the truth by their wickedness, since what may be known about God is plain to them, because God has made it plain to them.*
>
> *For since the creation of the world God's invisible qualities—his eternal power and divine nature—have been clearly seen, being understood from what has been made, so that men are without excuse. For although they knew God, they neither glorified him as God nor gave thanks to him, but their thinking became futile and their foolish hearts were darkened.*
>
> *Although they claimed to be wise, they became fools and exchanged the glory of the immortal God for images made to look like mortal man*

and birds and animals and reptiles. Therefore God gave them over in the sinful desires of their hearts to sexual impurity for the degrading of their bodies with one another. They exchanged the truth of God for a lie, and worshiped and served created things rather than the Creator—who is forever praised. Amen (Romans 1:18-25).

Paul wrote that "God gave them over." That makes me think of Moses and his dealings with Pharaoh. At first, the Bible says that Pharaoh hardened his heart (see Exodus 8:15 and 32). As time went on, it says that God hardened Pharaoh's heart (see Exodus 9:12).

13:7 *He was given power to make war against the saints and to conquer them. And he was given authority over every tribe, people, language and nation.*

The beast's authority will be total, in that he will have an influence on the whole world. He will actually seem to prevail against the Church! Any victory he has, however, will be short-lived, since he is under God's control. This seeming defeat of the Church will give him and his followers increased confidence of their ultimate victory, even against God. They of course will be defeated, not by the power of the Church but by the power of God.

God rules and reigns in all things. Is there something in your life today that you need to accept as coming from the hand of God? How can you apply this truth to what you are going through?

13:8 *All inhabitants of the earth will worship the beast— all whose names have not been written in the book of life belonging to the Lamb that was slain from the creation of the world.*

As I mentioned above, it's all about worship for the devil. The beast and the dragon want worship; they want what only belongs to God.

No one can be neutral where God is concerned. If they do not worship the true God, they will worship something. Many are looking for some end time government to fulfill this verse. There is no need. That is the way it's been since the beginning. You either worship God or something and someone else.

I am glad my name is in the book. God has a sharp pencil and a big book, and He has knowledge of all those who are His. Just like He protected Israel living in Goshen during the time of Moses, He will protect and preserve His church in the midst of the world system in which the Church functions. There will always be tough times, for the world system of the beast and dragon hate God and His Church. God is in control, however, and He and His people will rule and reign forever.

13:9 *He who has an ear, let him hear.*

The choice is yours. Will you fear the future and the power of the beast, or will you fear God, who is more powerful than any created being?

I choose to follow and fear God. I have no fear of any beast, although I know the world system has great power that can inflict great suffering on anyone who follows God. I am not naïve of the danger, but I have made a choice to put my faith in the power of God. For that reason, I do not fear the beast and I do not appreciate any teaching or philosophy that instills fear in the hearts of God's people by making the beast the focus instead of Christ.

13:10 *If anyone is to go into captivity, into captivity he will go. If anyone is to be killed with the sword, with the sword he will be killed. This calls for patient endurance and faithfulness on the part of the saints.*

When I took my first missions trip in 1989, I went to Guyana, South America, where I was traveling on piranha-infested waters. Later I traveled to Cali, Colombia, at that time considered the most dangerous city in the world. Since then, I have been to many "hot spots" full of danger and trouble.

I gave my life to the Lord and will not take it back from Him. If He chooses to take my life in some jungle or on a plane trip, that is none of my business. As we serve God, some of us may suffer hardship, imprisonment, or even death. That doesn't mean God has failed to live up to His promises. God has a plan not only for our lives but also for all the earth. Our death will be part of that plan to reveal His purpose and glory.

In the midst of circumstances that are personally difficult, we must be patient and faithful. That is what God requires. The message to the Revelation churches and to us is to endure hardship for our faith, even persecution. Jesus said that the world would hate us. The world hated and killed Jesus; can we expect any better treatment?

Study 31: Revelation 13:11-18

13:11 *Then I saw another beast, coming out of the earth. He had two horns like a lamb, but he spoke like a dragon.*

The Lord opened John's eyes to see the reality of evil and its intelligent nature. The kingdom of darkness is powerful and clever. The first beast was fierce looking, but this second was more like a lamb. If the first beast was not able to overwhelm, then the second beast would woo the earth with its more gentle appearance and demeanor.

This second beast spoke like a dragon, for it was speaking out of its true nature. The devil is religious. He understands spiritual things and even quotes the Bible. Look at the temptation of Jesus, where the devil appeared to be spiritual but spoke "like a dragon":

> *Then Jesus was led by the Spirit into the desert to be tempted by the devil. After fasting forty days and forty nights, he was hungry. The tempter came to him and said, "If you are the Son of God, tell these stones to become bread." Jesus answered, "It is written: 'Man does not live on bread alone, but on every word that comes from the mouth of God.'"*
>
> *Then the devil took him to the holy city and had him stand on the highest point of the temple. "If you are the Son of God," he said, "throw yourself down. For it is written: "He will command his angels concerning you, and they will lift you up in their hands, so that you will not strike your foot against a stone.'" Jesus answered him, "It is also written: 'Do not put the Lord your God to the test.'"*
>
> *Again, the devil took him to a very high mountain and showed him all the kingdoms of the world and their splendor. "All this I will give you," he said, "if you will bow down and worship me." Jesus said to him, "Away from me, Satan! For it is written: 'Worship the Lord your God, and serve him only.'" Then the devil left him, and angels came and attended him* (Matthew 4:1-11)

The tempter was persuasive and persistent. He was offering great power that would have enabled Jesus to do some good things. Jesus, however, understood that power wasn't the issue but rather the source of the power. The devil's power came apart from God; Jesus' power came from His submission to God and His Word. If that is where Jesus got His power and authority, from what source will you get yours?

Jesus resisted the devil and gives His church the same ability. The Holy Spirit provides the Church with discernment to understand what evil is doing. There is no need to fear:

Therefore put on the full armor of God, so that when the day of evil comes, you may be able to stand your ground, and after you have done everything, to stand. Stand firm then, with the belt of truth buckled around your waist, with the breastplate of righteousness in place, and with your feet fitted with the readiness that comes from the gospel of peace.

In addition to all this, take up the shield of faith, with which you can extinguish all the flaming arrows of the evil one. Take the helmet of salvation and the sword of the Spirit, which is the word of God. And pray in the Spirit on all occasions with all kinds of prayers and requests. With this in mind, be alert and always keep on praying for all the saints (Ephesians 6:13-18).

Evil days will come, but God equips His people for victory, even in death. That is the message of Revelation. What's more, Revelation is not a book about the devil. It is a book about the power of God to redeem and preserve His people.

13:12 *He exercised all the authority of the first beast on his behalf, and made the earth and its inhabitants worship the first beast, whose fatal wound had been healed.*

The devil is relentless. His aim is to draw as many people away from God as possible. Remember what was said in the previous study. All this is about worship; that is what the devil is after. He wants the worship that only belongs to God. He is a usurper who wants God's position. He seeks worshipers, yet when he has them, he destroys them. That is why he seeks more and more worshipers.

Our job is to secure as many worshipers for the true God as possible. That is why we must proclaim the gospel to the ends of the earth, for the devil is proclaiming his "bad news" in like manner.

Only one power is greater than the devil's and that is the power of God. You will either succumb to one or surrender to the other. There are no other options. Only one thing will defeat the devil once and for all, and that is the Second Coming of Christ. At other times, he will appear defeated, only to reappear in the form of some new government or philosophy. That is what is indicated by the image of the fatal wound that was healed. Before the Lord returns, Satan will always refigure himself and reappear as another movement of evil.

13:13 *And he performed great and miraculous signs, even causing fire to come down from heaven to earth in full view of men.*

God will accommodate people who repeatedly choose to reject Him and open themselves to counterfeit gods. Do you remember the story when Moses first came to see Pharaoh to secure the release of Israel?

So Moses and Aaron went to Pharaoh and did just as the Lord commanded. Aaron threw his staff down in front of Pharaoh and his officials, and it became a snake. Pharaoh then summoned wise men and sorcerers, and the Egyptian magicians also did the same things by their secret arts: Each one threw down his staff and it became a snake. But Aaron's staff swallowed up their staffs. Yet Pharaoh's heart became hard and he would not listen to them, just as the Lord had said (Exodus 7:10-13).

Moses and Aaron did just as the Lord had commanded. He raised his staff in the presence of Pharaoh and his officials and struck the water of the Nile, and all the water was changed into blood. The fish in the Nile died, and the river smelled so bad that the Egyptians could not drink its water. Blood was everywhere in Egypt. But the Egyptian magicians did the same things by their secret arts, and Pharaoh's heart became hard; he would not listen to Moses and Aaron, just as the Lord had said. Instead, he turned and went into his palace, and did not take even this to heart (Exodus 7:20-23).

The Egyptians had access to secret, evil arts that were able for a season to imitate the things that Moses and Aaron did. That gave Pharaoh confidence that he could resist Moses and God. Pharaoh hardened his heart but then God took over and hardened it for him: "But the Lord hardened Pharaoh's heart and he would not listen to Moses and Aaron, just as the Lord had said to Moses" (Exodus 9:12). When God hardens someone's heart, it is only after one has made repeated choices to harden his or her own heart.

Study 31: Revelation 13:11-18

13:14 *Because of the signs he was given power to do on behalf of the first beast, he deceived the inhabitants of the earth. He ordered them to set up an image in honor of the beast who was wounded by the sword and yet lived.*

All of life is a matter of obedience. Some will obey God, others will obey the spirit of the anti-God or antichrist. The beast ordered the people to set up an image. The earth is full of images that claim to be God that have power to heal, provide, or save. The early chapters of Revelation, however, established that there is only One who is worthy of worship—Jesus, the Lamb of God.

I am not insinuating that this power struggle is an easy one, for the enemy of the Church is cunning and deceitful. I have faith, however, that the Lord is able to protect me and bring me into what He has promised. That is what I have chosen to believe and will stand on for the rest of my life.

13:15 *He was given power to give breath to the image of the first beast, so that it could speak and cause all who refused to worship the image to be killed.*

Martyrdom is a fact of life and history. Many who served the Lord have given their lives to His service. Losing your life for God is not a sign of weakness on His or your part. You cannot love your life more than you love God. That was the message to the Revelation churches; that is the message to the modern Church.

I suppose the basic question is: Can you trust the Lord, even in hard times and death? In many places today if you proclaim faith in Christ, you will lose everything and perhaps even die. The same was true when John received the Revelation.

13:16 *He also forced everyone, small and great, rich and poor, free and slave, to receive a mark on his right hand or on his forehead*

No one can escape making a decision about who or what his or her God is. No one can stay neutral. You will either serve the Lord or His counterfeit. Everyone will be forced to make a decision. The Church must reach out to the world, for many still don't know the other option to what they are serving.

The mark of the beast as described in these last few verses of chapter 13 has consumed the imagination and attention of many people. There is speculation of when and how that mark will be administered.

I hope by now you understand that I believe Revelation is a book of symbols, given to a persecuted people so that their persecutors would not understand what was being said. I also hope you understand that Revelation is a book of victory—our God wins. With so much that is symbolic, why would we now take this mark of the beast to be literal? It is inconceivable to me that this could be the case.

I can conceive, however, of great pressure being brought upon the Church and her members that when they publicly proclaim faith in Christ, they will face great deprivation and even death. The Roman Empire certainly required that people worship Caesar or die. Other governments and systems, most recently the Soviet Union, North Korea and China, have found ways to mark people who don't serve their totalitarian systems.

They have done this without putting a literal stamp or mark on their citizens. Many people have been martyred by these regimes. Those who have the mark will be free to live in harmony with their cultural world system. Those who do not worship that culture will be ostracized, persecuted and maybe even killed. That happened in John's day and it is happening now.

13:17 *so that no one could buy or sell unless he had the mark, which is the name of the beast or the number of his name.*

In fundamentalist Islamic systems, Christians cannot own property and the ability to make a living can be greatly hindered. I am a marked man; my faith in Christ marks me. I must always maintain allegiance to Him. No government, employer or system provides for me. God does. If that will offend other systems, controlled by evil, who want to be seen as my source, so be it.

13:18 *This calls for wisdom. If anyone has insight, let him calculate the number of the beast, for it is man's number. His number is 666.*

I received an article this week claiming that Bill Gates, owner of Microsoft and the richest man in the world, is the antichrist. In my lifetime, I have heard the same said about Henry Kissinger, the Pope, Saddam Hussein, and Michal Gorbachev. This is silly speculation and obviously those reports were incorrect.

It is a waste of time to try and determine a literal meaning for the number 666. If the Bible wanted us to know, it would have indicated. Because this is the only mention of this concept (a mark on the forehead), then we must leave it alone. If you read back over the commentary on the verses above, you will understand that persecution and death for believers have been part of every generation somewhere on the earth. Those who belong to God can be easily distinguished; those who don't can as well.

I wear the marks of faith, and those who don't serve my God wear a mark of works or some other religious system. I wear the mark of joy and peace, and those who don't serve my God must wear the mark of sadness and torment.

Without question there is a systematic plot to wipe out Christians. That is nothing new. It was true in the days when Revelation was written; it is true today. What is also true is that God is still on the throne and the Church of Jesus is still here. It is also true that the devil is still trying, by every means possible, to thwart the work of God. The good news for us is that he has always and will always fail. To God be the glory!

Study 32: Revelation 14:1-11

14:1 *Then I looked, and there before me was the Lamb, standing on Mount Zion, and with him 144,000 who had his name and his Father's name written on their foreheads.*

When we ended Study 31, the mark of the beast was mentioned in 13:17. Much speculation has surrounded that one verse mentioning the sign 666. Yet the writer quickly returns the focus to the Lamb, where it should be. Where is your focus, on the mark of the beast or on the mark of the Lamb?

There were no chapters or verses in the original manuscript. Therefore, John saw the Lamb immediately after the warning about the beast. The central theme of Revelation is the ongoing and ultimate victory of God in Christ. The focus was not to be the beast, the dragon, or the antichrist.

A company of 144,000 was standing with Christ on Mt. Zion. They too had a mark on their forehead. Why isn't anyone speculating about what this mark is? They are not because most believe it is a spiritual symbol and not a literal mark. Then why would the mark of the beast be a literal mark? It makes no sense if you follow this logic.

There aren't literally 144,000 who are "saved" and standing with the Lamb. The number is symbolic. I have tried not to get immersed in the meaning of numbers in *The Revelation Project*. But 144,000 is 12 times 12 times 10 times 10 times 10—two 12s and three 10s. Let's just say these are all numbers with positive meaning and implication, so this 144,000 represents the totality of God's government on earth represented by the full number of the saved community.

Since the 144,000 are standing on Mt. Zion, a location on earth, the number represents the entire Church or number of saved on the earth at any one time. It is not a literal census but a picture of the fact that all those chosen by God are saved in every generation.

God's name is written on my forehead. He is always in front of me, always on my mind. When I look at myself closely, I am reminded to look at Him. When I get too into myself, I am reminded to think about Him.

14:2 *And I heard a sound from heaven like the roar of rushing waters and like a loud peal of thunder. The sound I heard was like that of harpists playing their harps.*

Here is another loud noise from heaven. As we said in earlier studies, heaven makes its message and voice heard. You must work not to hear what God is saying. He is a great communicator.

Even studying the sky and all of creation speaks to the existence of God. What we behold in nature is too magnificent for it to be an accident. This speaks loudly and clearly to anyone who is interested in hearing it.

Since harps are mentioned here (and later), some through history have depicted the saints in heaven playing harps. Notice it doesn't say there were harps; John wrote that the sound resembled that of harps playing.

14:3 *And they sang a new song before the throne and before the four living creatures and the elders. No one could learn the song except the 144,000 who had been redeemed from the earth.*

God is so magnificent and wonderful that we must always be searching for new ways and words to express His glory and majesty. Those who behold Him regularly still see parts of God that previously went unnoticed. These new insights require new songs. Those who do not know God don't know what all the singing is about.

Yet those that don't know God still sing, but they sing of their gods—

Study 32: Revelation 14:1-11

love, money, sex, history, learning or relationships. All the earth sings, but only the 144,000 (representing the Church) worship, for they are the only ones who know Him and worship Him as the Creator.

Are you singing a new song? Is your relationship with God fresh, thus causing you to see and declare new aspects of Him that you haven't seen previously? If not, what can you do to sing this new song? Can you fast and pray? Read a book about God? Read more of the Bible? Attend a retreat or special conference? Remember:

> *Come near to God and he will come near to you. Wash your hands, you sinners, and purify your hearts, you double-minded. Grieve, mourn and wail. Change your laughter to mourning and your joy to gloom. Humble yourselves before the Lord, and he will lift you up* (James 4:8-10).

You often determine how God will respond to you by your own approach to Him. If you seek Him, He will allow you to find Him.

> *The Lord has rewarded me according to my righteousness, according to the cleanness of my hands in his sight. To the faithful you show yourself faithful, to the blameless you show yourself blameless, to the pure you show yourself pure, but to the crooked you show yourself shrewd. You save the humble but bring low those whose eyes are haughty* (Psalm 18:24-27).

14:4 ***These are those who did not defile themselves with women, for they kept themselves pure. They follow the Lamb wherever he goes. They were purchased from among men and offered as firstfruits to God and the Lamb.***

These are not celibates in a natural sense, but they are celibate in that they have not joined themselves to anyone or anything but the Lamb of God. They have kept themselves pure from idolatrous and adulterous spiritual defilement.

Guidance should not be a problem for the 144,000. They simply follow the Lamb. Guidance should not be a problem for you either. You simply commit to do God's will before you know what it is, and He will show you if He expects you to do it.

Perhaps the problem is not that you don't know God's will, but rather that you don't want to do it or feel you cannot for some reason. Often,

God's will represents a radical departure from the norm, which can be frightening. You can then slow down your speed of obedience by praying or waiting for confirmation. I have done this many times in my own life and seen others do it too.

Are you delaying God's will in your life at this time? Is there anything you have ignored or for which you are waiting on additional confirmation, when you know already what you are to do? If so, then please take steps of obedience today.

14:5 *No lie was found in their mouths; they are blameless.*

The mouth is a focus of much of our walk with the Lord. The Bible has much to say about the power of the tongue and its potential for good and evil, for the mouth reveals the condition of the heart. Without any commentary from me, read the verses below and evaluate your own walk with the Lord as it pertains to your speech.

> *Likewise the tongue is a small part of the body, but it makes great boasts. Consider what a great forest is set on fire by a small spark. The tongue also is a fire, a world of evil among the parts of the body. It corrupts the whole person, sets the whole course of his life on fire, and is itself set on fire by hell. All kinds of animals, birds, reptiles and creatures of the sea are being tamed and have been tamed by man, but no man can tame the tongue.*
>
> *It is a restless evil, full of deadly poison. With the tongue we praise our Lord and Father, and with it we curse men, who have been made in God's likeness. Out of the same mouth come praise and cursing. My brothers, this should not be. Can both fresh water and salt water flow from the same spring? My brothers, can a fig tree bear olives, or a grapevine bear figs? Neither can a salt spring produce fresh water* (James 3:5-12).

You brood of vipers, how can you who are evil say anything good? For out of the overflow of the heart the mouth speaks. The good man brings good things out of the good stored up in him, and the evil man brings evil things out of the evil stored up in him. But I tell you that men will have to give account on the day of judgment for every careless word they have spoken. For by your words you will be acquitted, and by your words you will be condemned (Matthew 12:34-37).

There are six things the Lord hates, seven that are detestable to him: haughty eyes, a lying tongue, hands that shed innocent blood, a heart that devises wicked schemes, feet that are quick to rush into evil, a false witness who pours out lies, and a man who stirs up dissension among brothers (Proverbs 6:16-19).

Reckless words pierce like a sword, but the tongue of the wise brings healing. Truthful lips endure forever, but a lying tongue lasts only a moment (Proverbs 12:18-19).

The tongue has the power of life and death, and those who love it will eat its fruit (Proverbs 18:21).

14:6-7 *Then I saw another angel flying in midair, and he had the eternal gospel to proclaim to those who live on the earth—to every nation, tribe, language and people. He said in a loud voice, "Fear God and give him glory, because the hour of his judgment has come. Worship him who made the heavens, the earth, the sea and the springs of water."*

The "loud voice" in this verse refers to an angel who was declaring the "eternal gospel." This gospel is for everyone who inhabits the earth and it is composed of three commands: fear God, give Him glory, and worship Him.

The message of the gospel is simple. Don't make it difficult. Many people don't share their faith because they don't know what to say and don't have the answers to the questions that people ask. Just keep it simple and straightforward and you can't go wrong. You can always tell someone your testimony, which no one can dispute.

14:8 *A second angel followed and said, "Fallen! Fallen is Babylon the Great, which made all the nations drink the maddening wine of her adulteries."*

The second angel declared a different message than the first concerning the fall of Babylon the Great. The Babylon of Daniel's time was an idolatrous place, with a god for everything and everyone. This declaration can hardly be noteworthy if the angel was referring to literal Babylon, for Babylon had been reduced to nothing centuries before Revelation was written.

The angel must have been referring to something else. The truth is that the angel is declaring the end of any system that sets itself up against the Lord and His Anointed One. Once again I must ask you to keep in mind that the early church was under persecution from Rome. They were being told that the Roman system had already been judged and found lacking in God's sight. They were informed, however, in code so that the message of Revelation, if read by an unbelieving Roman, would make no sense.

The phrase "maddening wine of her adulteries" is accurate. People run into error as if drunk. What they do makes no sense, yet they pursue their false interpretations of God and their idolatries with reckless abandon.

14:9-10 *A third angel followed them and said in a loud voice: "If anyone worships the beast and his image and receives his mark on the forehead or on the hand, he, too, will drink of the wine of God's fury, which has been poured full strength into the cup of his wrath. He will be tormented with burning sulfur in the presence of the holy angels and of the Lamb."*

The third angel had another message, this time one pertaining to the beast and his worshipers. We see now that the mark of the beast can be carried on the forehead or the hand, through how one thinks or what one does.

Babylon had her wine, which men drank, and God has His wine as well. His wine is drunk from the cup of His wrath. God is slow to anger, but once angered, His actions are irrevocable.

The reference to sulfur is probably a reference to hell. Imagine the stench! Also think of the heat! And finally imagine the torment of it all carried out in the presence of the Lamb and His angels. What torment hell must carry. Hell is not a state of mind. It is a physical place of torment.

14:11 *"And the smoke of their torment rises forever and ever. There is no rest day or night for those who worship the beast and his image, or for anyone who receives the mark of his name."*

The work of the Church is for high stakes. Heaven and hell are the choices that people have and that is why we must urgently proclaim the message of His grace. What are you doing to lead people to the Lord?

I am not a particularly gifted soul winner, but I do all I can to promote new church planting efforts and missions work. I want to support those who are effective evangelists because their work is so important. There is no rest for the wicked, or so an old saying goes, and this verse supports that claim.

> *Those who worship the beast have no rest now, nor will they ever have any. It is hard not to serve the Lord. "Good understanding giveth favour: but the way of transgressors is hard"* (Proverbs 13:15 KJV).

Are you doing all that you can physically and financially to see that people do not spend eternity in hell? I hope you are. Also, how is your Revelation journal? Are you still writing down what you are seeing, learning, and hearing?

Study 33: Revelation 14:12-20

14:12 *This calls for patient endurance on the part of the saints who obey God's commandments and remain faithful to Jesus.*

God is not always going to deliver you from difficult situations, persecution, or even martyrdom. Instead, He will stand with you and bring you through those experiences by His power and grace. What you must do is patiently endure the suffering until He delivers you, as He promised He would.

"This" in 14:12 refers to what was written immediately before that verse, and the topic is the beast and the turmoil surrounding people worshiping it as opposed to God. Jesus explained this to His disciples when He was here, and nothing has changed since then.

> *"I have told you these things, so that in me you may have peace. In this world you will have trouble. But take heart! I have overcome the world"* (John 16:12).

Paul taught a great deal about the need to endure. You only need endurance when you are going through tough times. So if Jesus and Paul told you to endure, then hard times must be what they were warning you about.

Let's look at some of the endurance passages as we did in Study 10:

> *"Because of the increase of wickedness, the love of most will grow cold, but he who stands firm to the end will be saved"* (Matthew 24:12-13).

We work hard with our own hands. When we are cursed, we bless; when we are persecuted, we endure it (1 Corinthians 4:12).

We do not want you to be uninformed, brothers, about the hardships we suffered in the province of Asia. We were under great pressure, far beyond our ability to endure, so that we despaired even of life (2 Corinthians 1:8).

Endure hardship with us like a good soldier of Christ Jesus (2 Timothy 2:3).

Therefore I endure everything for the sake of the elect, that they too may obtain the salvation that is in Christ Jesus, with eternal glory. Here is a trustworthy saying: If we died with him, we will also live with him; if we endure, we will also reign with him. If we disown him, he will also disown us; if we are faithless, he will remain faithful, for he cannot disown himself (2 Timothy 2:10-13).

Endure hardship as discipline; God is treating you as sons. For what son is not disciplined by his father (Hebrews 12:7).

But how is it to your credit if you receive a beating for doing wrong and endure it? But if you suffer for doing good and you endure it, this is commendable before God (1 Peter 2:20).

14:13 *Then I heard a voice from heaven say, "Write: Blessed are the dead who die in the Lord from now on." "Yes," says the Spirit, "they will rest from their labor, for their deeds will follow them."*

Death is not the end for you as a Christian. It is only the beginning. That is why you can lose this life, because you are sure there is another life to come! I wonder if that is why the psalmist wrote, "Precious in the sight of the Lord is the death of his saints" (Psalm 116:15).

When you die, you rest from your labors, but God doesn't forget any of your past labors for and in Him. Figuratively speaking, God has a big book and a sharp pencil and He writes everything down that you do. The image I have of this is found in the book of Esther. God may not seem to notice what you do, or be in a hurry to reward you, but He doesn't forget.

But Mordecai found out about the plot and told Queen Esther, who in turn reported it to the king, giving credit to Mordecai. And when the report was investigated and found to be true, the two officials were hanged on a gallows. All this was recorded in the book of the annals in the presence of the king (Esther 2:22-23).

That night the king could not sleep; so he ordered the book of the chronicles, the record of his reign, to be brought in and read to him. It was found recorded there that Mordecai had exposed Bigthana and Teresh, two of the king's officers who guarded the doorway, who had conspired to assassinate King Xerxes.

"What honor and recognition has Mordecai received for this?" the king asked. "Nothing has been done for him," his attendants answered. The king said, "Who is in the court?" Now Haman had just entered the outer court of the palace to speak to the king about hanging Mordecai on the gallows he had erected for him.

His attendants answered, "Haman is standing in the court." "Bring him in," the king ordered. When Haman entered, the king asked him, "What should be done for the man the king delights to honor?" Now Haman thought to himself, "Who is there that the king would rather honor than me?"

So he answered the king, "For the man the king delights to honor, have them bring a royal robe the king has worn and a horse the king has ridden, one with a royal crest placed on its head. Then let the robe and horse be entrusted to one of the king's most noble princes. Let them robe the man the king delights to honor, and lead him on the horse through the city streets, proclaiming before him, 'This is what is done for the man the king delights to honor!'"

"Go at once," the king commanded Haman. "Get the robe and the horse and do just as you have suggested for Mordecai the Jew, who sits at the king's gate. Do not neglect anything you have recommended" (Esther 6:1-10).

God will judge everyone according to his or her deeds. You can find rest and peace in that fact, for God never forgets and He always sees.

14:14-16 *I looked, and there before me was a white cloud, and seated on the cloud was one "like a son of man" with a crown of gold on his head and a sharp sickle in his hand. Then another angel came out of* *the temple and called in a loud voice to him who was sitting on the cloud, "Take your sickle and reap, because the time to reap has come, for the harvest of the earth is ripe." So he who was seated on the cloud swung his sickle over the earth, and the earth was harvested.*

Jesus is seated on the throne with a crown on His head. He is the King and is holding a sharp sickle. A sickle was used to cut wheat and other tall grain at harvest time. He was obviously doing something there that represented the harvest of something that was ripe or mature.

Jesus told the following parables and statements that also explain the harvest alluded to in 14:15-16:

He also said, "This is what the kingdom of God is like. A man scatters seed on the ground. Night and day, whether he sleeps or gets up, the seed sprouts and grows, though he does not know how. All by itself the soil produces grain—first the stalk, then the head, then the full kernel in the head. As soon as the grain is ripe, he puts the sickle to it, because the harvest has come" (Mark 4:26-29).

"Once again, the kingdom of heaven is like a net that was let down into the lake and caught all kinds of fish. When it was full, the fishermen pulled it up on the shore. Then they sat down and collected the good fish in baskets, but threw the bad away. This is how it will be at the end of the age. The angels will come and separate the wicked from the righteous and throw them into the fiery furnace, where there will be weeping and gnashing of teeth" (Matthew 13:47-50).

"His winnowing fork is in his hand to clear his threshing floor and to gather the wheat into his barn, but he will burn up the chaff with unquenchable fire" (Luke 3:17).

Jesus told them another parable: "The kingdom of heaven is like a man who sowed good seed in his field. But while everyone was sleeping, his enemy came and sowed weeds among the wheat, and went away. When the wheat sprouted and formed heads, then the weeds also appeared.

"The owner's servants came to him and said, 'Sir, didn't you sow good seed in your field? Where then did the weeds come from?' 'An enemy did this,' he replied. The servants asked him, 'Do you want us to go and pull them up?' 'No,' he answered, 'because while you are pulling the

weeds, you may root up the wheat with them. Let both grow together until the harvest. At that time I will tell the harvesters: First collect the weeds and tie them in bundles to be burned; then gather the wheat and bring it into my barn"' (Matthew 13:24-30).

14:17-19 *Another angel came out of the temple in heaven, and he too had a sharp sickle. Still another angel, who had charge of the fire, came from the altar and called in a loud voice to him who had the sharp sickle, "Take your sharp sickle and gather the clusters of grapes from the earth's vine, because its grapes are ripe." The angel swung his sickle on the earth, gathered its grapes and threw them into the great winepress of God's wrath.*

A final judgment will take place, when all will be rewarded or punished according to their deeds. This was meant to encourage the churches receiving this letter from John. Some in those churches were going to lose their lives. They could be confident that God would preserve them and grant them their eternal reward as He had promised.

Are you in tough times? Have you doubted or questioned God's love or His ability to reward you? Have you wondered whether everything you are going through is worth it? The early church asked the same questions and its answers are your answer: Yes, it is worth it! God rewards those who diligently seek Him and who endure to the end (see Hebrews 11:6).

As difficult as it may be for you now, the wicked will have it far worse for all eternity. The image of winemaking here is graphic and would have been relevant to all who initially received the letter. It seems that everyone will feel the sickle of God's judgment. The writer of Revelation encouraged the readers to be in the first harvest of the righteous. That exhortation applies to you and me as well.

14:20 *They were trampled in the winepress outside the city, and blood flowed out of the press, rising as high as the horses' bridles for a distance of 1,600 stadia.*

This winepress was outside the city. Going outside the city was always a sign of judgment and isolation. Jesus was crucified outside the protection of the city walls and away from the community that those walls contained and represented.

These last few verses represent such a graphic image of judgment without ever explaining exactly what would happen in that judgment. These verses were meant to encourage the saved and inform them of the end that would come to all.

For we must all appear before the judgment seat of Christ, that each one may receive what is due him for the things done while in the body, whether good or bad (2 Corinthians 5:10).

For if God did not spare angels when they sinned, but sent them to hell, putting them into gloomy dungeons to be held for judgment; if he did not spare the ancient world when he brought the flood on its ungodly people, but protected Noah, a preacher of righteousness, and seven others; if he condemned the cities of Sodom and Gomorrah by burning them to ashes, and made them an example of what is going to happen to the ungodly; and if he rescued Lot, a righteous man, who was distressed by the filthy lives of lawless men (for that righteous man, living among them day after day, was tormented in his righteous soul by the lawless deeds he saw and heard)—if this is so, then the Lord knows how to rescue godly men from trials and to hold the unrighteous for the day of judgment, while continuing their punishment (2 Peter 2:4-9).

By the same word the present heavens and earth are reserved for fire, being kept for the day of judgment and destruction of ungodly men (2 Peter 3:7).

The end of the world, or at least of your world, is a certainty. At that time, all will be judged. Praise the Lord that we are washed in the blood of the Lamb and will survive the judgment deeds of God not because of our deeds, but to be rewarded according to the good deeds that He prepared beforehand for us to do.

Study 34: Revelation 15:1-8

15:1 *I saw in heaven another great and marvelous sign: seven angels with the seven last plagues—last, because with them God's wrath is completed.*

John saw things from a heavenly perspective. I wrote in an earlier study

Study 34: Revelation 15:1-8

that he saw reality more clearly on the island of Patmos than the churches to whom he was writing, and they weren't in exile as he was. Why was he able to see? He could see because he was "in the Spirit" on the Lord's Day.

Old Testament prophets were referred to as "seers." They saw things from God's perspective. Some people get strange with this, but the reality is that we all have the capability of seeing if we can understand how to walk and work in the Spirit. You may think seeing like this is only for a special few. That may be true, but only because most believers don't understand where they are. What do I mean? Let's allow Paul to explain:

But because of his great love for us, God, who is rich in mercy, made us alive with Christ even when we were dead in transgressions—it is by grace you have been saved. And God raised us up with Christ and seated us with him in the heavenly realms in Christ Jesus, in order that in the coming ages he might show the incomparable riches of his grace, expressed in his kindness to us in Christ Jesus (Ephesians 2:4-7).

You are seated in heavenly places. You must only look around where you live to be able to see the things of heaven. Have you been living below your position in Christ? How can you raise your living standard, so to speak?

Before we move on, I must comment once more on the number seven, used again in 15:1. That number is used forty-one times through chapter 15. I will not get into a study of numerology in *The Revelation Project*, but I want to remind you that the number seven is universally accepted as the number of spiritual perfection. That means when the number seven appears, it is representing a totality that goes beyond a literal number. Consider all the uses of seven up to this point:

- Seven churches—1:4,7
- Seven spirits—1:4, 3:1
- Seven lamp stands—1:12
- Seven stars—1:16
- Seven lamps—4:5
- Seven seals—5:1
- Seven horns and eyes—5:6
- Seven angels—8:2
- Seven trumpets—8:2
- Seven thunders—10:3
- Seven heads on the dragon—12:3
- Seven angels—15:1

- Seven plagues—15:1
- Seven bowls—15:6

Each example of seven represents God's spiritual perfection and completion in all that He is and does.

15:2 *And I saw what looked like a sea of glass mixed with fire and, standing beside the sea, those who had been victorious over the beast and his image and over the number of his name. They held harps given them by God*

In this verse there is a sea of glass mixed with fire. Glass reflects things and the Church is to reflect God's glory on earth. Furthermore, looking in glass shows you the reflection of who you are. Finally, hiding behind glass is not easy. The Church's deeds are to be pure and holy, done in such a way that the world will see and hopefully turn to Him.

A reward is coming to those who overcome the devil and his world system. God honors the overcomers, if not in this life, then certainly in the next. It is interesting that God gives them harps to play. A harp is a difficult instrument to master. Not many people on earth can actually play one. But if God gives you a harp—something seemingly complicated and hard to do—then He will equip you to play it! What is impossible for man is possible for God (see Luke 1:37).

Notice that the saints were rewarded for overcoming, yet it is the grace of God that enables you and me to overcome. Somehow it is a partnership. I must cooperate with God's grace and agree to allow it to work in my life. Yet I can never take credit for what God has done in my life; it is His work alone.

15:3 *and sang the song of Moses the servant of God and the song of the Lamb: "Great and marvelous are your deeds, Lord God Almighty. Just and true are your ways, King of the ages."*

The people who were victorious over the beast sang the song of Moses. It is interesting that they would sing this song. It is also interesting that plagues were mentioned in verse one. Why this reference to Moses and the plagues of Egypt?

God delivered Israel from all the plagues He brought upon Egypt, and then He delivered them from Egypt itself by the parting of the Red Sea.

Study 34: Revelation 15:1-8

After the Red Sea deliverance, Moses sang a song of thanksgiving to commemorate that event. Anyone familiar with the Old Testament who would read these words of John would be able to make the connection.

Let's read Moses' song from Exodus and see how the message applies to Revelation and to your life in the modern church:

Then Moses and the Israelites sang this song to the Lord: "I will sing to the Lord, for he is highly exalted. The horse and its rider he has hurled into the sea. The Lord is my strength and my song; he has become my salvation. He is my God, and I will praise him, my father's God, and I will exalt him.

"The Lord is a warrior; the Lord is his name. Pharaoh's chariots and his army he has hurled into the sea. The best of Pharaoh's officers are drowned in the Red Sea. The deep waters have covered them; they sank to the depths like a stone. Your right hand, O Lord, was majestic in power.

"Your right hand, O Lord, shattered the enemy. In the greatness of your majesty you threw down those who opposed you. You unleashed your burning anger; it consumed them like stubble. By the blast of your nostrils the waters piled up. The surging waters stood firm like a wall; the deep waters congealed in the heart of the sea.

"The enemy boasted, 'I will pursue, I will overtake them. I will divide the spoils; I will gorge myself on them. I will draw my sword and my hand will destroy them.' But you blew with your breath, and the sea covered them. They sank like lead in the mighty waters.

"Who among the gods is like you, O Lord? Who is like you—majestic in holiness, awesome in glory, working wonders? You stretched out your right hand and the earth swallowed them. In your unfailing love you will lead the people you have redeemed. In your strength you will guide them to your holy dwelling.

"The nations will hear and tremble; anguish will grip the people of Philistia. The chiefs of Edom will be terrified, the leaders of Moab will be seized with trembling, the people of Canaan will melt away; terror and dread will fall upon them.

"By the power of your arm they will be as still as a stone—until your people pass by, O Lord, until the people you bought pass by. You will bring them in and plant them on the mountain of your inheritance—the place, O Lord, you made for your dwelling, the sanctuary, O Lord, your hands established. The Lord will reign for ever and ever" (Exodus 15:1-18).

When God delivered His people in Revelation from the beast and his mark, the people worshiped and sang another song of deliverance, just as the Jews did after they crossed the Red Sea.

What song are you singing? Is it a song of deliverance? A song of freedom? You cannot sing a song of deliverance from the sidelines. God must deliver you from some real danger for you to sing a song of deliverance. Yet often when the trouble comes, you may want to be saved from it instead of being preserved through it.

15:4 *"Who will not fear you, O Lord, and bring glory to your name? For you alone are holy. All nations will come and worship before you, for your righteous acts have been revealed."*

God's focus is the nations. All the nations or ethnic groups of people will see and worship.

How committed are you to seeing the truth of God spread to all nations? In modern terms, that means a commitment to effective missions work. Everyone in every church can pray, give, or go in response to the command to reach the nations with the message of Jesus. He said to go into all the nations. I have asked many people, "What part of 'go' don't you understand?" It is a simple word that is challenging to do.

God loves all the nations. No particular culture is His favorite; no one language is His preferred means of communication. His objective is that as many people from as many ethnic groups as possible will worship Him. Remember, I said in an earlier study that the spiritual battle is over worship. Everyone worships someone and something. The options need to be reduced to one: Worship God!

15:5 *After this I looked and in heaven the temple, that is, the tabernacle of the Testimony, was opened.*

This verse has another Old Testament reference, this time to the tabernacle of the testimony. Let's examine why it is here and what it is saying to the reader:

> *Now the first covenant had regulations for worship and also an earthly sanctuary. A tabernacle was set up. In its first room were the lampstand, the table and the consecrated bread; this was called the Holy Place. Behind the second curtain was a room called the Most Holy Place,*

which had the golden altar of incense and the gold-covered ark of the covenant.

This ark contained the gold jar of manna, Aaron's staff that had budded, and the stone tablets of the covenant. Above the ark were the cherubim of the Glory, overshadowing the atonement cover. But we cannot discuss these things in detail now. When everything had been arranged like this, the priests entered regularly into the outer room to carry on their ministry.

But only the high priest entered the inner room, and that only once a year, and never without blood, which he offered for himself and for the sins the people had committed in ignorance. The Holy Spirit was showing by this that the way into the Most Holy Place had not yet been disclosed as long as the first tabernacle was still standing.

This is an illustration for the present time, indicating that the gifts and sacrifices being offered were not able to clear the conscience of the worshiper. They are only a matter of food and drink and various ceremonial washings—external regulations applying until the time of the new order.

When Christ came as high priest of the good things that are already here, he went through the greater and more perfect tabernacle that is not man-made, that is to say, not a part of this creation. He did not enter by means of the blood of goats and calves; but he entered the Most Holy Place once for all by his own blood, having obtained eternal redemption.

The blood of goats and bulls and the ashes of a heifer sprinkled on those who are ceremonially unclean sanctify them so that they are outwardly clean. How much more, then, will the blood of Christ, who through the eternal Spirit offered himself unblemished to God, cleanse our consciences from acts that lead to death, so that we may serve the living God! (Hebrews 9:1-14).

Old Testament worship was a type or shadow of heavenly realities. Back then the tabernacle was closed, now it is open. Before only one could enter, now all can enter. Thank You, Lord!

15:6 *Out of the temple came the seven angels with the seven plagues. They were dressed in clean, shining linen and wore golden sashes around their chests.*

The angels carrying the plagues were not some accident or coincidence;

they came from the temple itself, just as the plagues on Egypt came from God. It is interesting that while Pharaoh resisted God and his plagues, many Egyptians became sympathetic to and even joined the Israelites when they left Egypt. God's judgments, while fulfilling His holiness in judging sin, are also to bring people to Him.

Everything is bright and shiny in the presence of God. There is nothing dull or uninteresting. If God surrounds Himself with color, shouldn't we do so as well?

15:7 *Then one of the four living creatures gave to the seven angels seven golden bowls filled with the wrath of God, who lives forever and ever.*

I am glad that by His grace I know God and am not an object of His wrath! Notice how all heaven is involved in doing the will of God: the angels, the four living creatures, and the elders.

In earlier studies, we speculated whether or not the four living creatures represented the Church. If in fact they do, then somehow the Church will be involved in meting out God's judgment on the earth. Jesus alluded to this when He said "If you forgive anyone his sins, they are forgiven; if you do not forgive them, they are not forgiven" (John 20:23).

15:8 *And the temple was filled with smoke from the glory of God and from his power, and no one could enter the temple until the seven plagues of the seven angels were completed.*

There seems to be no end to the pictures in Revelation that were first described in the Old Testament. The smoke in the temple here is reminiscent of the same smoke or cloud that was described in 1 Kings:

> *When the priests withdrew from the Holy Place, the cloud filled the temple of the Lord. And the priests could not perform their service because of the cloud, for the glory of the Lord filled his temple. Then Solomon said, "The Lord has said that he would dwell in a dark cloud; I have indeed built a magnificent temple for you, a place for you to dwell forever"* (1 Kings 8:10-12).

The interesting thing in 15:8 is that the glory of the Lord appeared simultaneously with the plagues. Once again this indicates that the Lord was glorified through what occurred. The plagues were not a mistake or an attack of the enemy; they were the work of God! You and I can rest assured that history is in God's hands, and He is glorified through the events, whether or not man can understand or give God glory for what transpires.

Study 35: Revelation 16:1-7

16:1 *Then I heard a loud voice from the temple saying to the seven angels, "Go, pour out the seven bowls of God's wrath on the earth."*

We start Study 35 with a familiar phrase: "I heard a loud voice from heaven." When I was a pastor, I would almost always start my counseling sessions with people by asking, "What is the Lord saying to you?" Does that mean the people were hearing voices? Not necessarily, but I was looking for what the people were hearing through the Word, other people, or the voice of the Lord.

Most people get hung up on whether or not they are hearing the voice of God. As I have stated throughout this book, however, God is a great communicator. He speaks through His Word, circumstances, other people, and even some people who don't know that God is speaking to you through them. If your heart is to hear God, then He will make sure you hear Him.

In the past God spoke to our forefathers through the prophets at many times and in various ways, but in these last days he has spoken to us by his Son, whom he appointed heir of all things, and through whom he made the universe (Hebrews 1:1-2).

I can find five references in the book of Acts that state, "The Holy Spirit spoke or said." What is the Holy Spirit saying to you today, right now? It is important to be in touch with His voice at all times.

The seven angels were holding bowls of God's wrath. These bowls were not under their supervision and control. These bowls were under God's control. There were seven bowls, and since seven is the number of spiritual perfection and completion, God has a perfect plan to pour out His wrath on the earth.

I trust God. I have learned that He is just and merciful. For God to pour out judgment is an act that is pure. When God pours out His wrath, I know He is not being arbitrary or cruel. Not everyone agrees with that statement, as we will see a little later in *The Revelation Project*.

16:2 The first angel went and poured out his bowl on the land, and ugly and painful sores broke out on the people who had the mark of the beast and worshiped his image.

This is similar to one of the plagues that the Lord brought on Egypt through Moses:

Then the Lord said to Moses and Aaron, "Take handfuls of soot from a furnace and have Moses toss it into the air in the presence of Pharaoh. It will become fine dust over the whole land of Egypt, and festering boils will break out on men and animals throughout the land." So they took soot from a furnace and stood before Pharaoh. Moses tossed it into the air, and festering boils broke out on men and animals. The magicians could not stand before Moses because of the boils that were on them and on all the Egyptians (Exodus 9:8-11).

Anyone familiar with the Old Testament would recognize that the magicians in Egypt were powerless to withstand this plague. No matter what the early church was going through, no power could stand against God. If any power has seeming success or has the upper hand, so to speak, it is only with God's permission. He is sovereign and none can withstand His hand.

Those who don't worship God do not have the physical protection that the people of God do. When you think of it, we humans are so frail. A few days without water, a week without food, a month without sunlight and we are in bad shape. It is easy to take your physical well being for granted, but you ought to thank God regularly for health and wellness.

Notice in verse two that God marks the people who worship the beast with His own external mark, just as they had adopted their mark of 666 to identify with the beast. This causes me to think of Cain, another person whom God marked with a sign or seal (see Genesis 4:12-14).

The rise of any anti-Christian system, no matter how pervasive or world encompassing, is no match for the power of God. Every "ism" that every existed or will exist has or will be a "wasm."

God's power controls nature. The fact that He inflicts such judgments on natural resources shows His power and absolute control over all of life and creation. I fear no act of the beast because my faith is in God. Where is your faith?

16:3 The second angel poured out his bowl on the sea, and it turned into blood like that of a dead man, and every living thing in the sea died.

Study 35: Revelation 16:1-7

This second bowl resembled another plague that the Lord inflicted on Egypt:

This is what the Lord says: "By this you will know that I am the Lord: With the staff that is in my hand I will strike the water of the Nile, and it will be changed into blood. The fish in the Nile will die, and the river will stink; the Egyptians will not be able to drink its water." The Lord said to Moses, "Tell Aaron, 'Take your staff and stretch out your hand over the waters of Egypt—over the streams and canals, over the ponds and all the reservoirs'—and they will turn to blood. Blood will be everywhere in Egypt, even in the wooden buckets and stone jars."

Moses and Aaron did just as the Lord had commanded. He raised his staff in the presence of Pharaoh and his officials and struck the water of the Nile, and all the water was changed into blood. The fish in the Nile died, and the river smelled so bad that the Egyptians could not drink its water. Blood was everywhere in Egypt. But the Egyptian magicians did the same things by their secret arts, and Pharaoh's heart became hard; he would not listen to Moses and Aaron, just as the Lord had said (Exodus 7:17-22).

It is interesting that the Egyptians magicians were able to duplicate this phenomenon through their magic arts. The enemy of God will try to confuse God's message to the world so that people do not repent and turn to God. He will do this through seeming spiritual acts of power that sound and look convincing. The devil, God's enemy, will produce deceitful explanations of what God is doing to confuse and hide God's work of judgment. He will help men devise natural explanations for the intervention of God in the affairs of men.

The magicians had secret arts that turned the water into blood. We should not be naïve that evil has any legitimate spiritual power. All their power is that of a kingdom that is totally opposed to everything that God and His people represent.

The fact that the seas were turned to blood speaks of God doing something of judgment on a worldwide scale. The oceans cover more of the earth than dry land, so whatever God does on or in the oceans will be on a large scale. In Jesus' ministry, He turned water into wine and used it for celebration and joy. Here God turns water into blood. God is able to take the most basic experience, symbolized as water, and turn it into something that sustains life or takes it away.

16:4 *The third angel poured out his bowl on the rivers and springs of water, and they became blood.*

Rivers and springs speak to me of more localized judgments inflicted upon certain areas and peoples. God is specific as He moves in the affairs of men. He can judge (or bless) the world, nations, people groups, cities, communities, families, or individuals.

Now let's look at it from another perspective. There is a promise that the knowledge of the Lord will cover the earth like the waters cover the seas (see Isaiah 11:9). Let's assume that the seas and rivers symbolize knowledge systems or philosophies. Here the seas of the beast, his knowledge and teaching, become a source of poison in which nothing can live or prosper. That is where all false religions and philosophies end: in death. The very source that seemed to hold the promise of life and well being will ultimately take life away. The only true life that can be found is that which is found in the Lord, the true giver of life. It is so critical that we have a correct understanding of who God is and how He acts. God can be a source of life but not choosing God is a source of death.

16:5 *Then I heard the angel in charge of the waters say: "You are just in these judgments, you who are and who were, the Holy One, because you have so judged"*

God is just. When judgment comes, it is a last resort. You can be sure that God has reached out to speak and turn people from their wicked ways. In the fullness of time, however, He judges. Here heaven declares God's justice. Heaven not only acts but also interprets its own actions. We cannot understand God apart from Him! We cannot figure God out according to human thinking. We must allow God to explain Himself and His actions.

My role is not to defend God; He can defend Himself. My job is to tell people of His goodness and mercy, and let God reveal Himself to those with whom I am in contact.

16:6 *"for they have shed the blood of your saints and prophets, and you have given them blood to drink as they deserve."*

The water is turned to blood because the followers of the beast have killed God's people. They are now reaping what they have sown! In a sense, they determined their own method of being judged. They choose bloodshed and now blood was being returned to them many times over!

16:7 *And I heard the altar respond: "Yes, Lord God Almighty, true and just are your judgments."*

I have heard many people say at one time or another, "How could God do that, or allow that to happen?" We must not judge God or His actions; God judges us. We don't interpret God through our limited understanding; we interpret God through the revelation He gives us about Himself. To believe that God is anything but good and just is to believe a lie.

John continually saw and heard things from heaven. What are you hearing from heaven? If your "revelation" leads to any conclusion other than God is just and true, then you don't have a revelation from heaven.

Study 36: Revelation 16:8-16

16:8 *The fourth angel poured out his bowl on the sun, and the sun was given power to scorch people with fire.*

God is in control of nature. The power of nature may be awesome to me, but it isn't for God. While I may be scared in the midst of a storm or other natural upheaval, God is comfortable in them. I should have faith to ask God to intervene in weather and other natural conditions. Better yet, I should learn to relax and trust God when things are beyond my comprehension or control. I think of a few miracles that Jesus performed in the realm of nature.

> *After he had dismissed them, he went up on a mountainside by himself to pray. When evening came, he was there alone, but the boat was already a considerable distance from land, buffeted by the waves because the wind was against it. During the fourth watch of the night Jesus went out to them, walking on the lake. When the disciples saw him walking on the lake, they were terrified. "It's a ghost," they said, and cried out in fear* (Matthew 14:23-26).

> *He got up, rebuked the wind and said to the waves, "Quiet! Be still!" Then the wind died down and it was completely calm. He said to his disciples, "Why are you so afraid? Do you still have no faith?" They were terrified and asked each other, "Who is this? Even the wind and the waves obey him!"* (Mark 4:39-41).

Jesus also turned water into wine and took a few pieces of food and fed a multitude. Jesus' miracles were not only performed for human beings and bodies, He did miracles over nature to show the total power of God in all natural situations. We can put our trust in Him no matter what and can have faith to move mountains if need be.

16:9 *They were seared by the intense heat and they cursed the name of God, who had control over these plagues, but they refused to repent and glorify him.*

This verse contains one of the reasons that God pours out His "plagues." It is so people will repent and glorify Him. God may bring hard times to people so that they come to their senses and turn to Him. I know many people who have come to know the Lord through a bankruptcy, death of a loved one, or some other tragic event.

When they have come through that tough time and found Jesus, they then go on to see that their gain far outweighs their loss! They have found the true treasure, which is God. Others, however, will endure difficult times and stubbornly resist coming to God for help, refusing to repent.

Do you see God in all your circumstances? Do you glorify Him in any and all situations? I am not saying I always do. Those who know God is in control should praise Him no matter what happens to them.

This "plague" mentioned in the above verse differs from any of those found in Exodus that occurred during Moses' ministry. The plague of darkness in Egypt wast not one of searing heat. It is interesting that a balance of light and darkness in our lives is a necessity. Too much of either one can be detrimental to our health.

I think the same is true spiritually. We experience times of great light and insight into God and His works; then we experience seasons of darkness when God seems far away. It would seem that both are necessary for spiritual growth. I know some people who have too much "light." They always have an answer and know what God is doing. Then there are those with too much "darkness," who never figure out what God is up to or trying to say.

16:10-11 *The fifth angel poured out his bowl on the throne of the beast, and his kingdom was plunged into darkness. Men gnawed their tongues in agony and cursed the God of heaven because of their pains and their sores, but they refused to repent of what they had done.*

Here we have the plague of darkness, similar to the one found in Exodus:

Then the Lord said to Moses, "Stretch out your hand toward the sky so that darkness will spread over Egypt—darkness that can be felt." So Moses stretched out his hand toward the sky, and total darkness covered all Egypt for three days. No one could see anyone else or leave his place for three days. Yet all the Israelites had light in the places where they lived (Exodus 10:21-23).

The symbolism for the early church would not have been lost on those reading about this plague. While God plagues the kingdom of the beast with darkness, He will maintain His people in the light at the same time. While the world grovels in spiritual darkness, God sheds the light of His knowledge on His people.

We have another clue to the meaning of these plagues that the angels released. They were somehow connected to what the followers of the beast had done. Therefore, these plagues are not just God pouring out His wrath, but pouring it out in response to something that the people did that merited such pain and suffering.

Men must take into account that they will reap what they sow. If they sow wickedness, then they will reap death. There is no way around the principle of sowing and reaping. This is the same scenario we saw in Exodus. God repeatedly showed His power to Pharaoh in Egypt, but repeatedly Pharaoh refused to acknowledge the Lord. In the verses above, God afflicts the kingdom of the beast and its inhabitants with plagues to prove His power and sovereign rule, yet they, like the Egyptians, continued to resist Him. This has been the case throughout history. Kingdoms of the beast resist God and perish. God continues to rule and reign.

Repentance should be a way of life for you and me. We should evaluate regularly our mindset and thought processes. Is there any adjustment that God would like to make in your thinking? After all, repentance is literally a "changing of the mind." Do you know the Lord but still find that you need to repent of attitudes and ways of thinking that aren't in alignment with Him or His ways? I know I do, and I need to do it even more.

16:12 *The sixth angel poured out his bowl on the great river Euphrates, and its water was dried up to prepare the way for the kings from the East.*

This is the first mention of any "kings from the East." No one knows who they were for sure. For the Revelation churches, the power of Rome would have been from the west. So the kings would have been unknown to these Revelation churches, powers that did not yet exist or were unknown to the world of the Revelation churches.

As we stated earlier, God will actually assist those who stubbornly resist Him. He will eventually harden them in their own unbelief so they keep right on doing what they are doing. This sixth plague doesn't seem like much of a plague compared to the ones described earlier. Yet it was a plague nonetheless, for the Lord did not oppose their folly, which led to their eventual doom.

I want God to oppose me if my path is wayward and against Him. While it may seem harsh at first, it is really His gracious act designed to save me. When I lost a job years ago, it was a devastating experience. Yet months later I thanked God that He had worked things out for me to be with my dying father. If I had kept that job, I would not have been able to be with my father. I want and need God to oppose me.

> *Search me, O God, and know my heart; test me and know my anxious thoughts. See if there is any offensive way in me, and lead me in the way everlasting* (Psalm 139:23-24).

Can you trust God enough to allow Him to rule in all the affairs of your life, whether you see the benefit of those affairs at the present time? Can you praise Him for the promotion or raise you didn't receive? That is true faith.

16:13 *Then I saw three evil spirits that looked like frogs; they came out of the mouth of the dragon, out of the mouth of the beast and out of the mouth of the false prophet.*

Why would these evil spirits resemble frogs? Perhaps they are depicted as frogs because anyone who looked closely to examine them would see that they are simple creatures not worth following. Yet the followers of the beast obeyed these deluding spirits with eagerness. To anyone with spiritual discernment, however, the words of the dragon, beast and false prophet would be akin to listening to the words of a frog!

These spirits are not just harmless like frogs, but they are unclean and evil. There were frogs in the plagues of Egypt as well (see Exodus 8:1-15). They became a nuisance and ended up everywhere. When anyone accepts

Study 36: Revelation 16:8-16

the teaching of these "frogs" coming from the beast, dragon and false prophet, that teaching has a way of permeating (and fouling) all of life. False doctrines are not harmless little things; they have the power to make all of life unclean (frogs were unclean according to Old Testament law).

16:14 *They are spirits of demons performing miraculous signs, and they go out to the kings of the whole world, to gather them for the battle on the great day of God Almighty.*

Demons and the kingdom of evil can do miraculous signs. The Egyptian magicians could replicate some of the early plagues and signs that Moses performed. Once again the Lord seems to use these actions and events to help determine who is with Him and who is against Him. He allows some of these things to happen so that those whose hearts are against Him will be duped into believing a lie. Why would He do this? He does this because they have rejected the truth!

Will there be a literal battle on "the great day of the Almighty?" I think there have been many such battles throughout history. Every kingdom, government, and philosophy that sets itself up against the Lord and His rule has been or will be defeated. They will not be able to stand in the age to come. Yet they fight the people of God and the Lord Himself even though they are destined to defeat.

Do I believe in an end of this age, with a literal return of Jesus? Absolutely! Am I convinced that 16:14 represents one last, great battle? No.

16:15 *"Behold, I come like a thief! Blessed is he who stays awake and keeps his clothes with him, so that he may not go naked and be shamefully exposed."*

We must be "clothed" in a righteousness that only God can provide through the blood of Jesus. We cannot be clothed in any other doctrine or system of religious works and deeds. No matter how attractive other systems may be, we must stay awake and be clothed in garments that only God can supply.

The Lord comes like a thief to everyone who doesn't know Him. To those who know Him, however, His intervention, whether through deliverance or death, is a welcome event that leads to joyous union with the Father's love.

Paul wrote about the day of the Lord being like a thief:

> *Now, brothers, about times and dates we do not need to write to you, for you know very well that the day of the Lord will come like a thief in the night. While people are saying, "Peace and safety," destruction will come on them suddenly, as labor pains on a pregnant woman, and they will not escape. But you, brothers, are not in darkness so that this day should surprise you like a thief. You are all sons of the light and sons of the day. We do not belong to the night or to the darkness.*
>
> *So then, let us not be like others, who are asleep, but let us be alert and self-controlled. For those who sleep, sleep at night, and those who get drunk, get drunk at night. But since we belong to the day, let us be self-controlled, putting on faith and love as a breastplate, and the hope of salvation as a helmet. For God did not appoint us to suffer wrath but to receive salvation through our Lord Jesus Christ. He died for us so that, whether we are awake or asleep, we may live together with him. Therefore encourage one another and build each other up, just as in fact you are doing* (1 Thessalonians 5:1-11).

Was Paul writing about the second coming of Jesus in these verses, or was he referring to the sudden end of each human that comes through death? Whatever he was referring to, he urged the saints to use these verses as an encouragement to one another.

Peter also wrote about this day being a thief:

> *But the day of the Lord will come like a thief. The heavens will disappear with a roar; the elements will be destroyed by fire, and the earth and everything in it will be laid bare. Since everything will be destroyed in this way, what kind of people ought you to be? You ought to live holy and godly lives as you look forward to the day of God and speed its coming.*
>
> *That day will bring about the destruction of the heavens by fire, and the elements will melt in the heat. But in keeping with his promise we are looking forward to a new heaven and a new earth, the home of righteousness. So then, dear friends, since you are looking forward to this, make every effort to be found spotless, blameless and at peace with him* (2 Peter 3:10-14).

Here it seems that Peter was referring to the return of the Lord. Yet see that his conclusion is the same as Paul's. They were not trying to spell out a doctrine of the end times but rather exhort the Church to holy living now. So where should our emphasis be, do you think? On some doctrine of the end, or on holy living for today?

16:16 *Then they gathered the kings together to the place that in Hebrew is called Armageddon.*

I have been to the valley called Armageddon in Israel on numerous occasions. It is an impressive valley but hardly big enough for the kings to gather. This must be symbolic of something else, especially in the context of the preceding verses.

I recently read, for the first time, one of the end time novels written by a well-known Christian author. It was entertaining but pure fiction. Even knowing that, it produced some fear in me because of the elements of conspiracy, intrigue and mystery that surround the story line. Does Revelation point to a literal Armageddon? Or is it a symbolic Armageddon that represents the ongoing battle between good and evil, which of course is ultimately won by the Lord?

A final historical event will end history as we know it and usher us into the next age of a new heaven and earth. I do believe that a final establishment of the kingdom of God will occur when His enemies will be defeated once and for all. How? I don't know. Revelation tells us to have faith that it will happen, however. Even if we lose our lives in the process, God will be victorious over all our foes, no matter how powerful they seem to be. We are also warned to be ready for this to happen at any time. It is too late to prepare when it happens. We must get ready now for when it happens, as Jesus warned:

> *"At that time the kingdom of heaven will be like ten virgins who took their lamps and went out to meet the bridegroom. Five of them were foolish and five were wise. The foolish ones took their lamps but did not take any oil with them. The wise, however, took oil in jars along with their lamps. The bridegroom was a long time in coming, and they all became drowsy and fell asleep.*
>
> *"At midnight the cry rang out: 'Here's the bridegroom! Come out to meet him!' Then all the virgins woke up and trimmed their lamps. The foolish ones said to the wise, 'Give us some of your oil; our lamps are going out.' 'No,' they replied, 'there may not be enough for both us and you. Instead, go to those who sell oil and buy some for yourselves.'*

"But while they were on their way to buy the oil, the bridegroom arrived. The virgins who were ready went in with him to the wedding banquet. And the door was shut. Later the others also came. 'Sir! Sir!' they said. 'Open the door for us!' But he replied, 'I tell you the truth, I don't know you.' Therefore keep watch, because you do not know the day or the hour" (Matthew 25:1-13).

Study 37: Revelation 16:17-21

16:17 *The seventh angel poured out his bowl into the air, and out of the temple came a loud voice from the throne, saying, "It is done!"*

In case you were wondering, this is the seventeenth occurrence of the phrase "a loud voice" to this point in Revelation! Some people ask, "How can I hear the Lord?" My question is, "How can you miss hearing the Lord?" While God may at times direct you to seek Him, He will always allow your search to end by hearing from Him.

You may be going through a time of trial and suffering, but a loud voice from heaven at some point in time will say, "It is done!" You may be experiencing persecution or misunderstanding, but at some point, heaven will say, "It is done!" Does this phrase sound familiar? It should, for as Jesus was dying He said on the cross: "When he had received the drink, Jesus said, 'It is finished.' With that, he bowed his head and gave up his spirit" (John 19:30).

One other passage relates to this theme in 16:17 of the Lord finishing His judgments:

> *For his anger lasts only a moment, but his favor lasts a lifetime; weeping may remain for a night, but rejoicing comes in the morning. When I felt secure, I said, "I will never be shaken." O Lord, when you favored me, you made my mountain stand firm; but when you hid your face, I was dismayed.*
>
> *To you, O Lord, I called; to the Lord I cried for mercy: "What gain is there in my destruction, in my going down into the pit? Will the dust praise you? Will it proclaim your faithfulness? Hear, O Lord, and be merciful to me; O Lord, be my help." You turned my wailing into dancing; you removed my sackcloth and clothed me with joy, that my heart may sing to you and not be silent. O Lord my God, I will give you thanks forever* (Psalm 30:5-12).

Study 37: Revelation 16:17-21

During good times we can feel confident and secure that God is with us and nothing adverse will ever happen. That is what the psalmist felt when he said, "I will never be shaken." A few verses later he is crying out, "O Lord, be my help!" In good times, I have made faith professions that were severely tested in times of lack or suffering.

When I see "It is done!" in Revelation, I think of what Jesus said on the cross, as mentioned above. Jesus suffered through the worst form of death man has ever conceived against man. Yet His suffering had an end to it, and your suffering and trial will have an end, too! Like Jesus, you will be able to say, "It is finished! It is done!" After every trial, a time of tremendous blessing follows. The deeper the trial, the greater the eventual blessing will be.

> *Therefore, since Christ suffered in his body, arm yourselves also with the same attitude, because he who has suffered in his body is done with sin. As a result, he does not live the rest of his earthly life for evil human desires, but rather for the will of God. For you have spent enough time in the past doing what pagans choose to do—living in debauchery, lust, drunkenness, orgies, carousing and detestable idolatry.*
>
> *They think it strange that you do not plunge with them into the same flood of dissipation, and they heap abuse on you. But they will have to give account to him who is ready to judge the living and the dead. For this is the reason the gospel was preached even to those who are now dead, so that they might be judged according to men in regard to the body, but live according to God in regard to the spirit. The end of all things is near. Therefore be clear minded and self-controlled so that you can pray* (1 Peter 4:1-7).

Since Christ our Lord suffered in the flesh, Peter urged his followers to have the same readiness and attitude that Jesus had. Do you have that attitude? Are you ready to suffer for His sake? Why should Revelation ever be a source of anxiety or stress for the believer?

We know the world will be judged and that we live in the world. Therefore, we may experience difficult times, even martyrdom for some of us. Yet our victory is secure, held fast by the eternal life and promises of Jesus Christ, our Lord!

Peter told us plainly that the end is near. How the end will come is open to interpretation. That should not make us anxious but rather glad. I fear no end-time beast or conspiracy. The Lord is my shepherd!

16:18 *Then there came flashes of lightning, rumblings, peals of thunder and a severe earthquake. No earthquake like it has ever occurred since man has been on earth, so tremendous was the quake.*

Years ago I was in Hawaii and saw the lava flow from an active volcano. It was awesome and scary! Nature and its power expressed through storms, floods, earthquakes, and eruptions should cause man to realize how powerless and insignificant he is. Furthermore, what happens in the spiritual world may have effects in the natural world.

Revelation employs what is called apocalyptic language. Will there be a literal earthquake? Maybe. Will things happen in heaven that will upset the status quo on earth where men and women are totally unsettled and powerless to control it? Definitely! So an earthquake is an accurate metaphor to explain the tumult that would occur in the heavens and on earth.

16:19 *The great city split into three parts, and the cities of the nations collapsed. God remembered Babylon the Great and gave her the cup filled with the wine of the fury of his wrath.*

God has entered into judgment many times in history when great cities and civilizations were reduced to nothing. He will do the same one final time and will usher in a new age with a new heaven and earth. No one knows when that will be, and many generations have felt it would happen during their lifetimes. Obviously, it did not. Many people feel that we are living in the last generation. Only time will tell whether or not they are correct. In the meantime, we should live like the Lord is coming back any day by urgently spreading the gospel and living a holy life.

16:20 *Every island fled away and the mountains could not be found.*

This is an excellent example of apocalyptic language and images. Islands will not flee and mountains will not literally hide. This language told the early church that cataclysmic events would take place that were not the norm. When those events happened, the church was to know it wasn't due to natural causes; it was due to heaven's intervention.

This doesn't mean that some islands and mountains may not disappear or change due to certain natural disasters, but apocalyptic language is not to be taken literally. It is simply a style that is used to communicate upheaval and unusual events.

16:21 *From the sky huge hailstones of about a hundred pounds each fell upon men. And they cursed God on account of the plague of hail, because the plague was so terrible.*

In this verse we see another plague that was similar to one that came upon Egypt in Moses' time:

> *Therefore, at this time tomorrow I will send the worst hailstorm that has ever fallen on Egypt, from the day it was founded till now. Give an order now to bring your livestock and everything you have in the field to a place of shelter, because the hail will fall on every man and animal that has not been brought in and is still out in the field, and they will die.'" Those officials of Pharaoh who feared the word of the Lord hurried to bring their slaves and their livestock inside.*
>
> *But those who ignored the word of the Lord left their slaves and livestock in the field. Then the Lord said to Moses, "Stretch out your hand toward the sky so that hail will fall all over Egypt—on men and animals and on everything growing in the fields of Egypt." When Moses stretched out his staff toward the sky, the Lord sent thunder and hail, and lightning flashed down to the ground.*
>
> *So the Lord rained hail on the land of Egypt; hail fell and lightning flashed back and forth. It was the worst storm in all the land of Egypt since it had become a nation. Throughout Egypt hail struck everything in the fields—both men and animals; it beat down everything growing in the fields and stripped every tree. The only place it did not hail was the land of Goshen, where the Israelites were.*
>
> *Then Pharaoh summoned Moses and Aaron. "This time I have sinned," he said to them. "The Lord is in the right, and I and my people are in the wrong. Pray to the Lord, for we have had enough thunder and hail. I will let you go; you don't have to stay any longer"* (Exodus 9:18-28).

Egypt worshiped the elements of nature, and the Lord was proving His superiority to and control over those elements. Up to that point, Pharaoh refused to repent and let God's people go; but after this storm, he began to soften. God will prove His superiority over anything that man exalts above Him, whether nature, philosophy, learning, or technology. His purpose, as I have indicated in the past studies, is for men to repent and turn to Him. God's judgment is an expression of His love, so that sin may be exposed and men may turn to Him.

In Revelation, the people upon whom the hail fell refused to repent, and they even cursed God. This is how hard man's heart can become, that he will interpret God's objects of mercy as indications of God's cruelty.

My greatest challenge in my walk with the Lord is to see all He does in my life as motivated by love and in my best interest. Too often tough times have caused me to question God's faithfulness and love. As I study Revelation, I see how God was comforting the early church through the message given to John. And I also see God's great love as He acts to help men decide whom they will follow.

For this reason, I cannot understand why some use Revelation as a history book or as a tool to scare or unsettle people. Revelation is the last great expression of God's love for His people in the Bible, a love that was first shown in Genesis and now comes to a conclusion in Revelation.

> Thank You, Lord, for Your care and involvement in the affairs of the earth. I trust You, and I commit myself and my family to You for protection. No matter what happens, Lord, I declare my trust in You. Amen.

Study 38: Revelation 17:1-8

17:1-2 *One of the seven angels who had the seven bowls came and said to me, "Come, I will show you the punishment of the great prostitute, who sits on many waters. With her the kings of the earth committed adultery and the inhabitants of the earth were intoxicated with the wine of her adulteries."*

Who is the great prostitute mentioned in verse one? This prostitute, like the beast and antichrist, is no one particular person or movement in history. Rather she is the prevailing philosophy or cultural system of any age that sets itself up as an alternative to worshiping God.

A prostitute usually does what he or she does for money. A prostitute provides an alternative for what God intended to occur in a marriage relationship. Thus, this prostitute is a counterfeit spiritual system that promises pleasure and peace in return for some economic return. Under that definition, communism, capitalism, socialism, and any other "ism" that does not make God its central focus is the "prostitute." So are liberation theology, liberalism, and all the false sects and cults that don't make Jesus the center of attention and worship.

In my lifetime, I have seen many systems promise prosperity and the answer to human problems and suffering. To date, all have failed. Yet that has not prevented leaders (kings) and their followers (the inhabitants) from becoming infatuated (intoxicated) with the possibilities of these systems and their beliefs.

Not only is prostitution mentioned in these verses but adultery as well. These are descriptive of how intimate the kings and inhabitants become with their philosophies and systems. Because these systems do not focus on and glorify God, their intimacies are misdirected and offensive to God.

Are you putting your trust or "becoming intimate" with anything that does not honor God? Is your hope in politics, economics or the wisdom of men? If so, then you are flirting with a "girlfriend" or "boyfriend" that isn't your spouse! You are married to God and must be faithful to Him and His ways. Read what James had to say in his epistle about this:

> *What causes fights and quarrels among you? Don't they come from your desires that battle within you? You want something but don't get it. You kill and covet, but you cannot have what you want. You quarrel and fight. You do not have, because you do not ask God. When you ask, you do not receive, because you ask with wrong motives, that you may spend what you get on your pleasures.*
>
> *You adulterous people, don't you know that friendship with the world is hatred toward God? Anyone who chooses to be a friend of the world becomes an enemy of God. Or do you think Scripture says without reason that the spirit he caused to live in us envies intensely? But he gives us more grace. That is why Scripture says: "God opposes the proud but gives grace to the humble." Submit yourselves, then, to God. Resist the devil, and he will flee from you* (James 4:1-7).

James said it well: "adulterous people" are friends with the world and its systems, which are in direct opposition to the things of God.

17:3 ***Then the angel carried me away in the Spirit into a desert. There I saw a woman sitting on a scarlet beast that was covered with blasphemous names and had seven heads and ten horns.***

I have been to Israel on numerous occasions and have traveled through its deserts. They are desolate places but are at the same time beautiful and breathtaking. They are places of loneliness, for not many live there due to the heat. At night, these deserts are cold without the sun. Sometimes God will take you to a desert place in your life to speak to you and give you revelation and understanding about what He is doing or going to do. I am in a desert place in my life as I write this, but it is a good time.

God took Moses and David into the desert to speak and train them for leadership and ministry. God the Father also took Jesus to a desert as He began His public ministry. If Jesus spent some time in the desert, don't you think you will as well?

> *Jesus, full of the Holy Spirit, returned from the Jordan and was led by the Spirit in the desert, where for forty days he was tempted by the devil. He ate nothing during those days, and at the end of them he was hungry* (Luke 4:1-2).

It appears that this desert experience was an important time in Jesus' life and ministry, for Matthew, Mark, and Luke all record what happened when He was there. Make sure you take good notes of what God speaks to you in the desert as well.

It appears the devil is busy in the desert too. This is where Jesus encountered His temptations (see Matthew 4) and this setting is where John saw the woman riding on the scarlet beast. When you have your desert experience, carefully evaluate everything you hear and see. Make sure it is heaven speaking to you. I don't say that to scare you, but everything you receive, whether by prophetic word from others or through the still, small internal voice, must and should be checked out to make sure it is biblical and sound. It never hurts to share it with someone who knows you and is spiritually mature. At the same time, you can be confident that heaven will speak with a "loud voice" as we have seen throughout Revelation.

17:4 *The woman was dressed in purple and scarlet, and was glittering with gold, precious stones and pearls. She held a golden cup in her hand, filled with abominable things and the filth of her adulteries.*

This woman was dressed well, which would make her attractive to others at first glance. And we know this to be true of sin in general: "He [Moses] chose to be mistreated along with the people of God rather than to enjoy the pleasures of sin for a short time" (Hebrews 11:25).

We would do well to tell people that sin does bring pleasure; there is no denying that. Sin's pleasures are passing, however, and the rewards do not last as long as the rewards for righteousness. Sin brings pleasure at first, but what it costs in the long run is not worth what it gives in the short run.

It seems that everyone has a "cup" to drink, one offered by God and the

Study 38: Revelation 17:1-8

other offered by the world system. "Going a little farther, he fell with his face to the ground and prayed, "My Father, if it is possible, may this cup be taken from me. Yet not as I will, but as you will" (Matthew 26:39).

What cup are you drinking from at this point in your life? And what is your attitude as you drink? If you are drinking the cup of suffering, then you must do it as unto the Lord. If you are drinking any other cup, repent! Nothing can take the place of doing the will of God in the manner God desires.

17:5 *This title was written on her forehead: MYSTERY BABYLON THE GREAT THE MOTHER OF PROSTITUTES AND OF THE ABOMINATIONS OF THE EARTH.*

This woman has a mark on her forehead just like the other followers of the beast. Do you think this is a literal marking or do you think it is symbolic? If you think it is symbolic, then the "666" mark must also be symbolic. This woman represents all the anti-God systems and philosophies that ever have existed or ever will.

Remember to ask yourself what this could have meant to the early church to whom the book of Revelation was addressed. They were under the control of Rome and Rome was idolatrous, corrupt and anti-Christian. What does it mean for the modern church? For example, what would this book have meant to a believer in Eastern Europe decades ago? They were under the control of the Soviet communists, who were idolatrous, corrupt, and anti-Christian, just like Rome. The message to the early church and modern church is the same: opposition will come but do not fear. God is more powerful than anything that opposes Him.

The message of Revelation is that it is impossible to find refuge or solace in anything or anyone except God. You cannot expect any world system to be righteous unless it is based on the law of God. So why put your trust there? Your education cannot save, you, nor can your retirement fund or your family heritage.

17:6 *I saw that the woman was drunk with the blood of the saints, the blood of those who bore testimony to Jesus. When I saw her, I was greatly astonished.*

Institutions, economic systems, and political movements have fueled, promoted, and protected themselves by persecuting the Church. These movements have champions and celebrities who give credence to their belief systems and way of life. Certainly Rome in the time of John and Revelation were examples of what is described in 17:6. Figuratively speaking, they were intoxicated with power and tried to use it to thwart the Church. All their efforts were futile, however, with only short-term success. Why? Let's look one more time at Psalm 2 to find the answer:

> *Why do the nations conspire and the peoples plot in vain? The kings of the earth take their stand and the rulers gather together against the Lord and against his Anointed One. "Let us break their chains," they say, "and throw off their fetters."*
>
> *The One enthroned in heaven laughs; the Lord scoffs at them. Then he rebukes them in his anger and terrifies them in his wrath, saying, "I have installed my King on Zion, my holy hill." I will proclaim the decree of the Lord: He said to me, "You are my Son; today I have become your Father. Ask of me, and I will make the nations your inheritance, the ends of the earth your possession. You will rule them with an iron scepter; you will dash them to pieces like pottery."*
>
> *Therefore, you kings, be wise; be warned, you rulers of the earth. Serve the Lord with fear and rejoice with trembling. Kiss the Son, lest he be angry and you be destroyed in your way, for his wrath can flare up in a moment. Blessed are all who take refuge in him* (Psalm 2:1-12).

These anti-Christ movements are all doomed to failure. While they bring tremendous suffering and even martyrdom to the saints, those very activities are their undoing. God settles the score with anyone who persecutes His people, for in doing so, they are really opposing God.

Let's review: the message of Revelation is one of victory, not of fear or gloom. Many have opposed the Church, and some even tried to eradicate it. They have all ended in failure and have themselves been exterminated while the Church has continued. Even the most recent anti-Christian movement, Islam, as powerful as it is, cannot resist the purpose of God forever. They will end like very other movement that has opposed God and the Church.

John was astonished by what he saw, and the Church is often astonished at its enemies and their hatred. Yet the enemies of the Church are taking out their hatred of the invisible God on the visible Church. Their best efforts, however, will never succeed, for God is against them.

Study 38: Revelation 17:1-8

17:7 *Then the angel said to me: "Why are you astonished? I will explain to you the mystery of the woman and of the beast she rides, which has the seven heads and ten horns."*

The angel explained to John what he was seeing. As stated many times already, one of the best rules to follow for biblical interpretation is to find what the Bible has to say about itself. Don't make up your own interpretations but follow those that are provided. If the Bible gives no insight into what a particular passage says, and a word or symbol is obscure, then be careful about how you interpret it. You may have an opinion about what it says or find a practical application, but you must be careful not to insist that "the Lord showed you" what it meant.

17:8 *The beast, which you saw, once was, now is not, and will come up out of the Abyss and go to his destruction. The inhabitants of the earth whose names have not been written in the book of life from the creation of the world will be astonished when they see the beast, because he once was, now is not, and yet will come.*

A popular series of novels loosely based on Revelation and the end times mistakenly portrays this scenario as a literal person who will be killed and then raised from the dead. Do you think this is what the early church took this to mean? I doubt it.

Those who don't know our God, whose names are not written in the book of life, are susceptible to all kinds of spiritual misinterpretation and delusion. In my own lifetime, I have seen whole people groups follow a charismatic leader to their own destruction and pain. As soon as one anti-Christ movement ends, another raises up to take its place.

When communism in the Soviet Union fell apart, some people thought the world would be a safer place. Today, totalitarianism is alive and well, and the world is a more dangerous place. This astonishes some people but should not surprise the people of God.

The beast is always fathering new ideas and promoting new leaders. They are all part of the anti-Christ purpose that the devil promotes by any and all means. Even the thinking that all religions are the same and that there are many roads to salvation are part of this "beastly" anti-Christian system.

The only one answer for the world's problems is Jesus. Anything else, no matter how promising it may look, is a fraud. The book of Revelation focuses on the supremacy of Christ and the reality of the devil who opposes Him. The good news is that we in Christ are victorious, even through martyrdom.

Study 39: Revelation 17:9-18

17:9 *"This calls for a mind with wisdom. The seven heads are seven hills on which the woman sits."*

The angel declared that wisdom was needed. I would say that wisdom is still needed. Wisdom is not given, however, to understand obscure Bible passages. Wisdom is given to apply to everyday life situations. On the one hand, I have found some people who try to impress others with their insight into the Bible, and maybe God has indeed revealed something to them. On the other hand, I prefer someone with wisdom to raise a godly family, be a good employer or employee, or build a strong church.

I have tried to make a life study of the book of Proverbs, for Proverbs' focus is wisdom. I pray for wisdom as James directed in his epistle. When people seek me out for wisdom, I know that is an answer to my prayer. Do you pray for wisdom? Wisdom for what areas of life? Do you study the book of Proverbs to get wisdom?

The reference to seven hills in 17:9 is generally recognized as symbolic of the Roman Empire, for the city of Rome sits on seven hills. That is a real possibility, for that would have meant something to the churches first receiving the Revelation letter. Some commentators read a reference to the Vatican and the Catholic Church in this verse. While the Vatican is in Rome in our present day, it was probably not the emphasis of this particular vision.

But in an earlier study, we saw how often the number seven (the number of spiritual perfection) is used throughout Revelation. Could the seven here represent the perfection or power of the spiritual forces that align themselves against the Church? They always seem to have the high ground and loyalty of the ruling powers. The woman, who persecuted the church, seems to have all the power in most nations. The Church, by comparison, is weak and powerless in the natural but all-powerful with the Lord as its protector.

Study 39: Revelation 17:9-18

17:10 *They are also seven kings. Five have fallen, one is, the other has not yet come; but when he does come, he must remain for a little while.*

What does all this represent? If the Bible wanted us to know, it would tell us plainly. Therefore I must conclude that all this is shrouded in mystery for a reason.

If we knew all about the end, we would not have to trust in the Lord. The morbid and unusual infatuation that many have with the end times is similar to the following for horror movies. The story of Revelation is not one that focuses on the kingdom of darkness, but on the victory of the Lamb.

It doesn't matter who the kings are or are not. The ultimate meaning is that well-organized and powerful governments and movements will oppose God and His people. They will all lose and be reduced to nothing. It isn't important for the Church to understand all that is going on; it is only important that heaven understands and controls it all. The angel told John everything that was going on. That means that heaven is in control, not the powers symbolically represented.

17:11 *The beast who once was, and now is not, is an eighth king. He belongs to the seven and is going to his destruction.*

This is the key issue: the beast and the kings are heading to their destruction. They may persecute the Church and gain control of the governments of the earth, but they are doomed to failure. The Lord reigns.

Much of this will not make sense until after it all happens, not before. Imagine the confusion produced over the three seemingly conflicting prophecies surrounding the coming of the Messiah. It was said that He would be from Bethlehem, come out of Egypt and be a Nazarene. Prior to Jesus' life and death, not many would have understood how all that could be true about one man. Today, however, it makes perfect sense. Eventually, the symbolism of Revelation will make sense.

The question for you is, "What does any particular interpretation produce in your life?" If it stirs up fear, for example, then you must question your interpretation. I read these prophecies and images, and it causes me to worship the Lamb. While I am powerless to do anything about these scenarios, He is all powerful. I am glad my name is in His book!

17:12-14 *"The ten horns you saw are ten kings who have not yet received a kingdom, but who for one hour will receive authority as kings along with the beast. They have one purpose and will give their power and authority to the beast. They will make war against the Lamb, but the Lamb will overcome them because he is Lord of lords and King of kings—and with him will be his called, chosen and faithful followers."*

Thank You, Lord Jesus! The seven, the ten, the beast, and the prostitute are all overcome! Whenever that happens, I will be with Him. You will too! This is not a time for charts and pictures of creatures from the dark side. This is a time for celebration. The Lamb is victorious and that makes you and me victorious. Let's look at Paul's words to the Roman church one more time to make sure we understand:

And we know that in all things God works for the good of those who love him, who have been called according to his purpose. For those God foreknew he also predestined to be conformed to the likeness of his Son, that he might be the firstborn among many brothers. And those he predestined, he also called; those he called, he also justified; those he justified, he also glorified.

What, then, shall we say in response to this? If God is for us, who can be against us? He who did not spare his own Son, but gave him up for us all—how will he not also, along with him, graciously give us all things? Who will bring any charge against those whom God has chosen? It is God who justifies. Who is he that condemns?

Christ Jesus, who died—more than that, who was raised to life—is at the right hand of God and is also interceding for us. Who shall separate us from the love of Christ? Shall trouble or hardship or persecution or famine or nakedness or danger or sword? As it is written: "For your sake we face death all day long; we are considered as sheep to be slaughtered."

No, in all these things we are more than conquerors through him who loved us. For I am convinced that neither death nor life, neither angels nor demons, neither the present nor the future, nor any powers, neither height nor depth, nor anything else in all creation, will be able to separate us from the love of God that is in Christ Jesus our Lord (Romans 8:28-39).

God does not keep us from engaging in spiritual warfare but delivers us through and out of spiritual warfare. Revelation shows that warfare is inevitable, but then again so is the victory of the Lamb!

17:15 *Then the angel said to me, "The waters you saw, where the prostitute sits, are peoples, multitudes, nations and languages."*

I know I am repeating myself, but the most reliable interpretation for anything in the Bible is to find what the Bible provides to interpret itself. That applies to Revelation as well as any other book. In 17:15, the angel told John what the water stands for; it stands for the nations. Don't you think the angel could have said what the other symbols stood for, if he had been directed to do so? He did not, because these symbols—beast, kings, horns, and the prostitute—are recurring themes throughout history and do not represent any one person or philosophy.

I have been to forty-two nations in my lifetime so far and have seen masses of people going about their daily lives; many of them don't know God. They are just trying to live day to day, some enslaved by one of the religious anti-Christian sects. The anti-Christian world system has them in its grips and won't let go of them, at least not without a fight.

The fight to see them free is not natural, but spiritual, for all of life's problems have their roots in the spiritual. Therefore you and I must fight spiritual battles, which have natural implications.

> *For though we live in the world, we do not wage war as the world does. The weapons we fight with are not the weapons of the world. On the contrary, they have divine power to demolish strongholds. We demolish arguments and every pretension that sets itself up against the knowledge of God, and we take captive every thought to make it obedient to Christ. And we will be ready to punish every act of disobedience, once your obedience is complete* (2 Corinthians 10:3-6).

17:16-17 *The beast and the ten horns you saw will hate the prostitute. They will bring her to ruin and leave her naked; they will eat her flesh and burn her with fire. For God has put it into their hearts to accomplish his purpose by agreeing to give the beast their power to rule, until God's words are fulfilled.*

"God has put it into their hearts to accomplish his purpose." What a wonderful phrase that is. Throughout history, God has accomplished His purpose by using even those who don't acknowledge His existence, including those governments who try to oppose. He proves His power by using them to achieve His ends without their cooperation. The very thing they don't want to do—follow and obey the Lamb—they actually are doing.

How many instances can you think of that are similar to the one described in 17:17? Here are a few that come to my mind:

- **Samson**—"His father and mother replied, 'Isn't there an acceptable woman among your relatives or among all our people? Must you go to the uncircumcised Philistines to get a wife?' But Samson said to his father, 'Get her for me. She's the right one for me.' (His parents did not know that this was from the Lord, who was seeking an occasion to confront the Philistines; for at that time they were ruling over Israel)" (Judges 14:3-4).
- **Proverbs**—"The king's heart is in the hand of the Lord; he directs it like a watercourse wherever he pleases" (Proverbs 21:1).
- **Caiaphas**—"Then one of them, named Caiaphas, who was high priest that year, spoke up, 'You know nothing at all! You do not realize that it is better for you that one man die for the people than that the whole nation perish.' He did not say this on his own, but as high priest that year he prophesied that Jesus would die for the Jewish nation, and not only for that nation but also for the scattered children of God, to bring them together and make them one" (John 11:49-52).

17:18 *"The woman you saw is the great city that rules over the kings of the earth."*

Here the angel identified the woman as the great city. What was that great city? If there is a city of God, the heavenly Jerusalem, it makes sense that there is a city of Satan, a heavenly entity where the government and power of Satan is concentrated. St. Augustine alluded to this in his classic work, *City of God*.

Once again we see that the woman is symbolic of something else, which is the literary tool used in the book of Revelation. Therefore to choose some of these symbols and interpret them as literal beings or specific events is not biblical, unless the Bible does so on its own behalf. You are on much safer and surer ground if you see this book as a cosmic play that has fictional characters that represent principles, trends and themes.

More importantly, you must not let any interpretation of Revelation detract from the Lamb's victory. I am at peace with the events of the present and future because Jesus is in control and will emerge victorious, over every "ism" and force that are against Him.

Study 40: Revelation 18:1-8

18:1 *After this I saw another angel coming down from heaven. He had great authority, and the earth was illuminated by his splendor.*

This angel did not speak with a loud voice as the others have. Yet it was still impossible for John to miss what heaven was doing and saying. This angel, while not loud like the others, was bright and had great authority. As I have said many times already, a person must work hard to ignore what heaven is doing, for God makes it plain to anyone who is interested to know. Could this angel be Jesus? Let's look at another passage to determine if this is possible.

> *In the past God spoke to our forefathers through the prophets at many times and in various ways, but in these last days he has spoken to us by his Son, whom he appointed heir of all things, and through whom he made the universe. The Son is the radiance of God's glory and the exact representation of his being, sustaining all things by his powerful word.*
>
> *After he had provided purification for sins, he sat down at the right hand of the Majesty in heaven. So he became as much superior to the angels as the name he has inherited is superior to theirs. For to which of the angels did God ever say, "You are my Son; today I have become your Father"?*
>
> *Or again, "I will be his Father, and he will be my Son"? And again, when God brings his firstborn into the world, he says, "Let all God's angels worship him." In speaking of the angels he says, "He makes his angels winds, his servants flames of fire." But about the Son he says, "Your throne, O God, will last for ever and ever, and righteousness will be the scepter of your kingdom.*
>
> *"You have loved righteousness and hated wickedness; therefore God, your God, has set you above your companions by anointing you with the oil of joy." He also says, "In the beginning, O Lord, you laid the foundations of the earth, and the heavens are the work of your hands. They will perish, but you remain; they will all wear out like a garment. You will*

roll them up like a robe; like a garment they will be changed. But you remain the same, and your years will never end."

To which of the angels did God ever say, "Sit at my right hand until I make your enemies a footstool for your feet"? Are not all angels ministering spirits sent to serve those who will inherit salvation? (Hebrews 1:1-14)

I would conclude that this angel could be Jesus because the Word provides a clue that it is possible. Hebrews states that He is the "radiance of God's glory" and is far superior in authority to the angels. Peter gave us this principle for biblical interpretation when he wrote:

We did not follow cleverly invented stories when we told you about the power and coming of our Lord Jesus Christ, but we were eyewitnesses of his majesty. For he received honor and glory from God the Father when the voice came to him from the Majestic Glory, saying, "This is my Son, whom I love; with him I am well pleased."

We ourselves heard this voice that came from heaven when we were with him on the sacred mountain. And we have the word of the prophets made more certain, and you will do well to pay attention to it, as to a light shining in a dark place, until the day dawns and the morning star rises in your hearts.

Above all, you must understand that no prophecy of Scripture came about by the prophet's own interpretation. For prophecy never had its origin in the will of man, but men spoke from God as they were carried along by the Holy Spirit (2 Peter 1:16-21).

Peter was referring to being present at what we call the transfiguration (see Matthew 17:1-7). At that time, he heard the voice of the Father from heaven. Yet he said in his epistle that we have the "word more certain" in the written word of God! No voice, impression, opinion, or idea is superior to the written Word. The Bible is not based on my opinions or impressions. I must be open to the Word, but the Word is not open to my personal interpretations.

The more I become familiar with God's Word, the more restricted I feel interpreting it. I must be true to the meaning the Holy Spirit intended and not try to make the Word say what I want it to say, think it should say, or hope it says. I want to walk in the light of heaven, don't you? I don't mean when I get to heaven, but right now. I can do that by following Jesus and obeying His Word. Jesus Himself said that He was the light.

In him was life, and that life was the light of men. The light shines in the darkness, but the darkness has not understood it (John 1:4-5).

When Jesus spoke again to the people, he said, "I am the light of the world. Whoever follows me will never walk in darkness, but will have the light of life" (John 8:12).

18:2-3 *With a mighty voice he shouted: "Fallen! Fallen is Babylon the Great! She has become a home for demons and a haunt for every evil spirit, a haunt for every unclean and detestable bird. For all the nations have drunk the maddening wine of her adulteries. The kings of the earth committed adultery with her, and the merchants of the earth grew rich from her excessive luxuries."*

There it is: another mighty, loud voice speaking heaven's perspective. What is this loud voice from heaven saying to you? Can you tell someone in a sentence or two? What are you learning these days from God's Word?

Old Testament Babylon had literally fallen as verse two described: it was desolate and deserted, never to be rebuilt or reinhabited. This is the same fate in store for any antichrist system that tries to establish itself in opposition to God and His Christ.

Whole people groups along with their governments have tried and will try to establish a government and worldview that opposes God's kingdom. They have failed and will continue to fail. Their economic systems were assisted in the short run by their alliance with the antichrist spirit, all to no avail.

18:4 *Then I heard another voice from heaven say: "Come out of her, my people, so that you will not share in her sins, so that you will not receive any of her plagues"*

It is difficult not to be affected by the prevailing culture in which you live. Every generation can look back at the things done by previous generations and wonder, *How could they have participated in that?* or *How could they have thought that?* Yet often "that" (racism, materialism, greed) was the dominant thinking of the age, and most people—even believers—went along with it or did not actively oppose it. It was difficult for them to see it let alone break out of the cultural norms in which they lived. That is why Paul wrote:

> *Therefore, I urge you, brothers, in view of God's mercy, to offer your bodies as living sacrifices, holy and pleasing to God—this is your spiritual act of worship. Do not conform any longer to the pattern of this world, but be transformed by the renewing of your mind. Then you will be able to test and approve what God's will is—his good, pleasing and perfect will* (Romans 12:1-2).

You must have your mind renewed so that you can be transformed and therefore not conform to the pattern of this world. I find God challenging my way of thinking more often than anything else. I don't see things from His perspective, and that leads me to follow the prevailing mindset of my generation while being a believer.

Ask the Lord to examine your heart and mind to see where you need renewal and transformation. Have you bought into any prevailing mindset of the age? What is the remedy if you have? Renewal and repentance!

18:5 *for her sins are piled up to heaven, and God has remembered her crimes.*

God may seem like He doesn't see or remember, but He does! I think the psalmist effectively expressed this fear of God's forgetfulness on several occasions. Here is one of them:

> *For I envied the arrogant when I saw the prosperity of the wicked. They have no struggles; their bodies are healthy and strong. They are free from the burdens common to man; they are not plagued by human ills. Therefore pride is their necklace; they clothe themselves with violence.*
>
> *From their callous hearts comes iniquity; the evil conceits of their minds know no limits. They scoff, and speak with malice; in their arrogance they threaten oppression. Their mouths lay claim to heaven, and their tongues take possession of the earth. Therefore their people turn to them and drink up waters in abundance.*
>
> *They say, "How can God know? Does the Most High have knowledge?" This is what the wicked are like—always carefree, they increase in wealth. Surely in vain have I kept my heart pure; in vain have I washed my hands in innocence. All day long I have been plagued; I have been punished every morning. If I had said, "I will speak thus," I would have betrayed your children.*
>
> *When I tried to understand all this, it was oppressive to me till I entered the sanctuary of God; then I understood their final destiny.*

Study 40: Revelation 18:1-8

Surely you place them on slippery ground; you cast them down to ruin. How suddenly are they destroyed, completely swept away by terrors! As a dream when one awakes, so when you arise,

O Lord, you will despise them as fantasies. When my heart was grieved and my spirit embittered, I was senseless and ignorant; I was a brute beast before you. Yet I am always with you; you hold me by my right hand (Psalm 73:3-23).

Have you ever envied or do you envy the wicked? Have you considered being more like them while maintaining your relationship with the Lord? Remember, God doesn't forget their wickedness and He will repay them, in due time. You must be patient and remember what is written to you:

Do not be deceived: God cannot be mocked. A man reaps what he sows. The one who sows to please his sinful nature, from that nature will reap destruction; the one who sows to please the Spirit, from the Spirit will reap eternal life. Let us not become weary in doing good, for at the proper time we will reap a harvest if we do not give up. Therefore, as we have opportunity, let us do good to all people, especially to those who belong to the family of believers (Galatians 6:7-10).

Don't give up trusting the Lord and doing what He wants you to do. He is watching, although it may not seem like it at the time.

18:6-8 *Give back to her as she has given; pay her back double for what she has done. Mix her a double portion from her own cup. Give her as much torture and grief as the glory and luxury she gave herself. In her heart she boasts, 'I sit as queen; I am not a widow, and I will never mourn.' Therefore in one day her plagues will overtake her: death, mourning and famine. She will be consumed by fire, for mighty is the Lord God who judges her.*

Another psalm addressed the apparent rewards of the wicked:

I have seen a wicked and ruthless man flourishing like a green tree in its native soil, but he soon passed away and was no more; though I looked for him, he could not be found. Consider the blameless, observe the upright; there is a future for the man of peace.

But all sinners will be destroyed; the future of the wicked will be cut off. The salvation of the righteous comes from the Lord; he is their stronghold in time of trouble. The Lord helps them and delivers them; he delivers them from the wicked and saves them, because they take refuge in him (Psalm 37:35-40).

The early church was living under tense conditions. They feared for their lives and lived in increasing danger because they did not worship the emperor. The conditions described in Hebrews applied to them:

> *Remember those earlier days after you had received the light, when you stood your ground in a great contest in the face of suffering. Sometimes you were publicly exposed to insult and persecution; at other times you stood side by side with those who were so treated.*
>
> *You sympathized with those in prison and joyfully accepted the confiscation of your property, because you knew that you yourselves had better and lasting possessions. So do not throw away your confidence; it will be richly rewarded.*
>
> *You need to persevere so that when you have done the will of God, you will receive what he has promised. For in just a very little while, "He who is coming will come and will not delay. But my righteous one will live by faith. And if he shrinks back, I will not be pleased with him." But we are not of those who shrink back and are destroyed, but of those who believe and are saved* (Hebrews 10:32-39).

Does this apply to you in any way? Are you suffering or being persecuted for your faith? If so, then be encouraged! God has neither forgotten your suffering nor the misdeeds of your persecutors. He will give everyone his or her just reward, especially you, His child and servant!

Study 41: Revelation 18:9-24

18:9-10 *"When the kings of the earth who committed adultery with her and shared her luxury see the smoke of her burning, they will weep and mourn over her. Terrified at her torment, they will stand far off and cry: 'Woe! Woe, O great city, O Babylon, city of power! In one hour your doom has come!'"*

Let's do a quick review. Revelation was addressed to churches living under the rule of the Roman Empire. This Empire was increasingly hostile to Christians and had a history of persecution and violence. I have stated repeatedly that Revelation was written first to comfort them in their distress and second to any others in history who would face the same dilemma.

At the time of Revelation, Babylon did not exist as a city. The name Babylon was used as a symbol of an idolatrous, polytheistic society. Babylon in its prime under Nebuchadnezzar in the sixth century BC was a magnificent city. The walls were so wide that a chariot with six horses across could ride on them! The Hanging Gardens, one of the ancient wonders of the world, have yet to be replicated, and it is not even known how they were constructed. Babylon was a tremendous city, yet it was one polluted with gods.

Babylon, with all its splendor, existed for only two generations. Quick was its rise and quick was its fall. That is the message to the reader of Revelation. We are not to be fooled by the magnificence or power of any society, for it is only temporary. The kingdom of God is advancing, and it will absorb or overcome any and all opponents as Daniel clearly saw in his vision of the nine-foot statue (see Daniel 3).

This discussion of the city of Babylon precludes the description of the heavenly Jerusalem in the last few chapters of Revelation. It seems that God builds cities and Satan, who can only imitate God, tries to do the same.

18:11-13 *The merchants of the earth will weep and mourn over her because no one buys their cargoes any more—cargoes of gold, silver, precious stones and pearls; fine linen, purple, silk and scarlet cloth; every sort of citron wood, and articles of every kind made of ivory, costly wood, bronze, iron and marble; cargoes of cinnamon and spice, of incense, myrrh and frankincense, of wine and olive oil, of fine flour and wheat; cattle and sheep; horses and carriages; and bodies and souls of men.*

When you purchase something, it is usually a self-focused activity, not always in a negative sense. When you are in business, you are in it to make money, also an act of self-interest. When you buy a suit or dress, you want to make sure that it fits you and it is something you want or need. The focus of commerce is usually on you, unless you are buying a gift or running a charity.

It seems that when this spiritual Babylon is conquered, people will lose their appetite for the normal activity of commerce, which raises an interesting point. People are in business to make money and that is what motivates many of the world systems. Kingdom activity, on the other hand, is always generous and has a focus on other people.

We see in Acts that when Paul preached the gospel, it was bad for the idolatrous merchants in Ephesus, who made money off the goddess Diana. When people turned to the Lord, they stopped buying statues of Diana, and the merchants were upset and started to persecute the Christians. In some ways, God is bad for business in systems that oppose the Lord and His people.

In addition to all the products and commodities mentioned above, note that the merchants of the earth had a business in the "bodies and souls of men," as mentioned in 18:13. There are men and women today who earn money by trafficking children and women in sex slavery. Thus, you can safely say that the Church is involved in life and death situations as it tries to rescue people from darkness.

The Church is competing for the hearts and souls of men, as is every other philosophy, economic system, and political structure. I can be a Christian and still find that materialism has a hold of my mind and pocketbook. The kingdom of God cannot be a part-time pursuit; it requires a total surrender to Christ and His demands. Are you completely His? Or do you share your allegiance with capitalism, liberation theology, socialism, a political party or educational trends or fads? You are to be in the world but not of it. Babylon represents this world system. You and I, however, belong to Christ.

As an American, I realize that God isn't that interested in my politics or my free enterprise. He has His own agenda and I must align myself with that agenda. He is not a Republican, Democrat or a capitalist. It is fine that I choose a political party, but I must not confuse my allegiance to a political party and my loyalty to Jesus. Jesus is my priority and He must be yours as well.

James clearly explained the end result for any person or system that was interested only in things and business:

> *What causes fights and quarrels among you? Don't they come from your desires that battle within you? You want something but don't get it. You kill and covet, but you cannot have what you want. You quarrel and fight. You do not have, because you do not ask God. When you ask, you do not receive, because you ask with wrong motives, that you may spend what you get on your pleasures.*

Study 41: Revelation 18:9-24   203

> *You adulterous people, don't you know that friendship with the world is hatred toward God? Anyone who chooses to be a friend of the world becomes an enemy of God. Or do you think Scripture says without reason that the spirit he caused to live in us envies intensely? But he gives us more grace.*
>
> *That is why Scripture says: "God opposes the proud but gives grace to the humble." Submit yourselves, then, to God. Resist the devil, and he will flee from you. Come near to God and he will come near to you. Wash your hands, you sinners, and purify your hearts, you double-minded.*
>
> *Grieve, mourn and wail. Change your laughter to mourning and your joy to gloom. Humble yourselves before the Lord, and he will lift you up* (James 4:1-10).

18:14-16 *"They will say, 'The fruit you longed for is gone from you. All your riches and splendor have vanished, never to be recovered.' The merchants who sold these things and gained their wealth from her will stand far off, terrified at her torment. They will weep and mourn and cry out: 'Woe! Woe, O great city, dressed in fine linen, purple and scarlet, and glittering with gold, precious stones and pearls!'"*

Throughout history many conspiracies and alliances with evil have enriched people. Jesus taught that riches are a bad foundation upon which to build a life. I was recently watching an interview on public television with a woman who became a multimillionaire as a pornographer! She was defending herself before the American public as a legitimate businesswoman. In the language and imagery of Revelation, she has made an alliance with the "great prostitute" (being one as well), and one day her riches and fame will fade and die, just as she will.

I have also watched the rich and powerful exposed for their duplicity and greed. Recent business scandals have made significant headlines. Those businesspeople made an alliance with the spirit of the age and they were brought to ruin. Only one alliance doesn't lead to disappointment or destruction, and that is an alliance with God.

The message of Revelation is that every alliance, except for the one between God and His people, will be rendered null and void. You can put your trust in God! Trust in anything else is like building a house on sinking sand as described in Matthew 7.

18:17-19 *"In one hour such great wealth has been brought to ruin! Every sea captain, and all who travel by ship, the sailors, and all who earn their living from the sea, will stand far off. When they see the smoke of her burning, they will exclaim, 'Was there ever a city like this great city?' They will throw dust on their heads, and with weeping and mourning cry out: 'Woe! Woe, O great city, where all who had ships on the sea became rich through her wealth! In one hour she has been brought to ruin!'"*

These verses make me think of Psalm 107, for God brings down those who exalt themselves against Him so they will call out to Him for help. He will then hear their cry and save them.

> *Others went out on the sea in ships; they were merchants on the mighty waters. They saw the works of the Lord, his wonderful deeds in the deep. For he spoke and stirred up a tempest that lifted high the waves.*
>
> *They mounted up to the heavens and went down to the depths; in their peril their courage melted away. They reeled and staggered like drunken men; they were at their wits' end.*
>
> *Then they cried out to the Lord in their trouble, and he brought them out of their distress. He stilled the storm to a whisper; the waves of the sea were hushed. They were glad when it grew calm, and he guided them to their desired haven. Let them give thanks to the Lord for his unfailing love and his wonderful deeds for men* (Psalm 107:23-31).

A city is a place where people congregate for purposes of employment, protection and community. This is not a literal city mentioned here in Revelation but rather a concentration of power that speaks of the grandeur of some world systems. Past and present civilizations have built cultural and economic systems that were the marvel of their day. Each one has said in their mind and heart, "Was there ever a city like this great city?" Yet they have all come to an end. Only the "city" of God has survived and will survive.

18:20 *"Rejoice over her, O heaven! Rejoice, saints and apostles and prophets! God has judged her for the way she treated you."*

Many economic and political systems have not simply ignored the Church but have also actively opposed it. Modern governments make the same mistake and contribute to their own demise. Take the Soviet Union for example. They tried to wipe out the Church; instead the government was destroyed. China, North Korea, and the Islamic countries will meet the same fate. That is the message of Revelation.

The Church has never had to take an active part in overthrowing any oppressive government, although some saints have been martyred while they actively preached the gospel. The Lord has brought down these kingdoms. Our focus should be on building God's kingdom on earth, not opposing the anti-Christian political forces. The best way to oppose evil is to do good: "Do not be overcome by evil, but overcome evil with good" (Romans 12:21).

18:21-23 *Then a mighty angel picked up a boulder the size of a large millstone and threw it into the sea, and said: "With such violence the great city of Babylon will be thrown down, never to be found again. The music of harpists and musicians, flute players and trumpeters, will never be heard in you again. No workman of any trade will ever be found in you again. The sound of a millstone will never be heard in you again. The light of a lamp will never shine in you again. The voice of bridegroom and bride will never be heard in you again. Your merchants were the world's great men. By your magic spell all the nations were led astray."*

We serve a mighty God! When He moves, no one can resist Him—not even whole civilizations or armies. The Bible and history are replete with stories describing how the mighty have fallen. Nations that were intoxicated with their own heresies and anti-Christian doctrine have vanished from the face of the earth or been reduced to irrelevance. What's more, God delights in using those who oppose Him to do His will! He is sovereign over all!

Think of what this message meant to the Revelation churches that were under such tremendous pressure from the Roman Empire equipped with powerful armies, a global economic system, a common language, and a worldwide justice and legal system. What was the Church compared to that mighty Roman force? Yet in less than two hundred years, this Empire was reduced to nothing, and the Church was a force to be reckoned with.

18:24 *"In her was found the blood of prophets and of the saints, and of all who have been killed on the earth."*

God is not mocked or fooled. He watches and judges the actions of entire people groups and nations and judges them according to how they treat the Church. He has harshly judged those who have not treated the Church well. Jesus warned his followers of what to expect. Do you think you and I are any different?

> *"Be on your guard against men; they will hand you over to the local councils and flog you in their synagogues. On my account you will be brought before governors and kings as witnesses to them and to the Gentiles.*
>
> *"But when they arrest you, do not worry about what to say or how to say it. At that time you will be given what to say, for it will not be you speaking, but the Spirit of your Father speaking through you. Brother will betray brother to death, and a father his child; children will rebel against their parents and have them put to death.*
>
> *"All men will hate you because of me, but he who stands firm to the end will be saved. When you are persecuted in one place, flee to another. I tell you the truth, you will not finish going through the cities of Israel before the Son of Man comes"* (Matthew 10:17-23).

> *"But before all this, they will lay hands on you and persecute you. They will deliver you to synagogues and prisons, and you will be brought before kings and governors, and all on account of my name. This will result in your being witnesses to them. But make up your mind not to worry beforehand how you will defend yourselves.*
>
> *"For I will give you words and wisdom that none of your adversaries will be able to resist or contradict. You will be betrayed even by parents, brothers, relatives and friends, and they will put some of you to death. All men will hate you because of me. But not a hair of your head will perish. By standing firm you will gain life* (Luke 21:12-19).

> *"If you belonged to the world, it would love you as its own. As it is, you do not belong to the world, but I have chosen you out of the world. That is why the world hates you. Remember the words I spoke to you: 'No servant is greater than his master.' If they persecuted me, they will persecute you also.*
>
> *"If they obeyed my teaching, they will obey yours also. They will treat you this way because of my name, for they do not know the One who sent me. If I had not come and spoken to them, they would not be*

guilty of sin. Now, however, they have no excuse for their sin. He who hates me hates my Father as well" (John 15:19-23).

"I have given them your word and the world has hated them, for they are not of the world any more than I am of the world. My prayer is not that you take them out of the world but that you protect them from the evil one. They are not of the world, even as I am not of it. Sanctify them by the truth; your word is truth. As you sent me into the world, I have sent them into the world" (John 17:14-18).

Where is your heart? Is it with the Church of Jesus Christ with all her imperfect people or with the systems of the world, such as education, commerce, politics, or finance? Are you committed to build the Church and extend God's kingdom, or are you content with simply attending a church every once in a while? My heart is with the Church! If the world doesn't like me, as Jesus predicted they would not, that is to be expected.

Study 42: Revelation 19:1-8

19:1-2 *After this I heard what sounded like the roar of a great multitude in heaven shouting: "Hallelujah! Salvation and glory and power belong to our God, for true and just are his judgments. He has condemned the great prostitute who corrupted the earth by her adulteries. He has avenged on her the blood of his servants."*

It has been a few chapters since John reminded us how loud heaven can be. It is impossible not to hear what heaven is doing and saying. You can ignore it, but you can't miss it. When Jesus was born, heaven spoke loudly and clearly. A star appeared for the Magi (see Matthew 2:1-12) and the angels came to visit the shepherds (see Luke 2:8-20).

What is God saying to you? I'm not asking you whether or not you hear His voice, but rather to identify the main theme of what the Holy Spirit is doing in your life. You should always be able to identify that without a problem. And have you figured out yet how God speaks to you? Does He use circumstances, other people or any other predictable and reliable pattern? What is saying to you from His Word?

Guidance is not (or should not be) a problem for the believer. If you commit to do God's will before you know what it is (surrendering the power to veto or ignore it), then you will know what God wants you to do (see John 7:17). How can God expect you to do His will if He doesn't tell you what that will is? God is a great communicator. He speaks every language and isn't limited to spoken words to get His message across. Listen carefully if for nothing else than God speaking through the life of Jesus as revealed in His Word:

> *In the past God spoke to our forefathers through the prophets at many times and in various ways, but in these last days he has spoken to us by his Son, whom he appointed heir of all things, and through whom he made the universe* (Hebrews 1:1-2).

When God acts on behalf of His people, the end result is not only deliverance for His people. The end result is worship! The multitudes in heaven, who are watching redemption history unfold, can only watch, marvel and worship as they see the power and majesty of God. And God judges the great prostitute out of His righteousness. His judgments are just and true and the great world systems, represented by the prostitute, are not anything like God.

19:3 *And again they shouted: "Hallelujah! The smoke from her goes up for ever and ever."*

The inhabitants of heaven shouted, "Hallelujah!" God obviously isn't intimidated or upset by loud sounds of worship. Are you?

This scenario reminds me of Israel as they watched Pharaoh's army destroyed at the Red Sea. Their only legitimate response was worship. The "smoke" from what God did there has gone up for all generations to learn from and behold. Yet God always has enemies who array in battle formation against Him, His anointed and His Church. Their end is always the same, going as far back as Pharaoh in Moses' day:

> *Pharaoh's chariots and his army God has hurled into the sea. The best of Pharaoh's officers are drowned in the Red Sea. The deep waters have covered them; they sank to the depths like a stone.*
>
> *"Your right hand, O Lord, was majestic in power. Your right hand, O Lord, shattered the enemy. In the greatness of your majesty you threw down those who opposed you. You unleashed your burning anger; it consumed them like stubble. By the blast of your nostrils the waters piled up.*
>
> *"The surging waters stood firm like a wall; the deep waters con-*

gealed in the heart of the sea. The enemy boasted, 'I will pursue, I will overtake them. I will divide the spoils; I will gorge myself on them. I will draw my sword and my hand will destroy them.'

"But you blew with your breath, and the sea covered them. They sank like lead in the mighty waters. Who among the gods is like you, O Lord? Who is like you—majestic in holiness, awesome in glory, working wonders? You stretched out your right hand and the earth swallowed them.

"In your unfailing love you will lead the people you have redeemed. In your strength you will guide them to your holy dwelling. The nations will hear and tremble; anguish will grip the people of Philistia" (Exodus 15:4-14).

If you are currently in a difficult place, be encouraged. It's not that God can't deliver you; it's that He is doing something else in your life, building something inside you. He is using your enemies to develop you and conform you to the image of Christ! Rejoice! When you no longer need your enemies, God will remove them. You will go looking for them but will be unable to find them.

19:4 *The twenty-four elders and the four living creatures fell down and worshiped God, who was seated on the throne. And they cried: "Amen, Hallelujah!"*

The book of Psalms is at the center of the Bible. The psalms teach us many things, but especially how to worship. The proper response to who God is and what He does is to worship Him. Worship is truly the central theme of the Bible and Jesus is the central focus, so worshiping Jesus is the goal for all creation!

We have not seen the elders or living creatures since chapter 14. Yet they have been there all along, watching the work of God unfold on the earth. I am reminded of another passage in Hebrews:

Therefore, since we are surrounded by such a great cloud of witnesses, let us throw off everything that hinders and the sin that so easily entangles, and let us run with perseverance the race marked out for us. Let us fix our eyes on Jesus, the author and perfecter of our faith, who for the joy set before him endured the cross, scorning its shame, and sat down at the right hand of the throne of God (Hebrews 12:1-2).

It seems that the citizens and creatures of heaven have the ability to see what is happening on earth. Perhaps they are cheering us on! If nothing else, their memory and legacy of faith in God spur us on to serve Him in our own generation. We are not alone, and I'm not talking about aliens from another planet. We are part of a spiritual family that has served God through the ages.

19:5 *Then a voice came from the throne, saying: "Praise our God, all you his servants, you who fear him, both small and great!"*

You are commanded to praise and worship. Praise is not a matter of how you feel or how well your circumstances are going. Your feelings and circumstances change, but God never does. If your focus is on Him, you will worship because He is worthy of worship.

What is heaven saying today? Heaven is telling you to worship Him. Worship is both a public, congregational exercise, and also a private and family one as well. You can and should praise and worship as an individual or as families.

19:6-7 *Then I heard what sounded like a great multitude, like the roar of rushing waters and like loud peals of thunder, shouting: "Hallelujah! For our Lord God Almighty reigns. Let us rejoice and be glad and give him glory! For the wedding of the Lamb has come, and his bride has made herself ready.*

Some things only God can do for you and then some things only you can do for Him. Your preparations are likened to a bride preparing for her bridegroom. A wedding is such a festive occasion. Everyone looks their best and under normal circumstances acts their best. The bride works hard to look her very best on that day. The church must work hard to prepare itself as well. How? The next verse tells you.

19:8 *"Fine linen, bright and clean, was given her to wear." (Fine linen stands for the righteous acts of the saints.)*

The Church and her members can prepare by wearing the fine linen that the Lord provides.

> *For it is by grace you have been saved, through faith—and this not from yourselves, it is the gift of God—not by works, so that no one can boast.*

Study 42: Revelation 19:1-8

For we are God's workmanship, created in Christ Jesus to do good works, which God prepared in advance for us to do (Ephesians 2:8-10).

Salvation is a gift of God, given to all those who believe in Him and trust in His name. Once saved, He expects you to do good works, but He provides the good works for you to do. He provides the garments, so to speak, but expects you to put them on. What are the good works that He has prepared for you to do? Are you doing them?

You do not have to work to find the works to perform (He will show them to you), but you must work to accomplish and complete the works He gives you. Paul described some of these good works toward widows when he wrote:

No widow may be put on the list of widows unless she is over sixty, has been faithful to her husband, and is well known for her good deeds, such as bringing up children, showing hospitality, washing the feet of the saints, helping those in trouble and devoting herself to all kinds of good deeds (1 Timothy 5:9-10).

These good works are practical and directed toward relieving the suffering or lack that others are experiencing. You are to be mindful that God will present these opportunities to you. A study of Revelation should not include you spending time trying to understand who the antichrist is. A study of the Bible should lead you to perform good works. These works do not earn your salvation; they prove the validity of your salvation. The rich are especially commanded to do good deeds.

Command those who are rich in this present world not to be arrogant nor to put their hope in wealth, which is so uncertain, but to put their hope in God, who richly provides us with everything for our enjoyment. Command them to do good, to be rich in good deeds, and to be generous and willing to share (1 Timothy 6:17-18).

At times, the more Bible someone knows, the more rigid and legalistic he or she can be! Knowledge of the Bible does not qualify you to be God's watchdog but should prepare you for love and good works. Does the Bible make you a better Christian in deeds or just through knowledge?

All Scripture is God-breathed and is useful for teaching, rebuking, correcting and training in righteousness, so that the man of God may be thoroughly equipped for every good work (2 Timothy 3:16-17).

Can you find any other references or examples of good works in the Bible? Are you doing good works? Are you dressing yourself as a bride for her husband? You need to be aware that God is bringing these good works to you. He has actually prepared them beforehand for you to accomplish. You need to be watching for them and then be ready to do something about them.

We of all people should be generous and gracious for we know that God is in control. We worship Him, acknowledging what He has done for us, when we do the things He sets before us to do. See how practical Revelation is. It doesn't only provide us with knowledge of who God is and what He is doing. It describes for us a life we now live that is to be both practical and sane.

Dear reader, I pray that you will clothe yourself in the good deeds that God has for you. *The Revelation Project* is not intended to make you more intelligent but to make you more like Him. *The Revelation Project* is also not geared to study the Antichrist, but the Christ. The knowledge of Jesus should make you a better spouse, obedient child, efficient worker and cooperative church member. Be careful not to make Revelation a book of bizarre interpretations but of godly knowledge that leads to righteous deeds!

Study 43: Revelation 19:9-13

19:9 *Then the angel said to me, "Write: 'Blessed are those who are invited to the wedding supper of the Lamb!'" And he added, "These are the true words of God."*

The angel said: "Write!" And that is the command, in my opinion, to many people today, maybe even you. You should write and record what the Lord is doing and saying in your life. Maybe you should even have a personal website or blog site where you can publish what you write so that people from all over the world can read it and give glory to God. You may even publish booklets, fliers, and books. To do any of that, however, means that you first must write! Is this something that the Lord is directing you to do?

I wonder if John understood that people would be reading what he wrote two thousand years after he wrote it. For that matter, I wonder if any of the writers of Scripture understood this. I am not saying that your material will last this long, but it could! It will never happen, however, until you do write. You must give God something to use before He can bless and distribute it.

Is there anything more joyous than a wedding feast? What an appropriate metaphor this is of the relationship between the Lamb and His bride, His people.

All God's words are true. I find it interesting that the angel would endorse God's words in such a manner. The human heart in its current fallen and sinful condition tends to doubt the words of God and attribute truth to other words. This is a mistake. If God said it, you can believe it!

19:10 *At this I fell at his feet to worship him. But he said to me, "Do not do it! I am a fellow servant with you and with your brothers who hold to the testimony of Jesus. Worship God! For the testimony of Jesus is the spirit of prophecy."*

Angels are not to be worshiped. Satan, however, distorted this truth and desired to be worshiped, which led to his downfall. This particular angel in 19:10, loyal to God and his purpose, refused to receive the worship, or at least the honor, that John tried to give.

There is a lesson here for leaders. People will have a tendency to fall down and worship at the feet of whoever brings the truth, or whoever is the most eloquent or powerful. Leaders must work to deflect man's praise and worship and focus their worship on God. That means developing lifestyles, spending habits, and church traditions that keep the focus on Jesus and not on the messengers of Jesus. Paul and Barnabas provide an example of this being done in Acts:

> When the crowd saw what Paul had done, they shouted in the Lycaonian language, "The gods have come down to us in human form!" Barnabas they called Zeus, and Paul they called Hermes because he was the chief speaker.
>
> The priest of Zeus, whose temple was just outside the city, brought bulls and wreaths to the city gates because he and the crowd wanted to offer sacrifices to them. But when the apostles Barnabas and Paul heard of this, they tore their clothes and rushed out into the crowd, shouting:
>
> "Men, why are you doing this? We too are only men, human like you. We are bringing you good news, telling you to turn from these worthless things to the living God, who made heaven and earth and sea and everything in them. In the past, he let all nations go their own way.

> *Yet he has not left himself without testimony: He has shown kindness by giving you rain from heaven and crops in their seasons; he provides you with plenty of food and fills your hearts with joy." Even with these words, they had difficulty keeping the crowd from sacrificing to them* (Acts 14:11-18).

Jesus did not deflect the worship that came His way. This is a key issue for those religions who claim that Jesus is only a prophet. If Jesus was "only" a prophet and He allowed men to worship Him, He was a false prophet and nothing He said can be trusted. Of course, this is not the case. Jesus allowed men to worship Him because He is God!

"When they saw him, they worshiped him; but some doubted" (Matthew 28:17). Even in the midst of worship, some doubted. Worship and doubt can coexist. Some act like God cannot do anything unless there is pure faith with no doubt. That is not the case.

The aim of prophecy is to exalt Jesus. All that the Church does and will do should be about Him, not about the messenger. We aren't really sure who recorded this Revelation. Many think it was the apostle John, as do I. Why isn't who wrote it more evident? He was not more prominently mentioned because it's not about who wrote it, it's about Jesus! Yet the authorship has some importance, for John's authority as an apostle who walked with Jesus would provide great credibility for the reader and listener.

The Church is built by personalities, but these personalities must work hard (harder than some are presently working) to shift the focus away from themselves and on to Jesus. Jesus is the message of the prophecy. Worship Him! Talk about Him! Adore Him! This was a challenge for leaders even before Jesus came:

> *They love to be greeted in the marketplaces and to have men call them "Rabbi." But you are not to be called "Rabbi," for you have only one Master and you are all brothers. And do not call anyone on earth "father," for you have one Father, and he is in heaven. Nor are you to be called "teacher," for you have one Teacher, the Christ. The greatest among you will be your servant. For whoever exalts himself will be humbled, and whoever humbles himself will be exalted* (Matthew 23:7-12).

19:11 *I saw heaven standing open and there before me was a white horse, whose rider is called Faithful and True. With justice he judges and makes war.*

John saw heaven standing open. What did he see? He saw Jesus! That reinforces the point made above, that Jesus is the message of and from heaven. Jesus needs to be the message of the Church.

A white horse, even in modern movies, is symbolic of the good guy or the hero. Jesus is the best man that ever lived, and now He is seated at the right hand of the Father. He is worthy of a white horse.

We know that Jesus is praying for the Church at the right hand of the Father. Here John tells us that He also judges and makes war. So prayer, at least for Jesus, must involve judgment and spiritual warfare. It is interesting that Jesus is in heaven, but He is working. You will work in heaven too.

Who is he that condemns? Christ Jesus, who died—more than that, who was raised to life—is at the right hand of God and is also interceding for us (Romans 8:34).

Which he exerted in Christ when he raised him from the dead and seated him at his right hand in the heavenly realms, far above all rule and authority, power and dominion, and every title that can be given, not only in the present age but also in the one to come. And God placed all things under his feet and appointed him to be head over everything for the church, which is his body, the fullness of him who fills everything in every way (Ephesians 1:20-23).

19:12 *His eyes are like blazing fire, and on his head are many crowns. He has a name written on him that no one knows but he himself.*

Jesus has a name written on Him that only He knows. That means we don't know everything there is to know about Jesus. We have been given all that we need to know, but His ways and being are beyond our human comprehension. Anyone who can figure God out, so to speak, would be God. We, however, are finite beings worshiping an infinite God; we can know Him intimately, but we cannot know Him in all His glory and majesty.

Why am I making this point? I do so because some people try to reduce God to a system, a set of principles. If you can reduce God to a system, then the system becomes God! God is not controlled by anyone or anything. God rules His principles; His principles do not rule Him!

Jesus has the power to look at something with eyes of fire. He cannot be fooled and His eyes can judge a situation accurately and with righteousness. He also wears many crowns; that is why He is the King of kings.

> *In the sight of God, who gives life to everything, and of Christ Jesus, who while testifying before Pontius Pilate made the good confession, I charge you to keep this command without spot or blame until the appearing of our Lord Jesus Christ, which God will bring about in his own time—God, the blessed and only Ruler, the King of kings and Lord of lords* (1 Timothy 6:13-15).

Paul stated that God was the King of kings. Since Jesus wears many crowns, He can be designated the King of kings. Therefore, Jesus is God!

19:13 *He is dressed in a robe dipped in blood, and his name is the Word of God.*

Besides being a warrior, Jesus is also a priest, the High Priest of heaven. What does this have to do with 19:13? Let's look at the Old Testament:

> *Then Moses took some of the anointing oil and some of the blood from the altar and sprinkled them on Aaron and his garments and on his sons and their garments. So he consecrated Aaron and his garments and his sons and their garments* (Leviticus 8:30).

The magnificent garments of Aaron were sprinkled with blood! That would be like a fine, expensive wedding dress being spotted with blood! What's the lesson here? No matter how magnificent the blessings that you enjoy today, you must not lose sight of the fact that they were earned through the blood of Jesus. He was and is our High Priest before God.

> *But we see Jesus, who was made a little lower than the angels, now crowned with glory and honor because he suffered death, so that by the grace of God he might taste death for everyone. In bringing many sons to glory, it was fitting that God, for whom and through whom everything exists, should make the author of their salvation perfect through suffering.*
>
> *Both the one who makes men holy and those who are made holy are of the same family. So Jesus is not ashamed to call them brothers. He says, "I will declare your name to my brothers; in the presence of the congregation I will sing your praises." And again, "I will put my trust in him." And again he says, "Here am I, and the children God has given me."*
>
> *Since the children have flesh and blood, he too shared in their hu-*

Study 43: Revelation 19:9-13

manity so that by his death he might destroy him who holds the power of death— that is, the devil—and free those who all their lives were held in slavery by their fear of death. For surely it is not angels he helps, but Abraham's descendants.

For this reason he had to be made like his brothers in every way, in order that he might become a merciful and faithful high priest in service to God, and that he might make atonement for the sins of the people. Because he himself suffered when he was tempted, he is able to help those who are being tempted (Hebrews 2:9-18).

Jesus is also the Word of God!

In the beginning was the Word, and the Word was with God, and the Word was God. He was with God in the beginning. Through him all things were made; without him nothing was made that has been made (John 1:1-3).

The Word became flesh and made his dwelling among us. We have seen his glory, the glory of the One and Only, who came from the Father, full of grace and truth (John 1:14).

The book of Revelation is about Jesus, not about the dragon, prophet, beast or antichrist. He is the main focus. Revelation was written to encourage people who were being persecuted by reminding them that Jesus was still on the throne.

Revelation was also written in symbolic language with many metaphors so that non-Christians would not understand what was being written about them. God speaks to His people in ways that the world cannot understand.

In every generation, powers rise up to challenge Jesus' authority. They have some measure of success and may gain a large following. They are destined to fail and perish, however, unless they repent. God is in control, yet He wishes that everyone would repent and come to the knowledge of His saving grace.

This means that He is in control of your life and circumstances as well. You can be encouraged in your difficulties by the fact that God will take care of you. You may even lose your life; but in another age to come, you will be exalted. God will not forget His people. Jesus is Lord to the glory of God the Father. Be encouraged today and every day.

Study 44: Revelation 19:14-21

19:14 *The armies of heaven were following him, riding on white horses and dressed in fine linen, white and clean.*

I'm glad there is an army in heaven fighting on my side. That makes me think of the story of Elisha and his assistant in the Old Testament.

> *Then he sent horses and chariots and a strong force there. They went by night and surrounded the city. When the servant of the man of God got up and went out early the next morning, an army with horses and chariots had surrounded the city. "Oh, my lord, what shall we do?" the servant asked.*
>
> *"Don't be afraid," the prophet answered. "Those who are with us are more than those who are with them." And Elisha prayed, "O Lord, open his eyes so he may see." Then the Lord opened the servant's eyes, and he looked and saw the hills full of horses and chariots of fire all around Elisha* (2 Kings 6:14-17).

The Lord opened the servant's eyes so that he could see spiritual reality. Do your eyes need to be opened? Are you focusing on how bad things are in the natural? Are you surrounded by things that are trying to bring you down? The cure may be for you to see spiritual reality. There is an army, the army of God, that is fighting for you and this army is following the commands of Jesus, our all-powerful Captain!

This army is dressed in white and riding a white horse. They are holy and in one accord with Jesus. They cannot fail in their mission. If all that is true, then what are you concerned about? It's time to review an oft-quoted passage in *The Revelation Project*, for you need to be reminded of this truth again and again, and then live like you believe it:

> *What, then, shall we say in response to this? If God is for us, who can be against us? He who did not spare his own Son, but gave him up for us all—how will he not also, along with him, graciously give us all things? Who will bring any charge against those whom God has chosen? It is God who justifies.*
>
> *Who is he that condemns? Christ Jesus, who died—more than that, who was raised to life—is at the right hand of God and is also interceding for us. Who shall separate us from the love of Christ? Shall trouble or hardship or persecution or famine or nakedness or danger or sword?*

Study 44: Revelation 19:14-21

> *As it is written: "For your sake we face death all day long; we are considered as sheep to be slaughtered." No, in all these things we are more than conquerors through him who loved us. For I am convinced that neither death nor life, neither angels nor demons, neither the present nor the future, nor any powers, neither height nor depth, nor anything else in all creation, will be able to separate us from the love of God that is in Christ Jesus our Lord* (Romans 8:31-39).

So what can separate you from the love of God? The only person is you! Decide today to stay connected to God's love. Those who are for you are more numerous than those against you!

19:15 Out of his mouth comes a sharp sword with which to strike down the nations. "He will rule them with an iron scepter." He treads the winepress of the fury of the wrath of God Almighty.

This is the third reference in Revelation to ruling with an "iron scepter" (see also Revelation 2:27; 12:5). Why is the concept of Jesus ruling with an iron scepter so important? This iron scepter is first mentioned in Psalm 2, another passage that has been included many times in this devotional. Let's look at the truth contained therein one more time:

> *The One enthroned in heaven laughs; the Lord scoffs at them. Then he rebukes them in his anger and terrifies them in his wrath, saying, "I have installed my King on Zion, my holy hill." I will proclaim the decree of the Lord: He said to me, "You are my Son; today I have become your Father. Ask of me, and I will make the nations your inheritance, the ends of the earth your possession. You will rule them with an iron scepter; you will dash them to pieces like pottery"* (Psalm 2:4-9).

Iron always represents strength and is made from a combination of natural resources in intense heat. The Lamb, who is gracious and kind to His people, will at the same time rule His enemies with firmness and authority. He will break seemingly powerful kingdoms like pottery.

Someone knowledgeable of the Old Testament reading Revelation 19:15 would understand that this iron scepter referred to Psalm 2, which is a psalm promising the victory of God and His Son over any and all who opposed them. Psalm 2 also appealed for God's enemies to repent and make peace with God, or else risk destruction.

That is why the Church of Jesus is to engage in missions and outreach to the nations, to save them from the wrath of God that comes upon any who do not acknowledge God's ownership of the earth, its people and all its institutions.

Are you asking God for the nations as an inheritance? If not, you should be as directed in Psalm 2. What nation would you like to pray for?

There is also a sharp sword coming out of Jesus' mouth. For His enemies this is the sword of destruction. For those who know Him, it is a surgical instrument for good as described in Hebrews 4:

> *For the word of God is living and active. Sharper than any double-edged sword, it penetrates even to dividing soul and spirit, joints and marrow; it judges the thoughts and attitudes of the heart. Nothing in all creation is hidden from God's sight. Everything is uncovered and laid bare before the eyes of him to whom we must give account.*
>
> *Therefore, since we have a great high priest who has gone through the heavens, Jesus the Son of God, let us hold firmly to the faith we profess. For we do not have a high priest who is unable to sympathize with our weaknesses, but we have one who has been tempted in every way, just as we are—yet was without sin. Let us then approach the throne of grace with confidence, so that we may receive mercy and find grace to help us in our time of need* (Hebrews 4:12-16).

While the Word is likened to a sword, notice how it is described in the context of Jesus being such a gentle and patient High Priest, as we discussed in the previous study. Jesus uses His word not to destroy you but to build you up and to draw you to Him. When your motives and thoughts are revealed to be less than God's will, you can draw near to find help and grace. Jesus' sword cuts and destroys those who don't know Him, but the same sword is a tool of God's grace for those who do. Hallelujah!

19:16 *On his robe and on his thigh he has this name written: KING OF KINGS AND LORD OF LORDS.*

This seems to have been Jesus' seal or logo, the title that would set him apart from all the other leaders of the earth. He is not a peer of the kings of the earth; He stands out as supreme.

When Jesus walked the earth, He was meek and lowly, difficult to distinguish from others in the crowd. Judas had to kiss Him so that the soldiers coming to arrest Him would know who Jesus was. His dress and demeanor did not set Him apart from His peers. That is no longer the case.

Jesus is now seated at the right hand of the Father and He is Lord above all!

Why is this title written on Jesus' thigh? The thigh muscle is the biggest and strongest muscle in the body. Jesus' title is placed over His greatest strength, built up because He walked out the will of God. How strong is your thigh muscle? You don't get a big thigh muscle by praying for one; you get a strong muscle by walking and running while doing the will of God.

19:17-18 *And I saw an angel standing in the sun, who cried in a loud voice to all the birds flying in midair, "Come, gather together for the great supper of God, so that you may eat the flesh of kings, generals, and mighty men, of horses and their riders, and the flesh of all people, free and slave, small and great."*

Once again, John heard heaven speak in a loud voice. Heaven is always broadcasting. Are you listening for what heaven is trying to say? Do not harden your heart. Have faith to hear and you will hear.

The angel was inviting spectators to see the fulfillment of the Word of the Lord. The angel is so confident that the Lord will win that he invites onlookers. The outcome is guaranteed.

As the rain and the snow come down from heaven, and do not return to it without watering the earth and making it bud and flourish, so that it yields seed for the sower and bread for the eater, so is my word that goes out from my mouth: It will not return to me empty, but will accomplish what I desire and achieve the purpose for which I sent it (Isaiah 55:10-11).

God does not make idle promises or talk for the sake of hearing Himself speak. He does what He says He will do. So every reader of Revelation can be encouraged, even in the midst of dark times, to know that God will prevail. Also, God is not a respecter of persons. If your name is written in His book, you will attend the marriage supper of the Lamb. If your name is not in the book, no matter who you are or what your status is, you will attend another supper, but this one will be for eternal damnation. Everyone has a choice, so God cannot be blamed for which supper a man chooses to attend.

19:19 *Then I saw the beast and the kings of the earth and their armies gathered together to make war against the rider on the horse and his army.*

The beast will always try to make war against the Lord and His saints, and the beast will always lose!

> The Lord says to my Lord: "Sit at my right hand until I make your enemies a footstool for your feet." The Lord will extend your mighty scepter from Zion; you will rule in the midst of your enemies. Your troops will be willing on your day of battle. Arrayed in holy majesty, from the womb of the dawn you will receive the dew of your youth.
> The Lord has sworn and will not change his mind: "You are a priest forever, in the order of Melchizedek." The Lord is at your right hand; he will crush kings on the day of his wrath. He will judge the nations, heaping up the dead and crushing the rulers of the whole earth. He will drink from a brook beside the way; therefore he will lift up his head (Psalm 110:1-7).

The Lord promises to destroy His enemies; but that doesn't mean they won't try to win, so they continue to wage war against Jesus and His army. They are doomed to failure, but they try anyway. They are desperate foes. There is no way around the reality of God and His promises, however, and He is always victorious.

19:20-21 *But the beast was captured, and with him the false prophet who had performed the miraculous signs on his behalf. With these signs he had deluded those who had received the mark of the beast and worshiped his image. The two of them were thrown alive into the fiery lake of burning sulfur. The rest of them were killed with the sword that came out of the mouth of the rider on the horse, and all the birds gorged themselves on their flesh.*

There are several Old Testament references that refer to earthly kings, but which seem also to refer to Satan's judgment:

> On the day the Lord gives you relief from suffering and turmoil and cruel bondage, you will take up this taunt against the king of Babylon: How the oppressor has come to an end! How his fury has ended! The Lord has broken the rod of the wicked, the scepter of the rulers, which in

anger struck down peoples with unceasing blows, and in fury subdued nations with relentless aggression. All the lands are at rest and at peace; they break into singing (Isaiah 14:3-7).

All your pomp has been brought down to the grave, along with the noise of your harps; maggots are spread out beneath you and worms cover you. How you have fallen from heaven, O morning star, son of the dawn! You have been cast down to the earth, you who once laid low the nations! You said in your heart, "I will ascend to heaven; I will raise my throne above the stars of God; I will sit enthroned on the mount of assembly, on the utmost heights of the sacred mountain. I will ascend above the tops of the clouds; I will make myself like the Most High."

But you are brought down to the grave, to the depths of the pit. Those who see you stare at you, they ponder your fate: "Is this the man who shook the earth and made kingdoms tremble, the man who made the world a desert, who overthrew its cities and would not let his captives go home?" (Isaiah 14:11-17)

And then another reference in Ezekiel:

The word of the Lord came to me: "Son of man, take up a lament concerning the king of Tyre and say to him: 'This is what the Sovereign Lord says: 'You were the model of perfection, full of wisdom and perfect in beauty. You were in Eden, the garden of God; every precious stone adorned you: ruby, topaz and emerald, chrysolite, onyx and jasper, sapphire, turquoise and beryl.

"'Your settings and mountings were made of gold; on the day you were created they were prepared. You were anointed as a guardian cherub, for so I ordained you. You were on the holy mount of God; you walked among the fiery stones. You were blameless in your ways from the day you were created till wickedness was found in you.

"'Through your widespread trade you were filled with violence, and you sinned. So I drove you in disgrace from the mount of God, and I expelled you, O guardian cherub, from among the fiery stones. Your heart became proud on account of your beauty, and you corrupted your wisdom because of your splendor.

"'So I threw you to the earth; I made a spectacle of you before kings. By your many sins and dishonest trade you have desecrated your sanctuaries. So I made a fire come out from you, and it consumed you, and I re-

duced you to ashes on the ground in the sight of all who were watching. All the nations who knew you are appalled at you; you have come to a horrible end and will be no more'"* (Ezekiel 28:11-19).

These are important passages that explain Satan's magnificence and his fall. Remember this, for so is the fate of all who oppose our God.

Our God is an awesome God! He knows how to punish the wicked but protect and reward the righteous! Praise the Lord!

Study 45: Revelation 20:1-6

20:1 *And I saw an angel coming down out of heaven, having the key to the Abyss and holding in his hand a great chain.*

Whoever this angel is, he had great power and authority. The key and chain are of course symbolic and not literal. What angel came down from heaven? The Lord Jesus did, so this verse may very well depict Him. He is the only angel or messenger with sufficient power and authority to hold the key to the Abyss and spiritual strength to hold a great chain that could bind the devil.

20:2 *He seized the dragon, that ancient serpent, who is the devil, or Satan, and bound him for a thousand years.*

Jesus bound the devil! Hallelujah! Jesus referred to this dynamic in his earthly ministry. We see this when the Pharisees accused Jesus of casting demons out of people by the power and authority of the devil himself!

> *But when the Pharisees heard this, they said, "It is only by Beelzebub, the prince of demons, that this fellow drives out demons." Jesus knew their thoughts and said to them, "Every kingdom divided against itself will be ruined, and every city or household divided against itself will not stand. If Satan drives out Satan, he is divided against himself. How then can his kingdom stand?*
>
> *"And if I drive out demons by Beelzebub, by whom do your people drive them out? So then, they will be your judges. But if I drive out demons by the Spirit of God, then the kingdom of God has come upon you. Or again, how can anyone enter a strong man's house and carry off his possessions unless he first ties up the strong man? Then he can rob his*

house. He who is not with me is against me, and he who does not gather with me scatters" (Matthew 12:24-30).

Jesus has authority to bind and direct the devil and that, according to Matthew, means that the kingdom of God is here. The kingdom of God is now! It is part of the already/not yet interpretation of Scripture. The kingdom is already here, for sure, but it is not yet all that it will be.

Jesus' power is not equal to Satan's; it is greater than Satan's. That is why He can bind Satan with a great chain and lock him in the Abyss. When I see the phrase "kingdom of God," I think of a seminary professor who referred to the kingdom as the government of God. Do you agree with this meaning? What implications does God's government have for you? For the world? For Satan?

Think of what this meant to the early church and what it means for us today. The early church was facing threats backed by the power of the Roman Empire. All this was demonically and devilishly inspired. The message of Revelation, however, is that Jesus is more powerful than anything they were facing or that we face today.

You cannot be passive or casual, however, about this spiritual truth. Jesus closed His message in Matthew by stating that those who did not make a conscious decision to walk in the reality of His power would be scattered and subject to the devil's authority. The devil is a powerful, mean enemy and you are helpless to oppose him without Jesus. Even then, you must exercise diligence and wage war to resist him.

Any spiritual power I have is because Jesus has that power and allows me to access it in His name. The disciples were excited about the authority they had, but Jesus cautioned them (and you) in the passage below:

> *The seventy-two returned with joy and said, "Lord, even the demons submit to us in your name." He replied, "I saw Satan fall like lightning from heaven. I have given you authority to trample on snakes and scorpions and to overcome all the power of the enemy; nothing will harm you.*
>
> *However, do not rejoice that the spirits submit to you, but rejoice that your names are written in heaven." At that time Jesus, full of joy through the Holy Spirit, said, "I praise you, Father, Lord of heaven and earth, because you have hidden these things from the wise and learned, and revealed them to little children. Yes, Father, for this was your good pleasure.*
>
> *"All things have been committed to me by my Father. No one knows*

who the Son is except the Father, and no one knows who the Father is except the Son and those to whom the Son chooses to reveal him" (Luke 10:17-22).

Jesus saw Satan fall, and his fall was as quick and dramatic as lightning. Because of Satan's fall, Jesus has given His followers the authority to overcome all the power of the enemy! Nothing can harm you—not death, persecution, criticism, lack, or any conspiracy of evil men! This authority is not given for your personal benefit. The early church did not use this power to acquire new vehicles, homes or diamond rings. They used this power, as small and weak as they were in their own strength, to eventually overthrow the Roman government. Jesus finished His message in Luke (see above) by talking about people knowing Him.

That is how you are to use this power and authority: to bind Satan so that people can come to know Jesus! Satan blinds eyes, but Jesus opens them. Satan confuses them, but Jesus brings clarity in the power of the Spirit. Satan binds them, but Jesus looses them. Jesus uses us to do this work, and that is why He gave us this authority. We share His work on earth.

How are you using the authority that is yours in Christ? Are you using it at all? Using it for personal gain and comfort? Or are you advancing the kingdom of God by binding Satan in Jesus' name so men and women may come to know Him, in your nation and in the nations of the earth?

20:3 *He threw him into the Abyss, and locked and sealed it over him, to keep him from deceiving the nations anymore until the thousand years were ended. After that, he must be set free for a short time.*

Now what about the issue of a millennium or one thousand-year rule? As we have seen in the previous studies, much of Revelation was written using symbols. The entire book is a vision, a dream that the Spirit gave to one John. This book was written in metaphorical symbols so that the persecutors of the Church, if they were to read the book, would not understand what it meant. It is written in code, so to speak.

So why would we take this one thousand-year concept as literally as some people have done? The fact that Satan is locked into the Abyss for one thousand years speaks of Christ's rule. He is in control of the events of history. I don't believe that the millennium will begin on September 1, 2032 and end on August 31, 3031! Yet I do believe, and you should as well, that Jesus will return and reign on the earth for a period of time. How long? He will rule as long as He chooses to rule!

There have been many seasons of relative peace for the church throughout history. Then there have been seasons of persecution and difficulties. In fact, those different seasons can be going on at the same time in different parts of the world. No matter what is happening, you are not to panic and be concerned. Jesus is in control. If the devil is free for a short time, we worship the One who holds the key and the chain. One day, He will pull the devil's chain, and the devil will be unable to go any further or do any more.

20:4 *I saw thrones on which were seated those who had been given authority to judge. And I saw the souls of those who had been beheaded because of their testimony for Jesus and because of the word of God. They had not worshiped the beast or his image and had not received his mark on their foreheads or their hands. They came to life and reigned with Christ a thousand years.*

Some say the blood of the martyrs is the life-giving seed of the Church. We should honor those who paid with their lives to stand for and further the Gospel. We don't even know, however, all those who died for Christ. Only God knows! And God has rewarded, is rewarding and will reward them.

I formerly worried whether or not I would be able to give my life for Christ, if it came to that. Would I be able to face the firing squad, torture or deprivation? I came to the conclusion that I didn't really know. I gave my life to the Lord on May 18, 1973 and have made it this far by faith. I will finish my life in faith and even die in faith, whether by natural causes or martyrdom, I do not know.

I also know that the stories of the saints of old who gave their lives are a tremendous encouragement to the modern church. Saints who died have taken their place alongside Jesus to encourage us and will rule in spiritual affairs. Think of Paul, Peter and the apostles. They were killed, but they live on! Their words endure, as do their stories and letters.

The account of the faithful found in Hebrews 11 ends with the first few verses of chapter 12:

> *Therefore, since we are surrounded by such a great cloud of witnesses, let us throw off everything that hinders and the sin that so easily entangles, and let us run with perseverance the race marked out for us.*

> *Let us fix our eyes on Jesus, the author and perfecter of our faith, who for the joy set before him endured the cross, scorning its shame, and sat down at the right hand of the throne of God. Consider him who endured such opposition from sinful men, so that you will not grow weary and lose heart. In your struggle against sin, you have not yet resisted to the point of shedding your blood* (Hebrews 12:1-4).

We are surrounded by a cloud of witnesses, comprised both of those still alive who have served the Lord and those who have gone before us who left their mark in their generation. We read their stories, sing their songs, and endeavor to match their greatness and distinguished service to Christ.

I do believe in what the Catholic Church referred to as "the communion of the saints." I feel historically tied to those who have gone before me and I want to continue and pass on the legacy they handed my generation and me.

Hebrews 12 (quoted above) is what you and I need to do with the truths revealed in Revelation. We must:

- Throw off everything that hinders;
- Run the race with endurance;
- Fix our eyes on Jesus;
- Not grow weary and lose heart; and
- Struggle against sin, in our own lives and in the world.

Your job is not to figure out who the Antichrist is or isn't, or whether or not the millennium is to be taken literally. Your job is to impact the world for Christ in your generation, whether you face extreme persecution or relative freedom.

20:5 *(The rest of the dead did not come to life until the thousand years were ended.) This is the first resurrection.*

What is the first resurrection? You and I were dead in our sins before we met Jesus. Now we have experienced resurrection life! That's right. The same Holy Spirit who raised Christ from the dead lives inside you today. You have received this Spirit as a pledge, a down payment, on the resurrection and eternal life that is to come.

> *Now we know that if the earthly tent we live in is destroyed, we have a building from God, an eternal house in heaven, not built by*

human hands. Meanwhile we groan, longing to be clothed with our heavenly dwelling, because when we are clothed, we will not be found naked.

For while we are in this tent, we groan and are burdened, because we do not wish to be unclothed but to be clothed with our heavenly dwelling, so that what is mortal may be swallowed up by life. Now it is God who has made us for this very purpose and has given us the Spirit as a deposit, guaranteeing what is to come.

Therefore we are always confident and know that as long as we are at home in the body we are away from the Lord. We live by faith, not by sight. We are confident, I say, and would prefer to be away from the body and at home with the Lord. So we make it our goal to please him, whether we are at home in the body or away from it. For we must all appear before the judgment seat of Christ, that each one may receive what is due him for the things done while in the body, whether good or bad (2 Corinthians 5:1-10).

You and I were once dead, but now we are alive. This is the first resurrection, the first coming to life! And the best is yet to come!

When you were dead in your sins and in the uncircumcision of your sinful nature, God made you alive with Christ. He forgave us all our sins, having canceled the written code, with its regulations, that was against us and that stood opposed to us; he took it away, nailing it to the cross. And having disarmed the powers and authorities, he made a public spectacle of them, triumphing over them by the cross (Colossians 2:13-15).

20:6 Blessed and holy are those who have part in the first resurrection. The second death has no power over them, but they will be priests of God and of Christ and will reign with him for a thousand years.

Are you blessed to be part of the first resurrection? I know I am and I am sure you are too. I can face the ultimate judgment of Christ, the second death, because I have experienced the born-again phenomenon. I was dead, but now I live. I am a priest of Christ and I am reigning with Him now, with the best yet to come.

> *As you come to him, the living Stone—rejected by men but chosen by God and precious to him—you also, like living stones, are being built into a spiritual house to be a holy priesthood, offering spiritual sacrifices acceptable to God through Jesus Christ.*
>
> *For in Scripture it says: "See, I lay a stone in Zion, a chosen and precious cornerstone, and the one who trusts in him will never be put to shame." Now to you who believe, this stone is precious. But to those who do not believe, "The stone the builders rejected has become the capstone," and, "A stone that causes men to stumble and a rock that makes them fall."*
>
> *They stumble because they disobey the message—which is also what they were destined for. But you are a chosen people, a royal priesthood, a holy nation, a people belonging to God, that you may declare the praises of him who called you out of darkness into his wonderful light. Once you were not a people, but now you are the people of God; once you had not received mercy, but now you have received mercy* (1 Peter 2:4-10).

Will there be a literal one thousand-year reign on the earth? Perhaps. But that is not important. What is essential is that you, like your brothers and sisters who first received Revelation, will rule now regardless of the circumstances in which you find yourself. You are a priest now. You rule with Christ now. You are enjoying resurrection life now. Should the Lord tarry, I know I will die, but that death cannot affect me. I am alive in Christ forevermore!

I had another seminary professor who said that eternal life is a quality of life so good and pure that nothing can end it, not even death. On that basis, we have entered into eternal life now!

I refuse to spend one minute in foolish, useless speculation concerning obscure passages or concepts. If the Lord wanted me to know more about the millennium, He would have made it clear. He did not, so I choose to focus on the many, many things He did make clear. It is a much better and wiser investment of my life, time and ministry.

Study 46: Revelation 20:7-15

20:7-8 *When the thousand years are over, Satan will be released from his prison and will go out to deceive the nations in the four corners of the earth—Gog and Magog—to gather them for battle. In number they are like the sand on the seashore.*

Study 46: Revelation 20:7-15

Let me quote what I wrote from Study 45: "Your job is not to figure out who the Antichrist is or isn't, or whether the millennium is to be taken literally. Your job is to impact the world for Christ in your generation, whether you face extreme persecution or relative freedom."

Historically, there seem to be specific seasons for the gospel and the Church. Some seasons are abounding with great grace, influence, and peace; and then others are crammed with persecution and pressure. God uses both seasons to spread His Word. For instance, during the first three centuries, the more Rome tried to wipe out the Church, the more it seemed to flourish and prosper.

Reports from modern totalitarian countries speak of a vibrant Church, although the believers are "malnourished" and doctrinally ignorant due to lack of teaching and resources. God is not limited to work even when His enemies are as numerous as the "sand on the seashore."

It is important to recognize the times and seasons of God. According to the writer of Ecclesiastes:

There is a time for everything, and a season for every activity under heaven: a time to be born and a time to die, a time to plant and a time to uproot, a time to kill and a time to heal, a time to tear down and a time to build, a time to weep and a time to laugh, a time to mourn and a time to dance, a time to scatter stones and a time to gather them, a time to embrace and a time to refrain, a time to search and a time to give up, a time to keep and a time to throw away, a time to tear and a time to mend, a time to be silent and a time to speak, a time to love and a time to hate, a time for war and a time for peace (Ecclesiastes 3:1-8).

What time is it right now for you and the church? What season is your nation enduring? What are you doing about this season? Are you complaining or trying to use your spiritual authority to get out of that particular season? Or are you armed with the knowledge of what season it is, using the power of God to spread the gospel according to the reality of the moment?

It may be a time of great openness in one country, and a time of persecution and tension in another. Remember what we discussed in previous studies: Jesus is in control. No power, especially that of the devil, can oppose the Lamb on the throne. That doesn't mean that Satan has no power. He does and it should be feared to some extent, for no human without Jesus can withstand him. And he has helpers and followers as numerous as the sand on the seashore.

20:9 *They marched across the breadth of the earth and surrounded the camp of God's people, the city he loves. But fire came down from heaven and devoured them.*

Thank God for the fire from heaven! Sometimes the fire from heaven also engulfs the people of God while God's enemies are being burned up. When this happens, God uses the fire to do good things in our lives, to purge that which is unnecessary or even unclean. Consider Daniel's three friends:

> *Furious with rage, Nebuchadnezzar summoned Shadrach, Meshach and Abednego. So these men were brought before the king, and Nebuchadnezzar said to them, "Is it true, Shadrach, Meshach and Abednego, that you do not serve my gods or worship the image of gold I have set up? Now when you hear the sound of the horn, flute, zither, lyre, harp, pipes and all kinds of music, if you are ready to fall down and worship the image I made, very good. But if you do not worship it, you will be thrown immediately into a blazing furnace. Then what god will be able to rescue you from my hand?"*
>
> *Shadrach, Meshach and Abednego replied to the king, "O Nebuchadnezzar, we do not need to defend ourselves before you in this matter. If we are thrown into the blazing furnace, the God we serve is able to save us from it, and he will rescue us from your hand, O king. But even if he does not, we want you to know, O king, that we will not serve your gods or worship the image of gold you have set up."*
>
> *Then Nebuchadnezzar was furious with Shadrach, Meshach and Abednego, and his attitude toward them changed. He ordered the furnace heated seven times hotter than usual and commanded some of the strongest soldiers in his army to tie up Shadrach, Meshach and Abednego and throw them into the blazing furnace. So these men, wearing their robes, trousers, turbans and other clothes, were bound and thrown into the blazing furnace.*
>
> *The king's command was so urgent and the furnace so hot that the flames of the fire killed the soldiers who took up Shadrach, Meshach and Abednego, and these three men, firmly tied, fell into the blazing furnace. Then King Nebuchadnezzar leaped to his feet in amazement and asked his advisers, "Weren't there three men that we tied up and threw into the fire?" They replied, "Certainly, O king." He said, "Look! I see four men walking around in the fire, unbound and unharmed, and the fourth looks like a son of the gods."*

> *Nebuchadnezzar then approached the opening of the blazing furnace and shouted, "Shadrach, Meshach and Abednego, servants of the Most High God, come out! Come here!" So Shadrach, Meshach and Abednego came out of the fire, and the satraps, prefects, governors and royal advisers crowded around them. They saw that the fire had not harmed their bodies, nor was a hair of their heads singed; their robes were not scorched, and there was no smell of fire on them.*
>
> *Then Nebuchadnezzar said, "Praise be to the God of Shadrach, Meshach and Abednego, who has sent his angel and rescued his servants! They trusted in him and defied the king's command and were willing to give up their lives rather than serve or worship any god except their own God. Therefore I decree that the people of any nation or language who say anything against the God of Shadrach, Meshach and Abednego be cut into pieces and their houses be turned into piles of rubble, for no other god can save in this way." Then the king promoted Shadrach, Meshach and Abednego in the province of Babylon* (Daniel 3:13-30).

God used the fire to burn up the things that bound Daniel's three friends. Jesus also met them in the midst of the fire, while the men who carried them to the fire were consumed. I would like to be with Jesus, but not while I'm in the middle of a raging furnace. Yet that is how and where I will fellowship with Him at times.

Dear reader, when will you fully comprehend that God is in control and works good in all things for those who know and love Him? Revelation is not a book of fear, nor is fire from heaven something to dread. God can deal with His enemies through fire and use that same fire to deliver and cleanse His people.

20:10 *And the devil, who deceived them, was thrown into the lake of burning sulfur, where the beast and the false prophet had been thrown. They will be tormented day and night for ever and ever.*

In 20:10, we see the eternal judgment for the devil and his followers. They will spend eternity apart from God in the real torment of hell's fires. No matter how powerful the devil is, God can still pick him up and throw him into the lake of fire.

It appears that the devil is "God's devil," under His oversight. Consider what is written in the book of Job:

> *One day the angels came to present themselves before the Lord, and Satan also came with them. The Lord said to Satan, "Where have you come from?" Satan answered the Lord, "From roaming through the earth and going back and forth in it"* (Job 1:6-7).

I don't fully understand all this, and it leads to many questions about evil and how it occurs. Humans and the devil have a free will, but God has the last word. Someone once said, "God is playing chess with man; He matches his every move." God matched every one of Satan's moves in the life of Job and eventually brought great victory to Job's life. He will do the same in your life as well.

20:11 *Then I saw a great white throne and him who was seated on it. Earth and sky fled from his presence, and there was no place for them.*

When God acts and moves, where can anyone go to flee from His presence? He is all-powerful!

Revelation uses what is referred to as apocalyptic language. It is a vocabulary of vivid and sometimes bizarre images and metaphors that are not to be taken literally. The earth and sky won't try to escape God's presence. It is symbolic language that speaks of a tumultuous time when men will try everything they know to avoid God's judgment, but nothing will work.

20:12 *And I saw the dead, great and small, standing before the throne, and books were opened. Another book was opened, which is the book of life. The dead were judged according to what they had done as recorded in the books.*

Do you think there is a literal book of life, or does this present a vivid and lasting image of God's ability to remember all the deeds that men and women performed (or didn't perform)?

20:13 *The sea gave up the dead that were in it, and death and Hades gave up the dead that were in them, and each person was judged according to what he had done.*

There is a final judgment that everyone who has ever lived must pass through. This is an irrefutable tenet of the Christian faith: God will judge all men.

Study 46: Revelation 20:7-15

He commanded us to preach to the people and to testify that he is the one whom God appointed as judge of the living and the dead (Acts 10:42).

In the presence of God and of Christ Jesus, who will judge the living and the dead, and in view of his appearing and his kingdom, I give you this charge (2 Timothy 4:1).

But they will have to give account to him who is ready to judge the living and the dead (1 Peter 4:5).

At that point of final judgment, everyone will be assigned to their eternal reward, whether heaven or hell.

20:14 *Then death and Hades were thrown into the lake of fire. The lake of fire is the second death.*

We saw in the last study that the first resurrection is in this life when men and women are raised in Christ through faith in His name and blood. There is also a second resurrection and death, and that is the final judgment.

Paul provided insight into this great judgment time to the church at Thessalonica, which was being unnerved by false teachings that the resurrection had already taken place:

Brothers, we do not want you to be ignorant about those who fall asleep, or to grieve like the rest of men, who have no hope. We believe that Jesus died and rose again and so we believe that God will bring with Jesus those who have fallen asleep in him.

According to the Lord's own word, we tell you that we who are still alive, who are left till the coming of the Lord, will certainly not precede those who have fallen asleep. For the Lord himself will come down from heaven, with a loud command, with the voice of the archangel and with the trumpet call of God, and the dead in Christ will rise first.

After that, we who are still alive and are left will be caught up together with them in the clouds to meet the Lord in the air. And so we will be with the Lord forever. Therefore encourage each other with these words (1 Thessalonians 4:13-18).

The above passage has been used to develop a "rapture" theology that has led to much speculation as to when the believers will be removed from the earth. Many believe that this will happen prior to a great tribulation on the earth. What is my thought on this?

I am not excited about any doctrine that does not exalt the power and glory of God first and foremost. The focus of a lot of rapture theology is the power of the devil and the weakness of the church. I find this inconsistent with the teachings of Revelation, which is a book of absolute triumph and victory for Jesus and His followers, not just in the future, but also now. Revelation is clear that difficult times and even martyrdom will happen for some, but that is not the central theme as I have repeated in almost every study. The central theme is the supremacy of Christ over every earthly government and demonic power.

20:15 *If anyone's name was not found written in the book of life, he was thrown into the lake of fire.*

The book of life is referenced also in Revelation 3:5, 13:8 and 17:8. Jesus referred to this book of life when He said: "However, do not rejoice that the spirits submit to you, but rejoice that your names are written in heaven" (Luke 10:20). It is not a literal book, but a metaphor for God's exceptional record-keeping ability. He remembers everyone who has ever known or will ever know Him!

Jesus also referred to the reality of hell. If hell is only a folk tale (as some maintain) and Jesus "played along" with the beliefs of His contemporaries, then Jesus' entire message or gospel is rendered suspect. That of course is not the case. If Jesus believed in a literal hell, everyone should believe in hell! It is a real place reserved for those who are not in right standing with God through faith in Christ. Here are a few of Jesus' references to hell:

> *"But I tell you that anyone who is angry with his brother will be subject to judgment. Again, anyone who says to his brother, 'Raca,' is answerable to the Sanhedrin. But anyone who says, 'You fool!' will be in danger of the fire of hell"* (Matthew 5:22).
>
> *"If your hand or your foot causes you to sin cut it off and throw it away. It is better for you to enter life maimed or crippled than to have two hands or two feet and be thrown into eternal fire"* (Matthew 18:8).
>
> *"Then he will say to those on his left, 'Depart from me, you who are cursed, into the eternal fire prepared for the devil and his angels'"* (Matthew 25:41).

"And if your eye causes you to sin, pluck it out. It is better for you to enter the kingdom of God with one eye than to have two eyes and be thrown into hell, where 'their worm does not die, and the fire is not quenched'" (Mark 9:47-48).

Some say that Jesus was only catering to the superstitions of His audience when He referred to hell. If Jesus was willing to accommodate the ignorance of His audience on that topic, that would indicate the possibility that He did the same on other topics. If that is the case (which it isn't), then how could we know what was fact and what was fiction in Jesus' teaching?

It seems to me that people have a choice to meet God's fire in such a way that brings them new life or final death. The writer of Hebrews warned that God is a consuming fire. I wonder if hell isn't meeting God in that capacity with no hope of ever meeting Him in any other way?

Therefore, since we are receiving a kingdom that cannot be shaken, let us be thankful, and so worship God acceptably with reverence and awe, for our "God is a consuming fire" (Hebrews 12:28-29).

Study 47: Revelation 21:1-8

21:1 *Then I saw a new heaven and a new earth, for the first heaven and the first earth had passed away, and there was no longer any sea.*

I'm not sure that 21:1 and those verses following are about heaven as we commonly refer to it. I know that's what John would appear to be addressing, but I'm not so sure. My reason for doubt is that the language of Revelation, which we have described as apocalyptic, is given to exaggeration and graphic metaphors for effect. Could Revelation be talking about the here-and-now, about the Church rather than the sweet by-and-by of heaven?

I think of what happened when Jesus was crucified. There was a literal shaking on earth, which tells us that all creation was impacted by Jesus' death.

At that moment the curtain of the temple was torn in two from top to bottom. The earth shook and the rocks split. The tombs broke open and the bodies of many holy people who had died were raised to life. They came out of the tombs, and after Jesus' resurrection they went into the holy city and appeared to many people (Matthew 27:51-53).

Did John see a literal heavenly city, or was this a picture of the new order that was established through Jesus' death, the age of the Church of Jesus Christ? Imagine our earth without the oceans! What a dramatic difference that would be from what we have and know now. Isn't that in a sense the difference before and after Jesus' death? Didn't Jesus' life, death, and resurrection redefine how we understand heaven, our role on earth, and the relationship of God with His people? That sounds like a new heaven and new earth order to me.

21:2 *I saw the Holy City, the new Jerusalem, coming down out of heaven from God, prepared as a bride beautifully dressed for her husband.*

There is now a new city, a new Jerusalem, for all to behold. The challenge is that it can only be seen through spiritual eyes! This new city, the Church, is a heavenly phenomenon. It has its origins in heaven, even though it is manifest on earth.

I hear many people talk about the Church adorning and preparing herself as a bride for her bridegroom. This bride is dressed in heaven, however, not on earth. God adorns His bride. The bride cannot dress herself in clothes that are pleasing to God. Only God can provide the clothes, symbolic of the righteousness that pleases Him. Otherwise, you have a Church of works, populated with people who are trying to do things for God, instead of in and through God. The work has been done in and through Jesus. You now only have to put on the garments He provided for you.

There is a new Jerusalem, the old one belonging to the earth and the old covenant. Now there is a new covenant and that requires a new headquarters. This headquarters is in heaven, not in Rome, Constantinople, Washington DC, or Jerusalem.

21:3 *And I heard a loud voice from the throne saying, "Now the dwelling of God is with men, and he will live with them. They will be his people, and God himself will be with them and be their God."*

Study 47: Revelation 21:1-8

This voice is from the throne. It is an authoritative voice that emanates from God's place of government and the Church's headquarters. You must work hard not to hear what heaven is doing and saying. What is heaven saying to you at this point in your life? The message is that God is living with His people! God no longer lives among His people by living in a temple or tabernacle. He is now with His people in an intimate way through the power of the Holy Spirit. That is why I don't think these verses are about heaven (although if they are, they are still powerful and comforting).

Let's keep in mind that Revelation was written to a church under siege in the first century. I fail to see how a picture of heaven, of the "by-and-by," would be a comfort to them. This image shows that God is with His people now, in power and might. They, and therefore we, don't have to wait to see the victory of Jesus. It is ours now. And the Church, beleaguered and inept as it may be at times, is still the bride of Christ adorned beautifully. Hallelujah!

21:4 *"He will wipe every tear from their eyes. There will be no more death or mourning or crying or pain, for the old order of things has passed away."*

Now you may disagree with my interpretation here because of the reference to no more death or mourning or pain. There is certainly plenty in this lifetime. If God is going to wipe away tears, however, He can only do that now while we are alive. That is what makes me think this is a reference to the present and not the future.

I have seen the Lord comfort people now who are going through tremendous loss, even persecution. They have a joy that is beyond description or comprehension. God is with them and has wiped away every tear from their eyes. They aren't mourning as the world mourns; there is meaning and comfort in their pain.

It may not be the best example of what I'm referring to, but consider what happened to the apostles early in their ministry after Jesus:

His speech persuaded them. They called the apostles in and had them flogged. Then they ordered them not to speak in the name of Jesus, and let them go. The apostles left the Sanhedrin, rejoicing because they had been counted worthy of suffering disgrace for the Name. Day after day, in the temple courts and from house to house, they never stopped teaching and proclaiming the good news that Jesus is the Christ (Acts 5:40-42).

How did the apostles respond? They responded with joy! They continued to do what they had to do, not hiding or cowering in fear. They preached the Word. They were operating in a new order, the order of the Holy Spirit. That was the message to those churches in Revelation. They weren't supposed to hold on until heaven, they were to act as if they were in heaven already. It was a new heaven and earth for them. Consider that Phillip found himself being translated from one place to another in Acts 8:39. There was no "sea" for the early church, no insurmountable obstacle between them and accomplishing the will of God.

There was even a new economic order established after Pentecost:

After they prayed, the place where they were meeting was shaken. And they were all filled with the Holy Spirit and spoke the word of God boldly. All the believers were one in heart and mind. No one claimed that any of his possessions was his own, but they shared everything they had. With great power the apostles continued to testify to the resurrection of the Lord Jesus, and much grace was upon them all. There were no needy persons among them. For from time to time those who owned lands or houses sold them, brought the money from the sales and put it at the apostles' feet, and it was distributed to anyone as he had need (Acts 4:31-35).

It is counterproductive to put too much emphasis on getting to heaven. That is already taken care of. What's more critical is to accomplish what you must do now on the earth in the power of the Holy Spirit.

21:5 *He who was seated on the throne said, "I am making everything new!" Then he said, "Write this down, for these words are trustworthy and true."*

Jesus often said while He was on earth, "Verily, verily" or "Truly I say unto you." Here He was speaking from the throne and is continuing this same pattern of speech. He was saying that the words "I make everything new!" are trustworthy and true, but at times they may seem like only wishful thinking and exaggeration.

That is why I am concluding that this passage to be a reference to our life on earth now and not our life in heaven. There is no need to dry tears or make everything new there. Jesus is making things new now. Paul wrote:

Study 47: Revelation 21:1-8   241

We were therefore buried with him through baptism into death in order that, just as Christ was raised from the dead through the glory of the Father, we too may live a new life. If we have been united with him like this in his death, we will certainly also be united with him in his resurrection. For we know that our old self was crucified with him so that the body of sin might be done away with, that we should no longer be slaves to sin—because anyone who has died has been freed from sin (Romans 6:4-7).

Therefore, if anyone is in Christ, he is a new creation; the old has gone, the new has come! (2 Corinthians 5:17).

Neither circumcision nor uncircumcision means anything; what counts is a new creation (Galatians 6:15).

You were taught, with regard to your former way of life, to put off your old self, which is being corrupted by its deceitful desires; to be made new in the attitude of your minds (Ephesians 4:22-23).

Do not lie to each other, since you have taken off your old self with its practices and have put on the new self, which is being renewed in knowledge in the image of its Creator (Colossians 3:9-10).

Are you waiting for heaven to be a new creation, or are you walking in newness of life now? If you are, what are the implications for you in your walk with the Lord? In your walk with others?

21:6 *He said to me: "It is done. I am the Alpha and the Omega, the Beginning and the End. To him who is thirsty I will give to drink without cost from the spring of the water of life."*

Revelation was wrapping up its message as the vision came to an end. Jesus referred to Himself as the Alpha and Omega in Revelation 1:8 and He refers to Himself in that way again.

I had someone recently send me a song entitled "Working the Middle." The message of that song was that Jesus is the Alpha and Omega, the beginning and the end. That is His role, so to speak. Our role is to work out everything "in the middle," in between His start and finish, His being the Alpha and Omega. I thought that was an interesting application of the Alpha and Omega truth.

Jesus promised to give a drink to those who are thirsty. This reminds me of Jesus' encounter with the woman at the well:

Jesus answered her, "If you knew the gift of God and who it is that asks you for a drink, you would have asked him and he would have given you living water." "Sir," the woman said, "you have nothing to draw with and the well is deep. Where can you get this living water? Are you greater than our father Jacob, who gave us the well and drank from it himself, as did also his sons and his flocks and herds?"

Jesus answered, "Everyone who drinks this water will be thirsty again, but whoever drinks the water I give him will never thirst. Indeed, the water I give him will become in him a spring of water welling up to eternal life." The woman said to him, "Sir, give me this water so that I won't get thirsty and have to keep coming here to draw water" (John 4:10-15).

Here in Revelation, Jesus said, "It is done!" He also said that from the cross:

When he had received the drink, Jesus said, "It is finished." With that, he bowed his head and gave up his spirit (John 19:30).

Jesus' work on the cross is available free of charge to all those who thirst after God. There is no price; Jesus paid it all! The work that empowers anyone to come to God is finished in Christ.

21:7 *He who overcomes will inherit all this, and I will be his God and he will be my son.*

In 21:7, we revisit a word that was used frequently in the first three chapters and that word is *overcomes*. With Jesus' help, you can overcome the trials that come your way. When you do, you inherit "all this." Only family or those specified in a last will and testament can inherit anything. What is it that overcomers will inherit? Let's look at some other passages:

I declare to you, brothers, that flesh and blood cannot inherit the kingdom of God, nor does the perishable inherit the imperishable (1 Corinthians 15:50).

The acts of the sinful nature are obvious: sexual immorality, impurity and debauchery; idolatry and witchcraft; hatred, discord, jealousy, fits of rage, selfish ambition, dissensions, factions and envy; drunkenness, orgies, and the like. I warn you, as I did before, that those who live like this will not inherit the kingdom of God (Galatians 5:19-21).

Are not all angels ministering spirits sent to serve those who will inherit salvation? (Hebrews 1:14).

Listen, my dear brothers: Has not God chosen those who are poor in the eyes of the world to be rich in faith and to inherit the kingdom he promised those who love him? (James 2:5).

Your inheritance is not only heaven, but it is heavenly or eternal life now. Remember that Jesus said the kingdom of God is within you (see Luke 17:21). The kingdom is here, already in affect but not yet all that it will be.

Are you living in your inheritance? Are you experiencing righteousness, peace, and joy in the Holy Spirit? Why or why not?

21:8 *"But the cowardly, the unbelieving, the vile, the murderers, the sexually immoral, those who practice magic arts, the idolaters and all liars—their place will be in the fiery lake of burning sulfur. This is the second death."*

I can understand that the idolaters and murderers will be in the lake of fire, but what are the cowards doing there? What are the unbelievers doing there? I don't associate cowardice and unbelief as sins worthy of hell or in the same league as adultery and theft, but there they are! Maybe the fearful would have sinned, but their fear stopped them instead of their love for God!

The second death is the final judgment where all are assigned their eternal destination, either heaven or hell.

I am glad that heaven is my destination, but I'm also glad I don't have to wait until I get to heaven before I can enjoy God's blessings. That is another message of Revelation: No matter how bad things are now, you can live in the kingdom of God right here and now. Praise the Lord!

Study 48: Revelation 21:9-16

21:9 *One of the seven angels who had the seven bowls full of the seven last plagues came and said to me, "Come, I will show you the bride, the wife of the Lamb."*

Here we have another visit from the angel who carried one of the plague-filled bowls. These angels obviously did double duty. This one in particular carried one of the plagues to earth, but he also brought a revelation or message to John. He offered to take John to see the bride of Christ, the Church.

The angel told John to "come." That tells me that you have a role to play in anything that God wants to show you. You must come to the place where He wants to reveal Himself and His will. That may even be a particular place or geographic location. When I first wrote this study, I was in Asia. That was where God wanted me at the time. For me to learn what God had for me then, I had to be in Asia and not remain in Pittsburgh. That is my role in hearing from God: positioning myself where He wants me to be. Where does God want you to be?

This also tells me that you cannot see the Church with its glory and majesty unless God shows it to you. Are you discouraged about the state of the Church and all its human imperfections? Then allow God to show you His Church from His perspective, with all its glory and beauty.

Church leaders and members have offended and hurt many people throughout history, even today. I too have been hurt, and I have also hurt others. Yet I am not walking away from the Church, nor am I discouraged about her. The Church is the apple of God's eye and the bride of Christ. I must serve what He loves and be where He is. That is in the Church, more specifically a local church.

Are you a member of a church? Are you holding back? Have you been hurt and withdrawn your gifts and time from God's bride? I urge you to get healing for your wounds and then get back into the Church, into a local church, where you belong:

> *Let us hold unswervingly to the hope we profess, for he who promised is faithful. And let us consider how we may spur one another on toward love and good deeds. Let us not give up meeting together, as some are in the habit of doing, but let us encourage one another—and all the more as you see the Day approaching* (Hebrews 10:23-25).

When Jesus was raised from the dead, He met the women who were coming to the tomb. What did He tell them?

> *"Then go quickly and tell his disciples: 'He has risen from the dead and is going ahead of you into Galilee. There you will see him.' Now I have told you." So the women hurried away from the tomb, afraid yet filled with joy, and ran to tell his disciples. Suddenly Jesus met them.*

"Greetings," he said. They came to him, clasped his feet and worshiped him. Then Jesus said to them, "Do not be afraid. Go and tell my brothers to go to Galilee; there they will see me" (Matthew 28:7-10).

Jesus had all the disciples assembled there in Jerusalem, where He appeared to the women. Yet He told them to instruct the disciples to meet Him in Galilee, some distance north of Jerusalem. God determines where and how you will encounter Him. It is by His grace that He reveals Himself, but He also reveals Himself as part of His Lordship. His revelation is based on His terms, not yours.

Is God telling you to "come" or "go" somewhere? He may want to show you something that He will not show you if you stay where you are. It is not a matter of convenience but of obedience. I had a professor say once, "When God wants to say something to you, He often takes you on a trip." I agree.

21:10 *And he carried me away in the Spirit to a mountain great and high, and showed me the Holy City, Jerusalem, coming down out of heaven from God.*

God shows you all things "in the Spirit." You cannot comprehend the things of God through intellectual means, but only by spiritual means. Revelation began with John "in the Spirit on the day of the Lord." The book now comes to an end the same way: in the Spirit!

The Spirit always takes you "up." John was taken to a great and high mountain. We discussed this truth in previous studies: we are already seated in high places with Christ!

And God raised us up with Christ and seated us with him in the heavenly realms in Christ Jesus, in order that in the coming ages he might show the incomparable riches of his grace, expressed in his kindness to us in Christ Jesus (Ephesians 2:6-7).

What great thing did John see? He saw the Holy City coming down from heaven. As we saw in the previous study, the Church originates in heaven. The bride of Christ is born and adorned in heaven. The Church was and is God's idea, and He has clothed her in His righteousness. The Church has no claim to her own merits; she stands on the work of God.

This city that John saw is referred to as the bride of Christ. Notice how the metaphors are mixed here: first a bride, then a city. Both are accurate descriptions for God's people. The writer of Hebrews mentioned the concept of a city in reference to Abraham, Sarah, and other people of faith.

By faith Abraham, when called to go to a place he would later receive as his inheritance, obeyed and went, even though he did not know where he was going. By faith he made his home in the promised land like a stranger in a foreign country; he lived in tents, as did Isaac and Jacob, who were heirs with him of the same promise. For he was looking forward to the city with foundations, whose architect and builder is God (Hebrews 11:8-10).

All these people were still living by faith when they died. They did not receive the things promised; they only saw them and welcomed them from a distance. And they admitted that they were aliens and strangers on earth. People who say such things show that they are looking for a country of their own. If they had been thinking of the country they had left, they would have had opportunity to return. Instead, they were longing for a better country—a heavenly one. Therefore God is not ashamed to be called their God, for he has prepared a city for them (Hebrews 11:13-16).

21:11 *It shone with the glory of God, and its brilliance was like that of a very precious jewel, like a jasper, clear as crystal.*

"When Jesus spoke again to the people, he said, "I am the light of the world. Whoever follows me will never walk in darkness, but will have the light of life" (John 8:12). The city of God, the Church, has one source of light and that is Jesus! Those who try to walk in their own light have a promise of torment and confusion:

But now, all you who light fires and provide yourselves with flaming torches, go, walk in the light of your fires and of the torches you have set ablaze. This is what you shall receive from my hand: You will lie down in torment (Isaiah 50:11).

How often I have followed a good idea or something that made sense to me only to find that I was walking in my own light and not the light of God. I have set my own torches ablaze and their light was indeed fleeting. I am still learning how to hear from and follow God.

The work of God in your life is priceless, like that of a precious jewel. The price of Jesus' death is incomprehensible. This jasper jewel mentioned in verse 12, however, is also clear. Transparency is one characteristic of the relationship between God and His people. There are neither hidden agendas nor is there any impurity in the jewel to pervert its clarity. Here I think of what Paul wrote:

Unlike so many, we do not peddle the word of God for profit. On the contrary, in Christ we speak before God with sincerity, like men sent from God (2 Corinthians 2:17).

God expects a transparent relationship between Him and His people, and in their dealings with one another. He wants you and me to be honest with Him, to share our hearts and inner feelings without reservation. It should be like David described:

I pour out my complaint before him; before him I tell my trouble. When my spirit grows faint within me, it is you who know my way. In the path where I walk men have hidden a snare for me (Psalm 142:2-3).

Are you being honest with God? Being honest with God is not for His sake, it is for yours! Maybe you need to pour out your complaint to Him today. When you are honest with God, then that releases Him to be honest with you. Do you need to hear from your Father today? Then maybe He first needs to hear from you.

21:12 *It had a great, high wall with twelve gates, and with twelve angels at the gates. On the gates were written the names of the twelve tribes of Israel.*

The Church has a high wall around it. There is no way to sneak or break into the Church of Jesus. You cannot enter by human effort of cleverness. Only God can show you the entrance.

The names of the twelve tribes are written on the gates. That signifies a great salvation history of God's faithfulness to His people. Our God is a covenant-making and covenant-keeping God, and it is on this covenant basis that He provides an entrance into His kingdom. When you enter into God's kingdom, you inherit a rich history outlined in the Old Testament and continued in the New.

21:13 *There were three gates on the east, three on the north, three on the south and three on the west.*

God is also a God of order. There is nothing random or haphazard in what He does or how He does it. What's more, all people from all compass points of the earth have equal access into His Holy City and a relationship with Him.

21:14 *The wall of the city had twelve foundations, and on them were the names of the twelve apostles of the Lamb.*

Notice that the names of the apostles of the Lamb are part of the foundation, while the twelve tribes are a part of the walls. Continuity in the Church that began in the Old Testament runs through the New and culminates in this last book of Revelation.

The original twelve apostles who walked with Jesus are generally referred to as apostles of the Lamb. Yet they were not the last apostles, for the word *apostle* literally means "sent forth one." Many have been sent forth to plant and oversee churches, and to preach the good news of the gospel.

> *Consequently, you are no longer foreigners and aliens, but fellow citizens with God's people and members of God's household, built on the foundation of the apostles and prophets, with Christ Jesus himself as the chief cornerstone. In him the whole building is joined together and rises to become a holy temple in the Lord. And in him you too are being built together to become a dwelling in which God lives by his Spirit* (Ephesians 2:19-22).

Since Paul referred to the people of God as a building and temple, I assume that Revelation is talking about the same thing. While the verses you are studying could refer to heaven, there is enough evidence to show they are also references to the Church.

The early Church would have been greatly encouraged when John reminded them, in the midst of their persecution, that they were already a part of a dwelling in which God lived.

21:15-16 *The angel who talked with me had a measuring rod of gold to measure the city, its gates and its walls. The city was laid out like a square, as long as it was wide. He measured the city with the rod and* *found it to be 12,000 stadia in length, and as wide and high as it is long.*

I love the order the Lord built into His creation. We know every day what time the sun will rise and set. The seasons begin and end on fixed dates. Nothing is haphazard about God and His creation, including His work in the Church. While I may not be able to see all that God is doing, the angels can see and measure it. It is a good work, laid out with excellence.

God is a master Architect and Builder! This city is a square and is equal in length, height, and depth. That speaks of planning and building correctly. You are in good hands when you are in God's care. He does all things well. Are you anxious about something, dear reader? There is no need. God, who orders all things by His power and strength, has everything under control. Let the angels of God show you today just how beautiful His work is in your life. It is even and orderly, and God has built and is building you into a wonderful edifice to glorify His name.

Let that angel also restore your hope for the Church and show you her beauty. Don't put your faith in the leaders of the Church; you will always be disappointed. Put your faith in the Leader of the Church—Jesus Christ. Those who trust in Him will never be disappointed.

Study 49: Revelation 21:17-27

21:17 *He measured its wall and it was 144 cubits thick, by man's measurement, which the angel was using.*

This verse describes a thick wall. As we saw in the Study 48, the walls of the heavenly Jerusalem are also high. This represents the fact that there is no way to "break into" the things of God, whether into the Church, eternal salvation or any of God's blessings. By man's measurement, perspective, and ability, it is an impossible task. Even the disciples asked Jesus how it was possible for anyone to be saved, especially the rich.

> *Then Jesus said to his disciples, "I tell you the truth, it is hard for a rich man to enter the kingdom of heaven. Again I tell you, it is easier for a camel to go through the eye of a needle than for a rich man to enter the kingdom of God." When the disciples heard this, they were greatly astonished and asked, "Who then can be saved?" Jesus looked at them and*

said, "With man this is impossible, but with God all things are possible" (Matthew 19:23-26).

It isn't possible for man to conceive any plan that will earn him favor with God. What is impossible for man, however, is possible for God. Think of this: If it is impossible for man to "break into" the things of God, it is also impossible for those inside these walls to ever be snatched away. Someone living in a city with high and thick walls is safe. You and I are safe in God's hands. He is indeed a refuge for us! The word *refuge* is used forty-four times just in the book of Psalms! Why not take some time and look up a few of those references? Then apply them to your life. Remember, the lessons of Revelation are not only for the future; they are for you today!

There is no way to get into this impregnable city unless someone can find the door or gate. Do you know who that door is?

> *Someone asked him, "Lord, are only a few people going to be saved?" He said to them, "Make every effort to enter through the narrow door, because many, I tell you, will try to enter and will not be able to* (Luke 13:23-24).

> *Jesus answered, "I am the way and the truth and the life. No one comes to the Father except through me"* (John 14:6).

> *"All who ever came before me were thieves and robbers, but the sheep did not listen to them. I am the gate; whoever enters through me will be saved. He will come in and go out, and find pasture"* (John 10:8-9).

All who came before Jesus, and by implication all who came after Him, and claimed to be spiritual leaders showing a way to favor with God, are thieves and robbers. This isn't just referring to false Jewish messiahs predating Jesus, but any world religious leader like Buddha who came before Jesus and made claims that he knew the way. They didn't and don't. There is only One who knows the way and that is because He is the way!

The wall is thick to keep enemies out. The Lord is able to protect His people from all harm. The Lord is able to protect you from all harm. The psalmist understood this and wrote:

> *I will say of the Lord, "He is my refuge and my fortress, my God, in whom I trust." Surely he will save you from the fowler's snare and from the deadly pestilence. He will cover you with his feathers, and under his*

Study 49: Revelation 21:17-27

wings you will find refuge; his faithfulness will be your shield and rampart.

You will not fear the terror of night, nor the arrow that flies by day, nor the pestilence that stalks in the darkness, nor the plague that destroys at midday. A thousand may fall at your side, ten thousand at your right hand, but it will not come near you.

You will only observe with your eyes and see the punishment of the wicked. If you make the Most High your dwelling—even the Lord, who is my refuge—then no harm will befall you, no disaster will come near your tent. For he will command his angels concerning you to guard you in all your ways; they will lift you up in their hands, so that you will not strike your foot against a stone.

You will tread upon the lion and the cobra; you will trample the great lion and the serpent. "Because he loves me," says the Lord, "I will rescue him; I will protect him, for he acknowledges my name. He will call upon me, and I will answer him; I will be with him in trouble, I will deliver him and honor him. With long life will I satisfy him and show him my salvation" (Psalm 91:2-16).

The walls that protect you are secure, well-built, and eternal. Thank You, Lord!

21:18 *The wall was made of jasper, and the city of pure gold, as pure as glass.*

While the walls are thick to keep intruders and enemies out, the walls are also transparent. The Church is not to function in obscurity, but is to act in such a way that mankind can behold the goodness of God through the deeds and behavior of the members. "In the same way, let your light shine before men, that they may see your good deeds and praise your Father in heaven" (Matthew 5:16).

The world is watching the Church because God wants that to happen. What is the world seeing you and your church doing? The walls are also transparent because God's work in the world is obvious, although many choose to ignore it.

21:19-20 *The foundations of the city walls were decorated with every kind of precious stone. The first foundation was jasper, the second sapphire, the third chalcedony, the fourth emerald, the fifth* *sardonyx, the sixth carnelian, the seventh chrysolite, the eighth beryl, the ninth topaz, the tenth chrysoprase, the eleventh jacinth, and the twelfth amethyst.*

Foundations are important and the Bible has much to say about proper foundations. Here we see that the foundation of both the Church and the work of God are precious and priceless. That is because God Himself laid that foundation through Jesus. Let's examine some other foundation verses firsthand: "When the foundations are being destroyed, what can the righteous do?" (Psalm 11:3).

When this priceless foundation is undermined, when Jesus' authority and position are lessened in someone's life, what can the righteous do? The implied answer is, "Nothing!"

The rain came down, the streams rose, and the winds blew and beat against that house; yet it did not fall, because it had its foundation on the rock (Matthew 7:25).

It seems that your personal foundations must be laid with the same material that John saw in his heavenly vision. What is the foundation for your life? Is it made of precious stones or your own works?

By the grace God has given me, I laid a foundation as an expert builder, and someone else is building on it. But each one should be careful how he builds. For no one can lay any foundation other than the one already laid, which is Jesus Christ. If any man builds on this foundation using gold, silver, costly stones, wood, hay or straw, his work will be shown for what it is, because the Day will bring it to light. It will be revealed with fire, and the fire will test the quality of each man's work (1 Corinthians 3:10-13).

Paul used the building analogy, and it is similar to what John saw. That is another reason why I don't think what John saw was simply a picture of heaven. What he saw pertained to the here-and-now reality of the Church.

Fire will test your work, not to destroy it, (although that may happen), but to verify the secure foundation that God has laid in your life. Think of something that has happened to you recently. How would you have reacted to that ten years ago? Perhaps not very well.

The fact that this most recent problem hasn't devastated you is because you have a better foundation today than ten years ago. With that in mind, the thing that has happened to you has come to test and prove the reality of the good things God has deposited in your life. Hallelujah! That is why we can praise God for trials; they come to prove how real His work is in your life. "Built on the foundation of the apostles and prophets, with Christ Jesus himself as the chief cornerstone" (Ephesians 2:20).

If the apostles and prophets are the foundation, then think of how precious they are in God's sight, for the image that John saw of the Church's foundation was made of all kinds of precious stones. Yet the world despises what is precious in God's sight:

> *For it seems to me that God has put us apostles on display at the end of the procession, like men condemned to die in the arena. We have been made a spectacle to the whole universe, to angels as well as to men. We are fools for Christ, but you are so wise in Christ! We are weak, but you are strong! You are honored, we are dishonored!*
>
> *To this very hour we go hungry and thirsty, we are in rags, we are brutally treated, we are homeless. We work hard with our own hands. When we are cursed, we bless; when we are persecuted, we endure it; when we are slandered, we answer kindly. Up to this moment we have become the scum of the earth, the refuse of the world* (1 Corinthians 4:9-13).

I hear many talking about the apostolic and prophetic. Are you one of them? If so, are you ready to endure the treatment that Paul described above to be apostolic or prophetic? Some apostles and prophets want a life of honor and even luxury; Paul endured something totally different.

> *If I am delayed, you will know how people ought to conduct themselves in God's household, which is the church of the living God, the pillar and foundation of the truth* (1 Timothy 3:15).

The Church is the pillar and foundation of truth. Without the Church, there would be no truth, for the Church is the guardian and proclaimer of God's truth!

21:21 *The twelve gates were twelve pearls, each gate made of a single pearl. The great street of the city was of pure gold, like transparent glass.*

Once again, we see John utilizing apocalyptic language. Can you imagine a pearl big enough to make one gate? I think not! This is exaggerated language to create an effect. A pearl is made inside an oyster by a grain of sand being worked into something precious. While heaven and the Church are beautiful places, access to them is not without a great price that Jesus paid. We can think of Jesus' life as one valuable pearl, shaped and developed by means of great pressure and stress.

21:22 *I did not see a temple in the city, because the Lord God Almighty and the Lamb are its temple.*

The Church isn't a building. The Church is a people among whom God lives! Buildings are important, but they are not the essence of the Church. People are.

The tabernacle and temple were only shadows of what was to come. The eternal reality was God creating a living building with His people. I know I am including a lot of cross-references in this Study, but I can't help it! These Revelation verses are stirring me to think of other passages because the themes of the Bible are repeated in Revelation; new themes are not interjected. By looking at these cross references, you can see how Revelation ties the whole Bible together in one neat summary and conclusion:

> *As you come to him, the living Stone—rejected by men but chosen by God and precious to him—you also, like living stones, are being built into a spiritual house to be a holy priesthood, offering spiritual sacrifices acceptable to God through Jesus Christ.*
>
> *For in Scripture it says: "See, I lay a stone in Zion, a chosen and precious cornerstone, and the one who trusts in him will never be put to shame. Now to you who believe, this stone is precious. But to those who do not believe, "The stone the builders rejected has become the capstone," and, "A stone that causes men to stumble and a rock that makes them fall."*
>
> *They stumble because they disobey the message—which is also what they were destined for. But you are a chosen people, a royal priesthood, a holy nation, a people belonging to God, that you may declare the praises of him who called you out of darkness into his wonderful light. Once you were not a people, but now you are the people of God; once you had not received mercy, but now you have received mercy* (1 Peter 2:4-10).

What place do you have in God's temple and holy building? You have a purpose to live out as only you can live it.

21:23 *The city does not need the sun or the moon to shine on it, for the glory of God gives it light, and the Lamb is its lamp.*

You walk in the light of heaven, not the light that comes from men's understanding and wisdom. Once again, let's look at what the Bible has to say about this heavenly, godly light:

There he was transfigured before them. His face shone like the sun, and his clothes became as white as the light (Matthew 17:2).

"For my eyes have seen your salvation, which you have prepared in the sight of all people, a light for revelation to the Gentiles and for glory to your people Israel" (Luke 2:30-32).

In him was life, and that life was the light of men. The light shines in the darkness, but the darkness has not understood it. There came a man who was sent from God; his name was John. He came as a witness to testify concerning that light, so that through him all men might believe. He himself was not the light; he came only as a witness to the light. The true light that gives light to every man was coming into the world (John 1:4-9).

"This is the verdict: Light has come into the world, but men loved darkness instead of light because their deeds were evil. Everyone who does evil hates the light, and will not come into the light for fear that his deeds will be exposed. But whoever lives by the truth comes into the light, so that it may be seen plainly that what he has done has been done through God" (John 3:19-21).

When Jesus spoke again to the people, he said, "I am the light of the world. Whoever follows me will never walk in darkness, but will have the light of life" (John 8:12).

For this is what the Lord has commanded us: "I have made you a light for the Gentiles, that you may bring salvation to the ends of the earth" (Acts 13:47).

21:24 *The nations will walk by its light, and the kings of the earth will bring their splendor into it.*

This does not indicate that whole nations will follow the Lord, but that some portion of the nations and ethnic groups will find the light of God and follow it. I am not waiting or working to see entire nations discipled to become followers of Jesus. I don't think this will ever happen. I do think, however, that every nation and people group need to hear and have a chance to respond to the gospel.

21:25 *On no day will its gates ever be shut, for there will be no night there.*

Salvation is available to anyone, anywhere, twenty-four hours a day, seven days a week. No one will be shut out, if they come to the Lord with a contrite heart. God is always vigilant to save and receive the lost. Praise the Lord!

21:26-27 *The glory and honor of the nations will be brought into it. Nothing impure will ever enter it, nor will anyone who does what is shameful or deceitful, but only those whose names are written in the Lamb's book of life.*

God sets the standards for entrance into His heavenly city and that standard is faith in His Son, Jesus. There are no other entrance passes, secret passwords or credentials. God controls the book of life and has the pen in His hand. He puts in the names that He determines meet the criteria, and the main criterion is faith!

> *And without faith it is impossible to please God, because anyone who comes to him must believe that he exists and that he rewards those who earnestly seek him* (Hebrews 11:6).

Study 50: Revelation 22:1-7

22:1 *Then the angel showed me the river of the water of life, as clear as crystal, flowing from the throne of God and of the Lamb*

Heaven continued to show John picture after picture, metaphor after metaphor. This time it was a river. A river was mentioned early in Genesis: "A river watering the garden flowed from Eden; from there it was separated into four headwaters" (Genesis 2:10).

In Revelation a clear river is flowing from God's throne. A river in biblical times represented life, for it was a source of water for people, crops, and transportation in a dry region of the earth. This heavenly river would represent the same thing. The heavenly river is for the good of men so that God can water and sustain the growth that He has begun. God is able to finish what He started in your life.

To him who is able to keep you from falling and to present you before his glorious presence without fault and with great joy—to the only God our Savior be glory, majesty, power and authority, through Jesus Christ our Lord, before all ages, now and forevermore! Amen (Jude 1:24-25).

Being confident of this, that he who began a good work in you will carry it on to completion until the day of Christ Jesus (Philippians 1:6).

The river was crystal clear. God has no hidden agenda as He works in your life, although He does not always reveal the ultimate purpose of His work. He is working to see Christ formed in you. At the same time, He never apologizes for what He does in your life. The river comes from the throne, the seat of His government. You must never compare what you are going through to that of someone else. God is working in your life according to His desire and will for you: "For it is God who works in you to will and to act according to his good purpose. Do everything without complaining or arguing" (Philippians 2:13-14).

22:2 ***down the middle of the great street of the city. On each side of the river stood the tree of life, bearing twelve crops of fruit, yielding its fruit every month. And the leaves of the tree are for the healing of the nations.***

You cannot avoid the river of God. It runs through the center of what God is doing and where He lives, which is in the midst of His people.

Whoever believes in me, as the Scripture has said, streams of living water will flow from within him." By this he meant the Spirit, whom those who believed in him were later to receive. Up to that time the

Spirit had not been given, since Jesus had not yet been glorified (John 7:38-39).

God is working to bear fruit in your life in the Church. This fruit from trees planted and watered by God is for the healing of the nations. The nations won't need healing in heaven; that is why Revelation is talking about the here and now. What is the Spirit working into your life at this time?

But the fruit of the Spirit is love, joy, peace, patience, kindness, goodness, faithfulness, gentleness and self-control. Against such things there is no law. Those who belong to Christ Jesus have crucified the sinful nature with its passions and desires. Since we live by the Spirit, let us keep in step with the Spirit (Galatians 5:22-25).

The fruit of the Spirit is just that: of the Spirit. It comes from the Spirit; you can't will it or produce it in your own strength. It belongs to the Spirit; no one can take credit for the fruit that God produces in and through you. It is up to you to crucify the sinful nature, but only God can produce the Spirit nature in your life and behavior.

You can't rush fruit to harvest. It develops in its own time. The river nourishes the fruit development, but then again, fruit from a tree is not for the tree. The fruit is for someone else to eat and enjoy. God is always doing something in your life, the benefit of which will be for others, not you. And it will ultimately be for God's glory.

22:3 No longer will there be any curse. The throne of God and of the Lamb will be in the city, and his servants will serve him.

Revelation constantly focused on the work of Jesus. There is no longer any curse because Jesus removed the curse by becoming a curse Himself:

All who rely on observing the law are under a curse, for it is written: "Cursed is everyone who does not continue to do everything written in the Book of the Law." Clearly no one is justified before God by the law, because, "The righteous will live by faith." The law is not based on faith; on the contrary, "The man who does these things will live by them." Christ redeemed us from the curse of the law by becoming a curse for us, for it is written: "Cursed is everyone who is hung on a tree" (Galatians 3:10-13).

At times you must work to apply this truth and make it a reality in your life. You must sometimes go back and remove the curses that may be on your life due to the sins of your forefathers. Is there a recurring problem or tragedy in your family line? Then consider specifically praying and breaking the curse, for Jesus came to remove all curses. Better yet, have someone pray with you.

God's desire has always been to live among His people. Since Jesus has removed the curse, God is now free to live in the hearts of His people. At one time, God lived among His people by means of the tabernacle and then the temple. Now He lives in the hearts of men through the presence of the Holy Spirit.

They will know that I am the Lord their God, who brought them out of Egypt so that I might dwell among them. I am the Lord their God (Exodus 29:46).

As for this temple you are building, if you follow my decrees, carry out my regulations and keep all my commands and obey them, I will fulfill through you the promise I gave to David your father. And I will live among the Israelites and will not abandon my people Israel (1 Kings 6:12-13).

He said: "Son of man, this is the place of my throne and the place for the soles of my feet. This is where I will live among the Israelites forever. The house of Israel will never again defile my holy name—neither they nor their kings—by their prostitution and the lifeless idols of their kings at their high places (Ezekiel 43:7).

"Shout and be glad, O Daughter of Zion. For I am coming, and I will live among you," declares the Lord (Zechariah 2:10).

We must honor the Lord's presence by living holy lives. Are you doing anything that would cause your heavenly and divine houseguest to be uncomfortable?

And do not grieve the Holy Spirit of God, with whom you were sealed for the day of redemption. Get rid of all bitterness, rage and anger, brawling and slander, along with every form of malice. Be kind and compassionate to one another, forgiving each other, just as in Christ God forgave you (Ephesians 4:30-32).

22:4 *They will see his face, and his name will be on their foreheads.*

Facial expressions are an important part of communication between people. That is why letters and emails are somewhat limited, for you cannot see or hear the person. I have always thought that "seeing God's face," while impossible to do, referred to knowing God intimately. It meant to be sensitive to His most subtle wish or command.

I want to know if God is smiling or if He is raising His eyebrow at something I have said or done. I want to see Him nod His head in approval, even if He doesn't say anything. That requires being close to Him and watching Him. I know that this may sound strange, but can you get to know God so well that He can communicate with you without dramatic events taking place in your life?

I don't think that His name will literally be on our foreheads, but I do think God will constantly be on our minds:

Eat unleavened bread during those seven days; nothing with yeast in it is to be seen among you, nor shall any yeast be seen anywhere within your borders. On that day tell your son, "I do this because of what the Lord did for me when I came out of Egypt. This observance will be for you like a sign on your hand and a reminder on your forehead that the law of the Lord is to be on your lips. For the Lord brought you out of Egypt with his mighty hand" (Exodus 13:7-9).

When something is on your forehead, it is impossible to forget about it. You see it when you look in a mirror and feel it because usually nothing is there. I think the presence of the Spirit in your life serves a similar purpose, to remind you about God. It is impossible to go too far without thinking about Him.

22:5 *There will be no more night. They will not need the light of a lamp or the light of the sun, for the Lord God will give them light. And they will reign for ever and ever.*

We have discussed the issue of the light of God in previous studies. Yet there are many more references to light in the Bible. Let's look at a few from the Psalms:

Blessed are those who have learned to acclaim you, who walk in the light of your presence, O Lord (Psalm 89:15).

Blessed is he who comes in the name of the Lord. From the house of the Lord we bless you. The Lord is God, and he has made his light shine upon us. With boughs in hand, join in the festal procession up to the horns of the altar. You are my God, and I will give you thanks; you are my God, and I will exalt you. Give thanks to the Lord, for he is good; his love endures forever (Psalm 118:26-29).

Your word is a lamp to my feet and a light for my path (Psalm 119:105).

The unfolding of your words gives light; it gives understanding to the simple (Psalm 119:130).

If I say, "Surely the darkness will hide me and the light become night around me," even the darkness will not be dark to you; the night will shine like the day, for darkness is as light to you (Psalm 139:11-12).

And then there is one more important passage about light in the New Testament:

This is the message we have heard from him and declare to you: God is light; in him there is no darkness at all. If we claim to have fellowship with him yet walk in the darkness, we lie and do not live by the truth. But if we walk in the light, as he is in the light, we have fellowship with one another, and the blood of Jesus, his Son, purifies us from all sin (1 John 1:5-7).

Take two minutes and two minutes only to write down what these last six passages about light mean to you. Do it quickly! Do you make a regular confession of sin? Do you need to? Are there dark times of depression or loneliness in which you need to see God's light shining? Go ahead, spend some time and write down your impressions.

22:6 The angel said to me, "These words are trustworthy and true. The Lord, the God of the spirits of the prophets, sent his angel to show his servants the things that must soon take place."

We have not seen the word *soon* since the earliest chapters of this study. What does soon mean? Soon means, well, it means soon! Soon to the churches of Revelation would not be two thousand years later!

It is amazing how many times the Bible expresses that its message is true and trustworthy. Even Jesus reinforced what He was saying with the same endorsement, "Verily, verily" or "Truly, truly I say unto thee." Why is that? It is because falseness is so pervasive that the truth seems bizarre at times. We must be reminded that it is truth!

God is the God of the spirits of the prophets. He controls what they see, when they share it and to whom they share it. Some prophets today are "loose cannons." They are running around sharing words and prophecies that are premature or shared with the wrong people. May the Lord of the spirits of the prophets rule in prophecy and may the Lord be exalted in the prophecies and not the prophets themselves!

I believe in modern-day prophecy and prophets. The Church as a whole, however, must do a better job of judging prophecy. I take the prophecies I have received very seriously; I have written them down, and study and review them regularly. At the same time, I take the time to judge them and then take the time to do my part to see them come to pass, all with God's help.

I abide by the truth and guidelines in the following passages:

Early in the morning they left for the Desert of Tekoa. As they set out, Jehoshaphat stood and said, "Listen to me, Judah and people of Jerusalem! Have faith in the Lord your God and you will be upheld; have faith in his prophets and you will be successful" (2 Chronicles 20:20).

Surely the Sovereign Lord does nothing without revealing his plan to his servants the prophets (Amos 3:7).

Do not put out the Spirit's fire; do not treat prophecies with contempt. Test everything. Hold on to the good. Avoid every kind of evil (1Thessalonians 5:19-22).

22:7 "Behold, I am coming soon! Blessed is he who keeps the words of the prophecy in this book."

The book of Revelation is a prophecy. This doesn't mean it's some hidden, mystical book that is hard to grasp (although it is harder than most). A prophecy is a message from God, and God wants that message to be understood. Any message where the meaning is only available to a select few isn't a message from God.

What does it mean that the Lord is coming soon? Here are some of my thoughts:

- He is literally coming soon. Revelation was written two thousand years ago and He still hasn't returned. So that interpretation is out.
- The presence of the Spirit makes the return of the Lord feel like it will be soon. Almost every generation has felt that the Lord would return in their lifetime, this one included. When the Spirit comes into your life and lives in you, you feel the closeness of Jesus and His Word. It feels like He is coming soon.
- You will soon die, thus your end will be soon.
- We don't understand exactly how to interpret the phrase, "the return of the Lord soon."

Earlier in Revelation, John wrote:

Remember, therefore, what you have received and heard; obey it, and repent. But if you do not wake up, I will come like a thief, and you will not know at what time I will come to you (Revelation 3:3).

Could the return of the Lord be our death or some other visitation where the Lord works to set things straight? The return of the Lord in my life is "soon." What I have been waiting for the Lord to do seems to be taking place at a faster pace. Is this what He meant by His returning in my life soon?

Study 51: Revelation 22:8-13

22:8 *I, John, am the one who heard and saw these things. And when I had heard and seen them, I fell down to worship at the feet of the angel who had been showing them to me.*

John reported what he erroneously did when the angel showed him these things. He was so moved by the experience and vision that he fell down to reverence the angel who showed it to him. He made a mistake and the angel corrected him. Imagine that: in the midst of a heavenly revelation, John made a mistake and God still used him. What's more, John felt secure enough to share his mistake (the second time this happened) for everyone to know!

Have you ever made a mistake? I know you must have. Do you celebrate your mistakes or hide them? John certainly exposed his for all to see in this case. I annually write and proclaim a "Celebrate a Failure Week" the world over. I urge people everywhere to be less concerned about their failures and to celebrate the goodness of God in the midst of our human weakness and even foolishness! When you face your failures, you can learn the lessons that they came to impart. When you hide them or from them, you have too many shadows and dark places to be truly effective for God.

The revelation was so overwhelming to John that he fell down to worship, perhaps not knowing what else to do. An encounter with heaven doesn't come to fill your mind with knowledge but to lead you to worship the God of the encounter!

He fell at the feet of the angel. Does this mean that angels have feet? Angels are not the chubby little cherubs pictured in so many artists' renditions. They are powerful, awesome beings. Even the spiritual man John fell down to worship this angel because the angel and the experience were so physically overwhelming.

As Revelation comes to an end, it is almost like John is putting his personal signature on it. Tradition has it that John received this Revelation in a cave over a period of days, which began on the Lord's Day. You can actually visit the cave, where there is an indentation in the cave wall where John supposedly propped his arm at the elbow while dictating the vision to an assistant. If Revelation's John is the apostle John, then he would have indeed been an old man when he received this.

We are created to hear and see the things of God. I think of a verse in Proverbs that states: "Ears that hear and eyes that see—the Lord has made them both" (Proverbs 20:12).

The Lord wants you to see and hear things from His perspective, but that takes some work on you part. You cannot control what you see; God determines that. You can train yourself, however, to recognize that it is God who is speaking. "But solid food is for the mature, who by constant use have trained themselves to distinguish good from evil" (Hebrews 5:14).

So while discerning good and evil can be a special gift, it is the duty of every spiritual person to develop discernment of spiritual things:

And this is my prayer: that your love may abound more and more in knowledge and depth of insight, so that you may be able to discern what is best and may be pure and blameless until the day of Christ (Philippians 1:9-10).

> *The man without the Spirit does not accept the things that come from the Spirit of God, for they are foolishness to him, and he cannot understand them because they are only spiritually discerned. The spiritual man makes judgments about all things, but he himself is not subject to any man's judgment: "For who has known the mind of the Lord that he may instruct him?' But we have the mind of Christ"* (1 Corinthians 2:14-16).

Are you happy with your level of spiritual discernment? Do you chase every new whim of what some say is the Spirit? Or have you learned to wait on the Lord and to use the Spirit to help you discern spiritual things?

If you are discerning, are you now a bit cynical and critical? Do you not trust anything new that is beyond your ability to initially recognize God moving in a new way? There is a balance to being mature and having wisdom to judge each situation on its own merits. I want to be mature, but I also want to be like a little child in the kingdom. Help me, Lord, to have this balance!

22:9 But he said to me, "Do not do it! I am a fellow servant with you and with your brothers the prophets and of all who keep the words of this book. Worship God!"

What does it mean to keep the words of this book? It means to carry them out, not just to give them mental assent.

> *Anyone who listens to the word but does not do what it says is like a man who looks at his face in a mirror and, after looking at himself, goes away and immediately forgets what he looks like. But the man who looks intently into the perfect law that gives freedom, and continues to do this, not forgetting what he has heard, but doing it—he will be blessed in what he does* (James 1:23-25).

This is such a simple, basic analogy. Who could look in the mirror and then forget what he or she looks like? That is exactly what you and I do when we read and don't obey the words of this book, the Word of God. We are not just to know, but to know and do. That requires work and constant decisions to do what God commands, trusting in His help to fulfill your commitments.

The Bible uses the phrase "make every effort" on eight separate occasions. Study the list below and then decide if you are indeed making ever effort to keep the words of this book:

Make every effort to enter through the narrow door, because many, I tell you, will try to enter and will not be able to (Luke 13:24).

Let us therefore make every effort to do what leads to peace and to mutual edification (Romans 14:19).

Make every effort to keep the unity of the Spirit through the bond of peace (Ephesians 4:3).

Let us, therefore, make every effort to enter that rest, so that no one will fall by following their example of disobedience (Hebrews 4:11).

Make every effort to live in peace with all men and to be holy; without holiness no one will see the Lord (Hebrews 12:14).

For this very reason, make every effort to add to your faith goodness; and to goodness, knowledge; and to knowledge, self-control; and to self-control, perseverance; and to perseverance, godliness; and to godliness, brotherly kindness; and to brotherly kindness, love. For if you possess these qualities in increasing measure, they will keep you from being ineffective and unproductive in your knowledge of our Lord Jesus Christ (2 Peter 1:5-8).

And I will make every effort to see that after my departure you will always be able to remember these things (2 Peter 1:15).

So then, dear friends, since you are looking forward to this, make every effort to be found spotless, blameless and at peace with him (2 Peter 3:14).

22:10 ***Then he told me, "Do not seal up the words of the prophecy of this book, because the time is near."***

John was warned not to keep the words of this prophecy to himself. He wrote them down and sent them out. John was to have an urgency to deliver and act on what he had received. I think the same is true for us today. Are you writing down and publishing or broadcasting what the Lord is doing and saying?

I am not equating what you are seeing today with what John saw. John saw and wrote the inspired Word of God, but that doesn't mean you shouldn't honor what you are seeing and hearing by writing and sending.

That is why I developed a website and three blogs: to write and send what God is teaching me. By the way, have you enjoyed keeping your Revelation journal? Why not take some to go back and review what you have written?

The angel said that the time was near. I don't think "near" meant two thousand years later for other churches that have read this prophecy down through history. As we have seen time and again in *The Revelation Project*, the key to understanding Revelation is to understand what it meant to the early churches that first received it. They were being encouraged that nothing and no one could resist God and His kingdom for very long. Revelation has been fulfilled and is being fulfilled.

The time of the Lord is near for you. Your death or your deliverance from a difficult situation is near. You just don't know when.

22:11 *"Let him who does wrong continue to do wrong; let him who is vile continue to be vile; let him who does right continue to do right; and let him who is holy continue to be holy."*

The angel urged everyone to continue and excel in his or her state of holiness or un-holiness. Since the end is near for all of us, you should be actively and aggressively furthering what is important to the kingdom of God. For the sinner, he or she should pursue what is important to him or her. For the saint, he or she should pursue what is important to God.

Are you aggressively pursuing your holiness and its practical expression to the world around you? If you are convinced that the Lord is near, has that realization impacted your finances, relationships and missions work?

So it is with you. Since you are eager to have spiritual gifts, try to excel in gifts that build up the church (1 Corinthians 14:12).

But just as you excel in everything—in faith, in speech, in knowledge, in complete earnestness and in your love for us—see that you also excel in this grace of giving (2 Corinthians 8:7).

Finally, brothers, we instructed you how to live in order to please God, as in fact you are living. Now we ask you and urge you in the Lord Jesus to do this more and more (1 Thessalonians 4:1).

Now about brotherly love we do not need to write to you, for you yourselves have been taught by God to love each other. And in fact, you do love all the brothers throughout Macedonia. Yet we urge you, brothers, to do so more and more (1 Thessalonians 4:9-10).

By God's grace, I want to do more and be more godly deeds than ever before. If that's your desire, what plan do you have to do that? Stop now and spend two minutes writing down some thoughts about how you can do more and develop more fully in the power of the Spirit.

22:12 *"Behold, I am coming soon! My reward is with me, and I will give to everyone according to what he has done."*

Remember, soon doesn't mean in two thousand years! Soon means the time is at hand. Now this was Jesus talking, perhaps through the mouth of the messenger angel. After all, this was not the message of the angel. It was the message of Jesus!

Either Jesus will intervene soon or you will die soon. Either way, you win because of what Jesus has done in your life. And you will receive your reward from Jesus, as everyone will. So be encouraged for God is watching and mindful of your situation. If it is a difficult one and doesn't seem to be changing, be encouraged. God is in control and it will change soon! What's more, Jesus may return tomorrow! You must be ready and found doing His will when He does come. Live in the reality that He is coming soon!

22:13 *I am the Alpha and the Omega, the First and the Last, the Beginning and the End.*

This is the third time that Jesus referred to Himself as the Alpha and Omega. Why does Jesus say this three times? Did He think we would forget? Did He forget He said it? Was Jesus into repeating things to hear His own words? Of course, the answer is no to all three silly questions. The answer is that this is the main message of Revelation. It's all about Jesus! Worship Him! Listen to Him! Exalt Him! He is the ruler of the universe. He is the start and finish of all good works in and around your life. His life, death, and resurrection are the central themes of history. Everything else is irrelevant in the end.

What Jesus starts, He finishes. What He initiates, He culminates. That is certainly the good news of the Bible and the final message that we are left with as we read this last book.

Study 52: Revelation 22:14-21

22:14 *Blessed are those who wash their robes, that they may have the right to the tree of life and may go through the gates into the city.*

Again we see much of the truth that what was introduced in Genesis is revisited in Revelation. The tree of life was first mentioned in Genesis when man was barred from eating its fruit because of sin:

And the Lord God made all kinds of trees grow out of the ground—trees that were pleasing to the eye and good for food. In the middle of the garden were the tree of life and the tree of the knowledge of good and evil (Genesis 2:9).

And the Lord God said, "The man has now become like one of us, knowing good and evil. He must not be allowed to reach out his hand and take also from the tree of life and eat, and live forever" (Genesis 3:22).

All who "wash their robes" will have access to this tree, which of course imparts eternal life. I mentioned in an earlier study that a seminary professor I studied under interpreted eternal life to be life so good and pure that nothing can end it. I have always remembered that definition. That is what you receive when you wash your robes.

How is anyone supposed to wash his or her robes? We are told earlier in Revelation that this washing is done with and through the blood of Jesus.

I answered, "Sir, you know." And he said, "These are they who have come out of the great tribulation; they have washed their robes and made them white in the blood of the Lamb" (Revelation 7:14).

Entrance into eternal life and the Church is through one gate and that gate is Jesus! That is the message of Revelation. Christ is the focus of the book, not the antichrist. Life and holiness only come through Him.

22:15 *Outside are the dogs, those who practice magic arts, the sexually immoral, the murderers, the idolaters and everyone who loves and practices falsehood.*

Entrance into the city and access to the tree of life are reserved for those who are righteous, a righteousness that only God can provide. There is no other access to the things of God except through Jesus. Is He your all in all? Do you need to repent from any sin? Are you relying on anything else—the wisdom of men, riches, intelligence—to give you the things of God? Are you practicing any self righteousness? Paul wrote:

> *Do you not know that the wicked will not inherit the kingdom of God? Do not be deceived: Neither the sexually immoral nor idolaters nor adulterers nor male prostitutes nor homosexual offenders nor thieves nor the greedy nor drunkards nor slanderers nor swindlers will inherit the kingdom of God. And that is what some of you were. But you were washed, you were sanctified, you were justified in the name of the Lord Jesus Christ and by the Spirit of our God* (1 Corinthians 6:9-11).

What's more, we have such an important message, in fact the most important message, that we must spend our lives to see it spread to as many as possible. What are you doing to spread the gospel? Are you hesitant to share your faith?

The Bible is in harmony with itself. In the last few studies, I have tried to provide more cross-references from other books of the Bible that relate to or further explain the message of Revelation. Even though many different men wrote the Bible over a long period of time, the Bible is a book of amazing continuity and unity. That is because there were many writers but only one author. Someone once said the Bible is the oldest book in existence whose author is still alive!

You cannot invest in a more productive and meaningful spiritual discipline than the study of God's Word. I encourage you to make it your passion, with God's help and in His power, for the rest of your life. That is my commitment and desire.

22:16 *"I, Jesus, have sent my angel to give you this testimony for the churches. I am the Root and the Offspring of David, and the bright Morning Star."*

The Jews asked the question: "All the people were astonished and said, 'Could this be the Son of David?'" (Matthew 12:23) The answer is yes! He is the Offspring of David. Jesus is the Morning Star. What could that represent? It is interesting that a star appeared to lead the Magi to Jesus. I have read various interpretations of what that star was and why it appeared. I really don't think it's that complicated.

Study 52: Revelation 22:14-21

> *The heavens declare the glory of God; the skies proclaim the work of his hands. Day after day they pour forth speech; night after night they display knowledge. There is no speech or language where their voice is not heard. Their voice goes out into all the earth, their words to the ends of the world. In the heavens he has pitched a tent for the sun, which is like a bridegroom coming forth from his pavilion, like a champion rejoicing to run his course* (Psalm 19:1-5).

I am no astronomer and the constellations are a mystery to me. How can anyone see a ram, a man, or a crab from a pattern of stars in the sky? I know I can't. When I search the night or early morning sky, however, I generally have no trouble picking out the planet Venus, referred to as the morning star. I can do this because it is by far the brightest.

In the same manner, I can search the heavens and pick Jesus out from all the other so-called lights. He is the brightest and best. He is the radiance of God's glory; He is God!

If men search the spiritual heavens, figuratively speaking, they will find many stars in the sky. They will find that Jesus is the brightest. He stands out from all the rest. Mohammed, Buddha and all the other "stars" that have some light cannot compare to the Morning Star. Not only that, but Jesus is not only based in the heavens. He is also in the ground from the root of David. Many referred to Him as the Son of David during His earthly ministry. Jesus is both God and man, and Revelation reminds us of this fact as it comes to an end.

22:17 *The Spirit and the bride say, "Come!" And let him who hears say, "Come!" Whoever is thirsty, let him come; and whoever wishes, let him take the free gift of the water of life.*

The Spirit and the bride, the Church, need to be saying the same thing. Too often, however, the Church is not saying to the world, "Come." We have often said to the citizens of the world, "Come, but . . ." and have put too many stipulations around their coming. The Spirit wants and pleads with those who are outside the city to "Come." The Church needs to get her message in line with the Spirit's message.

Wait a minute. Why am I writing as if I'm not part of the Church of Jesus? If the Church has failed, it is because I have failed. I am to take the message of the Church to the world. I am to tell as many as possible to "Come." If I don't say that, who will? I can't wait for someone else to do it.

Are you in line with the Spirit's message? Are you representing God accurately in what you say and do? Or do you have a different message and agenda? Are you angry but God isn't? Are you condemning others while Jesus isn't? You are God's ambassadors and God's coworkers (see 2 Corinthians 6:1). An ambassador carries the message for the country or government he or she represents and not a personal message. We must be careful to represent the kingdom of God accurately.

For example, Moses did not represent God accurately and God prevented him from entering the Promised Land:

> *"Take the staff, and you and your brother Aaron gather the assembly together. Speak to that rock before their eyes and it will pour out its water. You will bring water out of the rock for the community so they and their livestock can drink." So Moses took the staff from the Lord's presence, just as he commanded him.*
>
> *He and Aaron gathered the assembly together in front of the rock and Moses said to them, "Listen, you rebels, must we bring you water out of this rock?" Then Moses raised his arm and struck the rock twice with his staff. Water gushed out, and the community and their livestock drank. But the Lord said to Moses and Aaron, "Because you did not trust in me enough to honor me as holy in the sight of the Israelites, you will not bring this community into the land I give them"* (Numbers 20:8-12).

Moses was to speak to the rock; instead he struck it. He made it appear that God was angry. Moses did not deliver the same message that the Spirit had in mind, and it cost him dearly. You must represent God when you speak and not voice your own opinions.

We referred to the tree of life in the beginning of this Study and now we see the water of life. Jesus referred to this water, too:

> *Jesus answered, "Everyone who drinks this water will be thirsty again, but whoever drinks the water I give him will never thirst. Indeed, the water I give him will become in him a spring of water welling up to eternal life." The woman said to him, "Sir, give me this water so that I won't get thirsty and have to keep coming here to draw water"* (John 4:13-15).

> *Then Jesus declared, "I am the bread of life. He who comes to me will never go hungry, and he who believes in me will never be thirsty"* (John 6:35).

If someone is spiritually thirsty, he or she still must choose to drink the water Jesus offers. I have known some thirsty people who steadfastly refused to quench their thirst with the water that God offers.

22:18-19 *I warn everyone who hears the words of the prophecy of this book: If anyone adds anything to them, God will add to him the plagues described in this book. And if anyone takes words away from this book of prophecy, God will take away from him his share in the tree of life and in the holy city, which are described in this book.*

Based on what we have learned in *The Revelation Project*, it is safe to say that some of my fellow servants over the years have added many words to this book. They have made comfortable livings concocting fantastic interpretations of the end times, using Revelation as their source. They are not theologians, but science fiction writers with vivid imaginations and good writing skills.

No matter how much I claim to know about God or the things of God, I still must face the reality of one truth:

For we know in part and we prophesy in part, but when perfection comes, the imperfect disappears. When I was a child, I talked like a child, I thought like a child, I reasoned like a child. When I became a man, I put childish ways behind me. Now we see but a poor reflection as in a mirror; then we shall see face to face. Now I know in part; then I shall know fully, even as I am fully known (1 Corinthians 13:9-12).

We all know in part and not in full. May we keep that in mind as we study, preach and debate with one another! Could it be that we all see a part of the whole and not the whole itself?

As we conclude *The Revelation Project*, our premise has been that an important key to understanding Revelation is to understand what it meant to the early church. The early church was under pressure from persecutors and was in a weakened state. The message of Revelation to them and consequently to us is that Jesus is on the throne. No power or authority will overcome His own. Therefore, the Church's focus is not to be on its enemies, but on Jesus, who is working in the midst of and through the Church no matter what the conditions.

Oh yes, and remember that the language of Revelation is also apocalyptic. It uses exaggerated images and metaphors to make a point and to hide the meaning from the "uninitiated," which in this case were the Roman government and citizens.

22:20 *He who testifies to these things says, "Yes, I am coming soon." Amen. Come, Lord Jesus.*

The Lord is coming soon—that has been the testimony of every generation of believers, whose lives and hearts have been quickened by the power of the Holy Spirit living in them. The Holy Spirit's presence causes everyone to feel like the Lord is near and is coming soon. In fact, the Lord is coming soon. All life goes by quickly and all governments, kingdoms, and empires seem as though they will last forever; they do not. They pass quickly. Is this what the Lord meant when He said that He would come quickly? I'm not sure, but it is a better interpretation than those who say that soon means in a few thousand years!

If you are in trouble or encountering trials or persecution, be encouraged. The Lord is going to come to your situation soon! Either the pressure will be removed, or you will change to be able to handle what you once thought impossible to endure—and it will happen soon!

> *So do not throw away your confidence; it will be richly rewarded. You need to persevere so that when you have done the will of God, you will receive what he has promised. For in just a very little while, "He who is coming will come and will not delay. But my righteous one will live by faith. And if he shrinks back, I will not be pleased with him." But we are not of those who shrink back and are destroyed, but of those who believe and are saved* (Hebrews 10:35-39).

> *Praise be to the God and Father of our Lord Jesus Christ! In his great mercy he has given us new birth into a living hope through the resurrection of Jesus Christ from the dead, and into an inheritance that can never perish, spoil or fade—kept in heaven for you, who through faith are shielded by God's power until the coming of the salvation that is ready to be revealed in the last time.*

> *In this you greatly rejoice, though now for a little while you may have had to suffer grief in all kinds of trials. These have come so that your faith—of greater worth than gold, which perishes even though refined by fire—may be proved genuine and may result in praise, glory and honor when Jesus Christ is revealed* (1 Peter 1:3-7).

Will the Lord return in your lifetime? Only God knows. No one else does and certainly no one can use Revelation to predict when He will return.

22:21 *The grace of the Lord Jesus be with God's people. Amen.*

The last prayer of the Bible is for grace to be with God's people. Are you a carrier and recipient of God's grace? Is your objective to see this grace reach as many people as possible? If you think the Lord is returning soon, do you fret about a retirement account? If you think He will return soon, do you spend every vacation day on a missions trip to reach the lost?

I would think that the so-called prophets of our age who predict the Lord's imminent return would not spend so much time with the people of God who do not really need to hear that message. We're ready to go! Those who do not know Him are the ones who need to hear that message!

My misguided brothers and sisters who are end-time zealots, however, are not my enemies. They are my family. I choose, however, to spend my time and effort spreading the good news that Jesus rules and reigns over all! He will come when He is ready and when the Father sends Him. The real question is: Will I be ready when He returns? I trust that *The Revelation Project* has made you a little more ready and eager to meet Jesus, who is coming soon, one way or another. There is no need to fear; God is in control.

There is no better way to end this book than to use the word that John used. So, my dear reader, I thank you for your time and effort that you expended on *The Revelation Project*, whether you read straight through or one study every week. Now it is time that I sign off, writing what John said when he ended the Revelation:

Amen!

Endnotes

1 *Vine's Expository Dictionary of Old and New Testament Words*, W. E. Vine (World Bible Publishers, Iowa Falls, Iowa), page 306.
2 *Let The Nations Be Glad*, John Piper (Baker Books, Grand Rapids, Michigan, 1993), page 11.
3 *Jesus and the Disinherited*, Howard Thurman; (Beacon Press: Boston, 1949), page 98.

SCRIPTURE REFERENCES

Text	Found In	Text	Found In
Genesis 2:9	Study 52	Psalm 19:1-5	Study 52
Genesis 2:10	Study 50	Psalm 23	Study 19
Genesis 3:22	Study 52	Psalm 29	Study 12, 29
Genesis 5:24	Study 10	Psalm 30:5-12	Study 37
Exodus 7:10-13	Study 31	Psalm 37:32-33	Study 16
Exodus 7:17-22	Study 35	Psalm 37:35-40	Study 40
Exodus 7:20-23	Study 31	Psalm 46:1-11	Study 17, 27
Exodus 9:8-11	Study 35	Psalm 72:14	Study 16
Exodus 9:12	Study 31	Psalm 73:3-23	Study 40
Exodus 9:18-28	Study 37	Psalm 89:15	Study 50
Exodus 10:21-23	Study 36	Psalm 91	Study 22, 49
Exodus 13:7-9	Study 50	Psalm 105:17-19	Study 16, 21
Exodus 15:1-18	Study 34	Psalm 107:23-31	Study 41
Exodus 15:4-14	Study 42	Psalm 110:1-7	Study 44
Exodus 16:4	Study 5	Psalm 116:15	Study 33
Exodus 19:16-19	Study 27	Psalm 118:26-29	Study 50
Exodus 29:46	Study 50	Psalm 119:105	Study 12
Leviticus 8:30	Study 43	Psalm 119:107	Study 50
Numbers 16:28-35	Study 8	Psalm 139:7-10	Study 6
Numbers 20:8-12	Study 52	Psalm 139:11-12	Study 50
Deuteronomy 8:16	Study 5	Psalm 139:23-24	Study 36
Joshua 10:23-25	Study 28	Psalm 142:2-3	Study 48
Judges 14:3-4	Study 39	Psalm 144:1	Study 28
1 Samuel 25:29	Study 116	Proverbs 3:11-12	Study 11
1 Kings 6:12-13	Study 50	Proverbs 3:34	Study 25
1 Kings 21:25	Study 7	Proverbs 6:16-19	Study 32
2 Kings 6:14-17	Study 15, 44	Proverbs 6:23	Study 11
2 Chronicles 20:5-6	Study 27	Proverbs 8:1-9	Study 19
2 Chronicles 20:20	Study 50	Proverbs 12:18-1	Study 32
Esther 2:22-23	Study 33	Proverbs 13:15	Study 32
Esther 6:1-10	Study 33	Proverbs 14:9	Study 5
Job 1:16-17	Study 46	Proverbs 18:20-21	Study 11, 32
Job 5:17	Study 11	Proverbs 20:11	Study 7 7
Psalm 2	Study 8, 27, 38	Proverbs 20:12	Study 9 15, 51
Psalm 2:4-9	Study 44	Proverbs 21:1	Study 39
Psalm 6:1-2	Study 11	Ecclesiastes 3:1-8	Study 46
Psalm 11:13	Study 459	Isaiah 11:9	Study 21
Psalm 18:24-27	Study 9, 32	Isaiah 14:3-7	Study 44

Reference	Study	Reference	Study
Isaiah 14:11-17	Study 44	Mark 11:24	Study 23
Isaiah 40:8	Study 20	Mark 13:12-13	Study 19
Isaiah 50:4-5	Study 11	Luke 2:30-32	Study 49
Isaiah 50:11	Study 48	Luke 3:22	Study 29
Isaiah 51:12	Study 20	Luke 4:1-2	Study 37
Isaiah 55:10-11	Study 44	Luke 8:12-15	Study 9
Isaiah 64:6	Study 9	Luke 8:16	Study 4
Jeremiah 5:14	Study 26	Luke 8:18	Study 5
Ezekiel 2:6-7	Study 22	Luke 10:17-22	Study 45
Ezekiel 3:1-7	Study 2, 25	Luke 10:19	Study 23
Ezekiel 28:11-19	Study 44	Luke 10:20	Study 46
Ezekiel 43:6-11	Study 25	Luke 13:23-24	Study 49, 51
Ezekiel 43:7	Study 50	Luke 18:10-14	Study 11
Daniel 3:13-30	Study 46	Luke 21:12-19	Study 41
Daniel 10:2-13	Study 23	John 1:4-5	Study 40
Haggai 2:8	Study 21	John 1:4-9	Study 49
Amos 3:7-8	Study 21, 24, 50	John 1:5-11	Study 23
Zechariah 1:18-21	Study 25	John 1:14	Study 43
Zechariah 2:10	Study 50	John 2:24-25	Study 4
Zechariah 4:11-14	Study 25	John 3:19-21	Study 49
Matthew 4:1-11	Study 30, 31	John 3:31-36	Study 13
Matthew 5:16	Study 49	John 4:10-15	Study 19
Matthew 5:22	Study 46	John 4:13-15	Study 52
Matthew 7:25	Study 49	John 6:35	Study 52
Matthew 8:23-27	Study 24	John 6:38-40	Study 18
Matthew 10:17-23	Study 41	John 7:38-39	Study 19, 50
Matthew 10:32-33	Study 9	John 8:12	Study 40, 48, 49
Matthew 11:15	Study 9	John 10:10	Study 23
Matthew 12:23	Study 52	John 10:14-16	Study 12
Matthew 12:24-30	Study 45	John 10:8-9	Study 49
Matthew 12:34-37	Study 32	John 11:25	Study 4
Matthew 13:10-16	Study 21	John 11:49-52	Study 39
Matthew 14:23-26	Study 36	John 12:28-29	Study 15, 29
Matthew 15:1-10	Study 9	John 12:47-50	Study 11
Matthew 16:19	Study 28	John 14:1-4	Study 18
Matthew 17:2	Study 49	John 14:6	Study 49
Matthew 17:5-6	Study 29	John 15:19-23	Study 41
Matthew 18:8	Study 46	John 16:7-11	Study 1
Matthew 19:23-26	Study 49	John 16:12	Study 33
Matthew 21:44	Study 17	John 17:14-18	Study 28, 41
Matthew 23:7-12	Study 43	John 17:9-15	Study 29
Matthew 23:30-35	Study 16	John 19:30	Study 37
Matthew 24:12-13	Study 33	John 20:23	Study 34
Matthew 25:1-13	Study 36	Acts 2:29-32	Study 4
Matthew 25:41	Study 46	Acts 2:33	Study 4
Matthew 26:39	Study 38	Acts 4:9-12	Study 14
Matthew 27:50-54	Study 27	Acts 4:31-35	Study 47
Matthew 27:51-53	Study 47	Acts 5:40-42	Study 47
Matthew 28:1-2	Study 27	Acts 7:51	Study 9
Matthew 28:7-10	Study 48	Acts 9:4-7	Study 29
Matthew 28:17	Study 14, 43	Acts 10:1-4	Study 14, 20
Matthew 28:18-20	Study 13, 14	Acts 10:42	Study 46
Mark 4:23-25	Study 9	Acts 13:47	Study 49
Mark 4:39-41	Study 36	Acts 14:11-18	Study 43
Mark 9:47-48	Study 46	Acts 14:21-22	Study 2, 19

Reference	Study
Acts 17:28	Study 10
Acts 26:33	Study 4
Romans 1:18-25	Study 30
Romans 6:4-7	Study 47
Romans 8:28-39	Study 28, 39
Romans 8:31-39	Study 17, 44
Romans 8:34	Study 43
Romans 8:35-39	Study 15
Romans 9:6-9	Study 18
Romans 12:1-2	Study 40
Romans 12:21	Study 41
Romans 14:19	Study 51
1 Corinthians 2:14-16	Study 51
1 Corinthians 3:10-13	Study 49
1 Corinthians 4:12	Study 10, 33
1 Corinthians 4:9-13	Study 49
1 Corinthians 6:1-9	Study 52
1 Corinthians 12:7, 18, 27	Study 8
1 Corinthians 13:9	Study 10
1 Corinthians 13:9-12	Study 52
1 Corinthians 14:12	Study 51
1 Corinthians 14:29-32	Study 21
1 Corinthians 15:42-46	Study 4
1 Corinthians 15:50	Study 47
1 Corinthians 15:54-58	Study 29
1 Corinthians 16:9	Study 9
2 Corinthians 1:8	Study 10, 33
2 Corinthians 2:15-16	Study 20
2 Corinthians 2:17	Study 48
2 Corinthians 4:1-12	Study 26
2 Corinthians 4:16-19	Study 10, 22
2 Corinthians 5:1-10	Study 45
2 Corinthians 5:10	Study 33
2 Corinthians 5:17	Study 47
2 Corinthians 8:7	Study 51
2 Corinthians 10:3-6	Study 22, 28, 39
Galatians 2:20	Study 10
Galatians 3:10-13	Study 50
Galatians 5:19-21	Study 47
Galatians 5:22-25	Study 50
Galatians 6:7-10	Study 40
Galatians 6:15	Study 47
Ephesians 1:20-23	Study 43
Ephesians 2:1-6	Study 10
Ephesians 2:4-7	Study 34
Ephesians 2:6-7	Study 48
Ephesians 2:8-10	Study 42
Ephesians 2:19-22	Study 48
Ephesians 2:20	Study 49
Ephesians 3:2-7	Study 24
Ephesians 4:3	Study 51
Ephesians 4:15	Study 11
Ephesians 4:22-23	Study 47
Ephesians 4:30-32	Study 50
Ephesians 5:1-2	Study 20
Ephesians 5:25-26	Study 29
Ephesians 6:10-18	Study 28, 31
Philippians 1:6	Study 50
Philippians 1:9-10	Study 51
Philippians 1:20-26	Study 18, 29
Philippians 1:21	Study 10
Philippians 2:5-11	Study 15
Philippians 2:9-11	Study 15
Philippians 2:13-14	Study 50
Philippians 3:10-12	Study 5
Philippians 4:4	Study 29
Philippians 4:18	Study 20
Colossians 2:13-15	Study 45
Colossians 3:1-6	Study 13
Colossians 3:3	Study 2, 9
Colossians 3:9-10	Study 47
Colossians 4:6	Study 11
1 Thessalonians 2:13	Study 25
1 Thessalonians 4:1	Study 51
1 Thessalonians 4:9-10	Study 51
1 Thessalonians 4:13-18	Study 46
1 Thessalonians 5:16-18	Study 2
1 Thessalonians 5:1-11	Study 36
1 Thessalonians 5:19-22	Study 7, 21, 50
1 Timothy 2:3-4	Study 24, 28, 33
1 Timothy 3:15	Study 49
1 Timothy 4:1-6	Study 6
1 Timothy 5:9-10	Study 42
1 Timothy 6:13-15	Study 43
1 Timothy 6:17	Study 42
2 Timothy 2:3, 10, 12	Study 10, 33
2 Timothy 3:16-17	Study 42
2 Timothy 4:1	Study 46
2 Timothy 4:3-4	Study 21
2 Timothy 4:5	Study 10
Hebrews 1:1-2	Study 35, 42
Hebrews 1:1-14	Study 40
Hebrews 1:14	Study 47
Hebrews 2:9-10	Study 11
Hebrews 2:9-18	Study 43
Hebrews 3:15	Study 29
Hebrews 4:9-13	Study 7, 23
Hebrews 4:11	Study 51
Hebrews 4:14-16	Study 11, 44
Hebrews 5:7-9	Study 11
Hebrews 5:14	Study 51
Hebrews 9:1-14	Study 34
Hebrews 9:23-28	Study 24, 27
Hebrews 10:23-25	Study 48
Hebrews 10:25	Study 8
Hebrews 10:32-39	Study 40
Hebrews 10:35-39	Study 52
Hebrews 11:8-10	Study 48
Hebrews 11:13-16	Study 48
Hebrews 11:25	Study 38

Hebrews 11:32-34	Study 9	1 Peter 3:21-22	Study 13
Hebrews 12:1-2	Study 42	1 Peter 4:1-7	Study 37
Hebrews 12:1-4	Study 45	1 Peter 4:5	Study 46
Hebrews 12:7	Study 10	1 Peter 4:17	Study 25
Hebrews 12:5-12	Study 11	1 Peter 5:1-4	Study 8
Hebrews 12:14	Study 51	1 Peter 5:5	Study 25
Hebrews 12:18-23	Study 12, 27	2 Peter 1:5-8	Study 51
Hebrews 12:26-29	Study 17, 27, 29	2 Peter 1:15	Study 51
Hebrews 12:28-29	Study 46	2 Peter 1:16-21	Study 40
James 1:2-12	Study 19	2 Peter 1:18-21	Study 29
James 1:12	Study 5	2 Peter 2:4-9	Study 33
James 1:23-25	Study 51	2 Peter 3:7	Study 33
James 2:5	Study 47	2 Peter 3:9	Study 8
James 3:1-2	Study 11	2 Peter 3:10-14	Study 36
James 3:5-12	Study 32	2 Peter 3:14	Study 51
James 4:1-7	Study 38	2 Peter 3:15-18	Study 29
James 4:1-10	Study 41	1 John 1:5-7	Study 50
James 4:6	Study 25	1 John 1:6-10	Study 7, 9
James 4:8-10	Study 32	1 John 1:8-10	Study 11
1 Peter 1:3-7	Study 52	Jude 1:24-25	Study 50
1 Peter 2:4-10	Study 45, 49		
1 Peter 2:20	Study 10, 33		

About the Author

John W. Stanko is the founder and president of PurposeQuest International, which creates resources and tools to help people around the world clarify their purpose and order their world. He is a sought-after conference speaker and consultant, and his website and blog are popular sites where people go to better understand who they are and how they can be more productive. John resides in Pittsburgh, PA and is currently pursuing a Doctor of Ministry degree from Reformed Presbyterian Theological Seminary while he continues to write.

You can stay in touch with John's world through the following sites:

www.purposequest.com • www.johnstanko.us
www.stankomondaymemo.com •
www.stankobiblestudy.com (where you can subscribe
to receive his weekly Bible studies)
or via email at johnstanko@att.net

PurposeQuest International
PO Box 91099 • Pittsburgh, PA 15221-7099
1.412.646.2780

www.ingramcontent.com/pod-product-compliance
Lightning Source LLC
Chambersburg PA
CBHW071304110426
42743CB00042B/1172